STATE POWER 2.0

This collection is dedicated to the international networks of activists, hacktivists, and enthusiasts leading the global movement for Internet freedom.

State Power 2.0

Authoritarian Entrenchment and Political Engagement Worldwide

Edited by

MUZAMMIL M. HUSSAIN
University of Michigan, USA

PHILIP N. HOWARD
University of Washington, USA

Routledge
Taylor & Francis Group
LONDON AND NEW YORK

First published 2013 by Ashgate Publishing

Published 2016 by Routledge
2 Park Square, Milton Park, Abingdon, Oxfordshire OX14 4RN
711 Third Avenue, New York, NY 10017, USA

First issued in paperback 2016

Routledge is an imprint of the Taylor & Francis Group, an informa business

British Library Cataloguing in Publication Data
A catalogue record for this book is available from the British Library

The Library of Congress has cataloged the printed edition as follows:
Howard, Philip N.
State Power 2.0 : Authoritarian Entrenchment and Political Engagement Worldwide / by Philip N. Howard and Muzammil M. Hussain.
pages cm
Includes bibliographical references and index.
ISBN 978-1-4094-5469-4 (hardback)
1. Internet--Political aspects. 2. Internet--Government policy. 3. Internet--Censorship. 4. Authoritarianism. 5. Social control. I. Hussain, Muzammil M. II. Title.
HM851.H69 2013
303.3'3--dc23

2013020296

ISBN 13: 978-1-138-25010-9 (pbk)
ISBN 13: 978-1-4094-5469-4 (hbk)

Contents

List of Figures

Notes on Contributors

Sheetal D. Agarwal is a doctoral candidate in the Department of Communication at the University of Washington, Seattle. Her research interests include the intersection of media, technology, and politics from a network perspective. Currently, she is evaluating the role of values, resources, and power distribution in technology development within networked organizations.

Fahed Al-Sumait is Assistant Professor and Department Chair of Communication at the Gulf University for Science and Technology in Kuwait. He was recently a post-doctoral research fellow at the National University of Singapore's Middle East Institute, and a Fulbright-Hays fellow from 2010–2011.

Gregory Asmolov is a doctoral student in the Media and Communications Department, at the London School of Economics and Political Science. He is a co-founder of HelpMap, a crowdsourcing platform which was used to coordinate assistance to victims of wildfires in Russia in 2010.

Jessica L. Beyer is a post-doctoral scholar in the Henry M. Jackson School for International Studies at the University of Washington, Seattle.

Matthew Carrieri is a researcher at the Citizen Lab, Munk School of Global Affairs, University of Toronto. He holds a BA in Middle East Studies from McGill University and an MA in Near Eastern Studies from New York University.

Ronald J. Deibert is Professor of Political Science and Director of the Canada Centre for Global Security Studies and the Citizen Lab at the Munk School of Global Affairs, University of Toronto.

David M. Faris is Assistant Professor of Political Science and Director of International Studies at Roosevelt University. He is author of *Dissent and Revolution in a Digital Age: Social Media, Blogging and Activism in Egypt* (I.B. Tauris).

Philip N. Howard is Professor of Communication, Information and International Studies at the University of Washington, Professor of Public Policy at the Central European University, and a fellow at the Center for Information Technology Policy at Princeton University.

Muzammil M. Hussain is Assistant Professor in International and Comparative Media Studies at the University of Michigan's Department of Communication Studies, Faculty Associate at the Institute for Social Research's Center for Political Studies, and directs the project on Comparative Digital Politics and Democratization (www.comparative-DPD.org).

Mohammed Ibahrine is Assistant Professor of Digital Advertising and Marketing Communication at the American University of Sharjah, UAE. He is a contributing member of the Open Society Global Project "Mapping Digital Media" and the ITU Global Cybersecurity Agenda (GCA).

David Karpf is Assistant Professor of Media and Public Affairs at the George Washington University. His primary research focus concerns online politics in the United States, and is the author of *The MoveOn Effect: The Unexpected Transformation of American Political Advocacy* (Oxford University Press).

Saad Omar Khan is a researcher at the Citizen Lab, Munk School of Global affairs, University of Toronto. He holds a master's degree from the London School of Economics, and completed his undergraduate studies at the University of Toronto.

Steven Livingston is Professor of Media and Public Affairs, and International Affairs at the George Washington University.

Katherine Maher is Director of Strategy and Engagement for the international digital rights organization "Access," and a fellow at the Truman National Security Project.

Catherine McKinley began her career as a reporter with the BBC World Service in London before moving to Shanghai and then Hanoi as Dow Jones Newswires' Bureau Chief for Vietnam. She later transitioned to media development consultancy, focusing on media skills, ethics, policy and legal reform and coordination between the international donors supporting media development in Vietnam. She also conducts research on the role of the media in combating corruption.

Babak Rahimi is Associate Professor of Communication, Culture and Religion at the Program for the Study of Religion, Department of Literature, University of California, San Diego.

Imad Salamey is Associate Professor of Political Science and International Affairs at the Lebanese American University in Beirut. He is President of the Center for Arab Research and Development (CARD), and Executive Board Member of the

Institute for the Study of Conflict, Security and Development (CSDS) at Richmond American International University in London.

Anya Schiffrin directs the Media and Communications Program at Columbia University's School of International and Public Affairs. She was Bureau Chief for Dow Jones Newswires in Amsterdam and Hanoi and wrote regularly for the *Wall Street Journal*. Her book *Bad News: How America's Business Press Missed the Story of the Century* (New Press) explores how the press covered the recent financial crisis.

Helga Tawil-Souri is Associate Professor in the Department of Media, Culture, and Communication at New York University. Her scholarship focuses on spatiality, technology, and politics in the Middle East with a particular focus on Israel-Palestine.

Jillian C. York is Director for International Freedom of Expression at the Electronic Frontier Foundation and sits on the board of directors of Global Voices Online.

Acknowledgments

We have received many different kinds of support for this work. This material is based upon work supported by the National Science Foundation under Grant No. 1144286, "RAPID—Social Computing and Political Transition in Tunisia," and Grant No. 0713074, "Human Centered Computing: Information Access, Field Innovation, and Mobile Phone Technologies in Developing Countries." Any opinions, findings, and conclusions or recommendations expressed in this material are those of the authors and do not necessarily reflect the views of the National Science Foundation. Support for Hussain's fieldwork was provided by the Department of Communication at the University of Washington, and the Horowitz Foundation for Social Policy. This research was conducted with the approval of the university's Human Subjects Division under Applications #32381 and #41115.

For helpful comments and feedback through the writing of this project, Hussain thanks the hosts and organizers of talks and workshops by the Center for Comparative and International Studies (ETH Zürich), the Media Change and Innovation Division (University of Zürich), and the Media Management and Transformation Centre (Jönköping International Business School). For helpful comments and feedback, Howard thanks the organizers of talks and workshops by the Free University of Berlin, Radcliffe Institute, Stanford University, and the US Institutes of Peace. Hussain and Howard are grateful for collegial conversations with Lance Bennett, Larry Diamond, Kirsten Foot, Steve Livingston, Joel Migdal, Malcolm Parks, and Gregor Walter-Drop.

Muzammil M. Hussain, University of Michigan, USA
Philip N. Howard, Princeton University, USA

Introduction: State Power 2.0

Muzammil M. Hussain, Philip N. Howard, and Sheetal D. Agarwal

There have been many studies of the different ways regimes censor the use of social media by their citizens, but shutting off digital networks altogether is something that rarely happens. However, it happens at the most politically sensitive times and has widespread—if not global—consequences for political, economic and cultural life. For democratic activists and international observers alike, 2011 was marked with hope and optimism. Digitally-enabled youth had successfully sparked nonviolent protests across North Africa and the Middle East, the likes of which had not been seen in these countries for many decades. In what is now referred to as the "Arab Spring" by hopeful observers, Tunisia and Egypt had successfully replaced decades-old dictatorships with the hopeful beginnings of writing new constitutions and building new democratic institutions. But fast forwarding to the end of 2013, the tasks of re-building new democracies from the ground up remain long-term processes still measured across years and decades, including ongoing moments of progress and setbacks.[1]

Since the removal of Ben Ali and Hosni Mubarak in 2011, Egypt had faced not some but several periods of social unrest and political uncertainty, most recently the July 2013 military coup and deposition of the Muslim Brotherhood-backed President Mohamed Morsi which has left the country in another sustained period of protest and turmoil. Tunisia's new government also moved snail-paced through much of 2012 in its new constitution writing and adoption process, but Tunisian civil society ready themselves for the country's second election after the "Jasmine Revolution" of 2011, schedule December 2013. Furthermore, in contrast to the relative high diffusion rates and vibrant online civil societies present in Egypt and Tunisia, the lack of Internet access, and regimes' heavy management of existing Internet infrastructure, particularly in Libya and Syria, have also vividly illuminated the ways in which unfriendly regimes use these same tools and infrastructures towards repressive ends. Syria's explicit and targeted violence against its citizens has garnered the regime routine international condemnations. But near the end of 2012, observers also took note of the regime's calculated methods of controlling its Internet infrastructure. While not as robust as Saudi

1 A longer version of this article was originally published as Howard, P.N., Agarwal, S.D., and Hussain, M.M. 2011. "When Do States Disconnect Digital Networks? Regime Responses to the Political Uses of Social Media." *The Communication Review*, 14(3): 216–232.

Arabia or China's well-financed Internet censorship platforms, nor as crude as Egypt's and Myanmar's national-level shutdowns in years before, Syria managed several times in 2011 and 2012 to do both. By acquiring sophisticated technologies from Western countries to censor and monitor political content, and also turning-off vast portions of its national Internet and physically targeting Internet activists, the regime is both learning and advancing its capacity to turn activists' digital tools against them. What might these two years following the Arab Spring tell us about how state powers and civil society actors find digital technologies to be politically consequential? How have Internet technologies been built and adopted by nondemocratic countries over the past two decades? Where do dictators acquire new technologies and skills to control digital infrastructure? And when do states disconnect their digital networks, and why?

Democratization movements have existed long before technologies such as mobile phones and the Internet came to nondemocratic countries. But with these technologies, people sharing an interest in democracy have built extensive networks, created social capital, and organized political action. With these tools, virtual networks have materialized in the streets. As a desperate measure, many states have tried to choke off information flows between activists, and between activists and the rest of the world. Mubarak tried to disconnect his citizens from the global information infrastructure in the last week of January 2011. It was a desperate maneuver with mixed impact. A small group of tech-savvy students and civil society leaders had organized satellite phones and dialup connections to Israel and Europe, so they were able to keep up strong links to the rest of the world. It appears that some of the telecommunications engineers acted slowly on the order to choke off Internet access. The first large Internet service provider was asked to shut down on Friday, January 28, but engineers didn't get to it until Saturday. Other providers responded quickly, but returned to normal service on Monday. The amount of bandwidth going into Egypt certainly dropped off for four days, but it was not the information blackout Mubarak had asked for. Taking down the nation's information infrastructure also crippled government agencies. The people most affected were middle-class Egyptians, who were cut off from Internet service at home. Some people certainly stayed there, isolated and uncertain about the status of their friends and family. But in the absence of information about the crisis, others took to the streets, eager to find out what was going on.

But this was not the first wave of incidents in which governments disconnected their citizens from global information flows. On Friday, June 12, 2009, Iran voted. When voters realized the election had been rigged, many took to the streets to protest. Social media such as Twitter, Facebook, and SMS messaging was actively used to coordinate the movements of protesters and to get images and news out to the international community. Compared to protests that occurred the last time elections were stolen, the social movement lasted longer, it drew in millions more participants, and there were more witnesses to the brutal regime crackdown. Social media had a clear role in extending the life of civil disobedience. While the theocratic regime did not fall, there were some important outcomes: the ruling mullahs were split in opinion about the severity of the crackdown. As part of the response, the regime attempted to disable national mobile phone networks. It disconnected the national Internet information infrastructure for several hours, and installed a deep packet inspection system that significantly slowed traffic.

For civil society actors around the world, digital media and online social networking applications have changed the way in which dissent is organized (Bimber 2005; Howard 2010; Still 2005). Social movement leaders from around the world use online applications and digital content systems to organize collective action, activate local protest networks, network with international social movements, and share their political perspective with global media systems (Byrne 2007; De Kloet 2002; Shumate 2006). In the past, authoritarian regimes easily controlled broadcast media in times of political crisis; by destroying newsprint supplies, seizing radio and television stations, and blocking phone calls. It is certainly more difficult to control digital media on a regular basis, but there have been occasions in which states have disabled a range of marginal to significant portions of their national information infrastructure. What situational tendencies cause state-powers to exercise specific acts of blocking Internet access and disabling digital networks? When do regimes resort to the more extreme measures of shutting off Internet access? And when they do not have the capacity to control digital networks, how do states respond offline to dissent and criticism? What is the impact of doing so, and who is most affected?

It is difficult to investigate patterns of state censorship. Many reports of censorship are essentially self-reports by technology users who assume there is a political reason behind their inability to connect to a digital network, whether they are mobile phone networks, gaming networks, or the Internet. Sometimes the state admits to acts of censorship, which makes it easier to learn why the government interfered and to what effect. Other times the state acts so clumsily or breaks the communication link between such large networks that many users can report being effected. While several researchers study the broad social impact of censorship, there are only a few who are able to provide evidence about both the shared perception that the state is surveilling its public, and specific incidents of censorship that involve disconnections in digital networks (Deibert and Rohozinski 2008; Deibert et al. 2010). Drawing from multiple sources, however, it is possible to do a comparative analysis of the myriad incidents in which government officials decide to censor their online publics. By collecting as many *known* incidents of state intervention in information networks, we are able to map out the contours of crisis situations, political risks, and civic innovations to understand the new intersections between state power and civil society.

Not all incidents involve authoritarian regimes, and not all acts of state censorship are easy to describe and classify. One of the first incidents occurred on December 29, 1995, when German prosecutors demanded that an Internet Service Provider (ISP) block four million worldwide subscribers from accessing sexually explicit content on portions of the Internet. This was the first instance of such drastic measures of state censorship, legislation, and regulation of information received online. Motivation for the shutdown came from a police investigation into child pornography in Bavaria, Germany. Though German officials were targeting 220,000 German subscribers when they asked for the block, CompuServe had no mechanism in place to limit just German users at the time, thus, they shut down service to all subscribers. In all, CompuServe restricted subscriber access to 200 newsgroups, specifically related to the site Usenet. Reaction to the censorship elicited varied responses from community and civic groups. The National Center for Missing and Exploited Children, for example, hailed it as a form of "electronic citizenship." Meanwhile, groups such as the Electronic Freedom Foundation indicated concern and resistance to the notion of state control over individual rights online.

This early incident of state intervention with Internet connectivity brought forth questions that we still struggle to answer today: Who controls Internet content? What are the legitimate reasons for state interference with digital networks? Over the last 15 years, states are increasingly willing to interfere with the links between nodes of digital infrastructure by shutting out particular users or shutting off particular servers, by breaking the links to sub-networks of digital media, and sometimes even by disconnecting national information infrastructure from global networks.

Recently, Research in Motion (RIM) was involved in a complex issue involving several states' requests to provide better access to the server nodes in Blackberry service networks. In the spring of 2010, a prominent political figure in the United Arab Emirates (UAE) used his Blackberry's mobile camera to record himself torturing a Bangladeshi migrant worker. The video was taken and posted online, causing outrage from human rights groups and embarrassing the country's ruling elites. The UAE's response has been to demand that RIM provide dedicated servers within their territory so that the regime could monitor traffic and disable services as needed. Eventually both Saudi Arabia and the United Arab Emirates threatened to ban the use of the popular Blackberry smart phone. The UAE threatened to block access to text messages, email, and web browsers if RIM did not allow government access for security investigations. The threat of censorship was still in place as of October 2010, potentially affecting over half a million users of the most popular smart phone in the UAE.

In 2010, India followed suit, also citing national security as the impetus for demanding RIM stop encrypting data sent through their phones. This incident illustrates a growing tension between governments and mobile Internet users' privacy today. Increasingly, over the past decade private companies and ISP providers like RIM are caught in between meeting the security and information needs of their citizen users, and obeying imposed government regulations by nation states. Most recently, Vodafone was under pressure from both Mubarak's regime to shut off Internet access, and civil society activists to keep the communication channels open. Concession by the ISP providers is more valuable to these states than a block however, as it will severely limit businesses run by citizens in these countries as well as those of visitors and tourists. After Vodafone complied with

Mubarak's regime to turn off Internet access, it cost the national economy an estimated $90 million and the country's reputation as a safe and stable place for technology firms to invest.

Since 1995—the year the National Science Foundation effectively privatized the Internet—there have been well over 500+ occasions in which governments intervened in the connections of a digital network. Of these, about half were enacted by authoritarian regimes. The three countries with the highest number of incidents, China, Tunisia, and Turkey, represent both authoritarian and democratic regimes. In times of political uncertainty, rigged elections, or military incursions, ruling elites are sometimes willing to interfere with information infrastructure as a way of managing crises. In many of these cases, the targets (victims) are active domestic civic society movements with international linkages. When these movements organize, authoritarian governments can react harshly and invasively by blocking access to the global Internet. Yet at the same time, these authoritarian regimes find that they cannot block Internet access for extended periods, both because doing so has an impact on the national economy and because of international political pressure. Shutting off the Internet for a country's network also has an impact on the capacity of the state to respond to the crisis—for example, Egyptian authorities did not expect that turning off Internet and SMS networks would draw out protesters in larger numbers to the street. Therefore, the decision tree for choking off Internet access also involves some willingness to incapacitate portions of the government's security apparatus. Increasingly, civil society groups find methods to circumvent the blocked social media. A significant corpus of literature has grown around the use of newer digital media by social movements against authoritarian regimes (Garrett 2006; Marmura 2008; McLaughlin 2003). While there is a healthy ongoing conversation by scholars on the issue of civil societies' uses of digital media for social and political mobilization, our investigation illuminates the impetuses, tactics, and impacts of state responses to online engagement.

In this collection of cases from around the world, our goal is to encourage the comparative analysis of occasions in which regimes have disconnected significant portions of their national digital infrastructure, including mobile phones and Internet access. Our goal is to define the range of situations in which states have actually disrupted large sections of their own national information infrastructure, as well as to uncover their long-term strategizing in managing new information infrastructure. Through grounded comparisons of incidents, we demonstrate the importance of understanding how information technologies have a role in political responses and counter-insurgency tactics of many kinds of regimes. Such comparative study will help explicate the meaning of contemporary state power in media systems of both advanced and developing countries. While some have argued that the state no longer has strong control of media production and consumption systems, there are a range of occasions in which state power over digital networks is noticeably strong.

Drawing on a range of sources, we built a detailed event catalog for major disruptions in digital networks of nations between 1995 and 2010. We collected information about incidents as reported in major news media, specialized news sources such as national security and information security blogs, and other online forums for discussing such topics. These sources include Google News, Lexus Nexus, Attrition.org, GlobalVoices.org, among others. A case is defined as an occasion where a government intervened in a digital network by breaking or turning off connections between national sub-networks and global information networks. Sometimes this meant blocking ports or access to a particular sub-network of digital media, such as content at the domains Facebook.com or YouTube.com. In times of significant political or military crisis, such as war or contested elections, the governments might disconnect SMS messaging services or block the entire country's access to global networks. Additionally, regimes may target individual actors in networks. But these incidents are more than general government threats of surveillance or intimidation (which are also forms of censorship). These are distinct incidents where government officials made the specific decision to disable the links or nodes in the portions of the information networks they can control.

Since the literature on digital censorship often makes a distinction between democracies, emerging democracies and authoritarian regimes, we rely on the Polity IV data about regime type (Marshall and Jaggers 2010). In addition, since several of the governments appearing in the event log are too fragile to sensibly be given one of these three categories, we rely on Polity IV data for a category of fragile regimes. As per Polity IV coding, if a state was recovering from civil war or foreign military invasion, experiencing a complex humanitarian disaster, or had effectively failed for other reasons, we code this state as fragile. A state's regime type was set according to the Polity IV score for that state in the year of the reported incident. Several countries had several incidents, and it is possible that regime types changed over time.

All in all, there have been at least 566 unique incidents involving 101 countries: 39 percent of the incidents occurred in democracies, 7 percent occurred in emerging democracies, 51 percent occurred in authoritarian regimes, and 2 percent occurred in fragile states. Each incident was coded for the name of the country in which a state agency intervened in digital networks, the year of the incident, the type of regime, and a precise date if available. We made general notes on the narrative of each incident, and mapped on the Polity IV score for the country in the year of the incident. Then we developed three standardized typologies for the kinds of incidents being reported. First, we developed a category that iteratively helped define the case, and a typology of actions that states take against social media. Second, we developed a category for why they took that action, sometimes relying on third-party reports if the state simply denied any interference. Finally, we developed a category for the impact of the interference.

While we might expect authoritarian regimes to more aggressively interfere with their digital infrastructure than other types of regimes, Figure I.1 reveals that democracies also substantively disconnect their communication networks. In recent years, there have been at least 80 incidents a year. Only a fraction of these involve emerging democracies. Over time, it appears that all types of regimes have

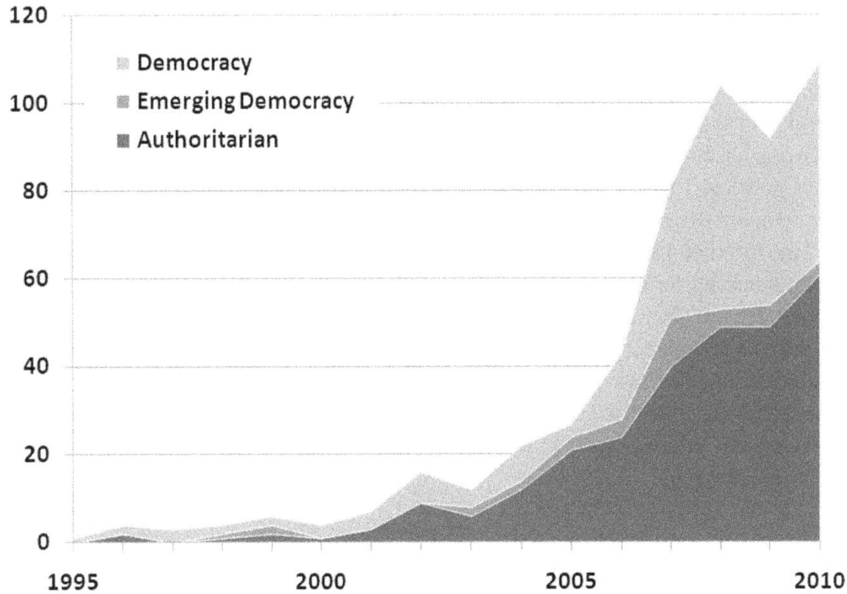

Figure I.1 Number of major incidents of state intervention in digital networks, by regime type, 1995–2011

become more and more willing to interfere with information access, particularly since 2006—the same year *Time Magazine* awarded "You" as the person of the year, recognizing the worldwide diffusion of participatory social media tools. As social media have diffused, they have become a fundamental infrastructure for collective action. Even though democracies appear just as aggressive as authoritarian regimes in disconnecting digital networks, are there differences in the ways in which such states intervene? What are the different reasons for such drastic interventions?

Decision Paths and Opportunity Structures

Civil society is often defined as the self-generating and self-supporting community of people who share a normative order and volunteer to organize political, economic or cultural activities that are independent from the state (Diamond 1994). Civil society groups are a crucial part of all elections because they represent diverse perspectives and promote those perspectives through communications media. Moreover, a key tenet of the shared normative order is that no one group can claim to represent the whole of society. Democracy is best served by a multitude of groups that contribute in different ways to conceiving public policy options and national development goals. Some governments work hard to censor digital media, but even in such countries the Internet is difficult to control. Governments might own nodes in the network, but rarely can they completely choke off network connections. This means that tools like YouTube, Twitter, Facebook, and email are useful, and at sensitive times, critical, organizational tools. In some of the toughest authoritarian regimes, these tools are crucial because face-to-face conversations about political life are so problematic. For civil society groups—these tools are often content distribution systems largely independent of the state.

The Internet has become an invaluable logistical tool for organization and communication for civil society groups. It is an information infrastructure mostly independent of the state, and since civil society groups are by definition social organizations independent of the state, the Internet has become an important incubator for social movements (radical and secular) and civic action. The Internet has altered the dynamics of political communication systems in many countries, such that the Internet itself is the site of political contestation between the state and civil society.

How do States Interfere with Digital Networks?

States interfere with digital networks using many tactics, with various levels of severity: online, by shutting down political websites or portals; offline, by arresting journalists, bloggers, activists, and citizens; by proxy, through controlling Internet service providers, forcing companies to shut down specific websites or denying access to disagreeable content; and, in the most extreme cases, shutting down access to entire online and mobile networks. Surprisingly, we find that while authoritarian regimes practice controlling full-networks, sub-networks, and nodes more than democracies, democracies are the most likely to target civil society actors by proxy by manipulating Internet service providers. Table I.1 presents cases where governments exercised control by targeting full-networks (shutting down the Internet), sub-networks (blocking websites), network-nodes (targeting individuals), and by proxy (pressuring Internet service providers).

The most extreme form of network control is when states shut down access to the Internet. Authoritarian regimes did so significantly more than fragile states and emerging democracies, and also twice as more as democracies. A clear illustration of this was when China shut down Internet services in the Xinjiang region after ethnic riots erupted in 2006. The riots resulted in 140 fatalities, and the state has since blocked access to Twitter and other social networking sites to control the conflict and dissent. More recently, Pakistan severely restricted the Internet after a Seattle-based cartoonist organized an "Everybody Draw Mohammed Day." After the event attracted 43,000 fans from around the world, the Pakistan government went into "banning mode" because the event invited members to draw and post pictures of the revered prophet. Similarly, emerging democracies, like Haiti and Thailand, have engaged in shutting down main Internet service providers, or entire online networks like YouTube, respectively. Thousands of Haitians lost Internet

Table I.1 How do states disconnect their digital networks? Incidents by regime type

	Democracy	Emerging democracy	Authoritarian	Fragile	Total
Complete network shut down (Full networks)	13	3	30	3	49
Specific site-oriented shut downs (Sub-networks)	140	25	210	8	383
Individual users (Nodes)	82	16	125	3	226
By proxy through ISP	47	4	41	4	96

Note: Total N = 754. Incident types are not mutually exclusive, as some incidents involved combinations of state tactics against social media use.

access in 1999 when the government attempted to allegedly silence dissent and consolidate power under the guise of punishing Alpha Network Communications for selling telephone cards and providing international telephone services. Bangladesh blocked YouTube and most other file sharing services after recordings of a meeting between the Prime Minister and army senior officers were leaked onto YouTube. Thailand, also an emerging democracy with a record of political online censorship, maintains a block on entire Internet services like YouTube. Bangladesh, a democracy, also blocked entire networks when a political crisis over the murder of a prominent lawyer raged on the WordPress network. These examples suggest that although complete network shut-downs are least common, they tend to materialize when states face national controversies and moments of severe social and political unrest, often (but by not exclusively) in authoritarian regimes.

Unlike the most extreme measure of shutting down entire online networks, states are most likely to target individual websites (online) or their producers and users (offline). Democracies are much more likely to engage in online content censorship than other tactics, though they also frequently target civil society members offline. The earliest case of a democracy shutting down online sub-networks was in 1995 when German authorities removed access to over 200 Internet newsgroups deemed indecent and offensive. In 1996, German authorities again removed access to banned material, such as a Netherlands' online magazine. More recently, advanced democracies like Australia, as of July 2010, was considering a mandatory Internet filter to censor a list of URLs associated with child sexual abuse, bestiality, sexual violence, crime, violence, drug use, and content advocating violence and extremism.

While socially questionable material and content promoting criminal activities are commonly cited reasons for blocking content in democratic states, some states have also used this as a tactic for foreign policy disputes. In August 2010, South Korea engaged in an online dispute with North Korea over social media when

South Korean citizens were threatened with arrests for accessing North Korea's Twitter feed. However, despite attempting to reroute requests from North Korea's Twitter page to a warning page, over 9,000 followers had accumulated.

In instances like this, when unable to block online content effectively, states are forced to go directly towards censoring individuals. Authoritarian states do this most often, and in many cases, with more severity. Bloggers, journalists, and social activists are the most common individual targets of offline censorship, often facing arrests and fines. For example, an Egyptian blogger was sentenced to four years in prison for insulting the Egyptian President Hosni Mubarak. Following Thailand's coup d'état in 2006, two cyber dissidents were arrested for comments made about the monarchy in online discussion boards, and face a minimum sentence of 15 years in prison. Another example of online activities leading to offline government reactions is Cuba's arrests of two online journalists working for CubaNet in 2005 and 2007. These journalists were arrested for engaging in "subversive propaganda" and "precriminal social danger." With authoritarian regimes, it is generally the case that criticisms of political elites are often dealt with the imposition of fines, searches, seizure of equipment, and imprisonment.

While democracies also engage in a heavy amount of censoring individual users, paralleling the conditions of authoritarian regimes, they also have a unique tendency to target individuals or agencies providing the infrastructure (a tactic that has increasingly been adopted by authoritarian regimes since the Arab Spring). In fact, democracies have a slightly higher rate of blocking content and controlling civil society actors through indirect measures, such as targeting Internet service providers. Turkey and Italy, both democracies, have legally pursued charges against both Internet service providers and their users. In March 2010, an Italian court convicted three Google executives for not removing violent video content that appeared on their online services. In August 2009, Malawi approved legal measures to pressure Internet service providers in monitoring social networking sites like Twitter and Facebook. Hungary and Belgium have also shared experiences where Internet service providers have received pressures to approve "notices of takedown" procedures from their governments. Surprisingly, while authoritarian regimes frequently fine and imprison civil society actors directly for criticizing the regime and its elites, democracies have more examples of regimes using legal frameworks and round-about institutionalized measures for targeting both Internet service providers and their users. As several of our contributors also document, successful authoritarian regimes today must not only punish civil society actors directly for using digital media in political ways, they must also create new legal, economic, and political relationships with infrastructure providers to ensure their control and survival.

Why do States Interfere with Digital Networks?

Looking across the range of known incidents, we have identified 12 categories representing two broader themes—protecting political authority and preserving the public good. The first broad theme of protecting leadership and state institutions included several reasons for state interference in public access to social media. These include: protecting political leaders and state institutions; election crisis; eliminating propaganda; mitigating dissidence; and national security. *National security* was the most commonly cited reason under this theme, where officials cited "terrorism threats" and preventing the spread of "state secrets" as reasons to intervene with Internet access. Information that undermined protection of authority figures was another sub-category oft attributed for intervention. In 2007 Kazakh officials shut down opposition web sites for three days, because of published transcripts and recordings related to a public battle between authoritarian President Nazarbayev and his estranged son-in-law. The *eliminating propaganda* sub-category included incidents where intervention occurred because of the spread of information aimed at serving an agenda undermining the standing regime. China in 2003 sentenced an individual to four years in prison for email discussions and postings in online forums and chat rooms related to democracy. The *mitigating dissidence* sub-category captures those cases in which intervention was attributed to an attempt to reduce dissident civic action, such as the US arresting two individuals who tweeted about police locations during G20 protests in Pittsburgh, Pennsylvania in 2009. Incidents included under the *election crisis* sub-category include cases in which a regime acted in response to events surrounding elections. This sub-category included times when the regime intervened prior to, during, or after elections. For example, in the aftermath of the highly contested Iranian elections in 2009, the regime first slowed and then shut down access to the Twitter network, which was heavily used by protestors to coordinate and share information about the contested elections.

The second over-arching theme for why states disabled social media was by claiming an urgent need to preserve the public good. Sub-categories of this theme include: preserving cultural and religious morals; preserving racial harmony; protecting children; cultural preservation; protecting individuals' privacy; and dissuading criminal activity. *Preserving cultural and religious morals* was the most cited reason for intervention across all themes and categories. This sub-category was used in incidents when officials attributed intervention to preventing the spread of blasphemous or offensive information that challenged the religious and cultural morality of the state. An overwhelming number of these cases involved targeting websites and individuals who accessed or distributed anti-Islamic or pornographic material (not including child pornography, which was captured in a separate category). An illustration of such an incident was from 2009, when Pakistan blocked access to 450 sites including Facebook and YouTube after an international event to depiction the prophet Mohammed was organized on Facebook.

Table I.2 Why do states disconnect their digital networks? Reasons by regime type

	Democracy	Emerging democracy	Authoritarian	Fragile	Total
Protecting authority					
Protecting political leaders and state institutions	30	7	23	1	61
Election crisis	4	3	9	0	16
Eliminating propaganda	5	1	24	0	30
Mitigating dissidence	8	5	11	3	27
National security	29	6	34	0	69
Preserving the public good					
Preserving cultural and religious morals	27	4	37	6	74
Preserving racial harmony	9	0	1	0	10
Protecting children	30	0	2	0	32
Cultural preservation	2	0	19	0	21
Protecting individual's privacy	3	0	2	0	5
Dissuading criminal activity	29	3	18	1	51
Alleged system failure, neither denied nor admitted	4	4	9	0	17
Censorship denied by state	3	1	11	0	15
Unknown, other	40	4	90	4	138
Total	**223**	**38**	**290**	**15**	**566**

Note: Total N = 566. Reasons for intervention are mutually exclusive.

Cultural preservation, included incidents in which interventions were attributed to the need to expel outside influence or threats to national interests were cited (but not related to terrorism or national security threats, which were captured by a separate category). In December 2006, Iran shut down access to websites such as YouTube and Amazon in order to "purge the country of Western influence." Though we encountered only a few cases that cited *preservation of racial harmony* as the impetus for action, these incidents are useful to separate from other categories as they focus interventions justified for protecting the public specifically from ethnic or racially motivated violence. For example, in 2008 Germany convicted a blogger for inciting hatred by denying the Holocaust.

Dissuading the public from *criminal activity* is another reason often cited by officials. Incidents under this category include arresting individuals for copyright infringement, distributing illegal information, and participating in activities deemed illegal by the state, such as online gambling. Cases in this sub-category included the arrests or criminal prosecutions of individuals whom authorities claimed were breaking the law. An example of such a case was when Polish authorities arrested the creators of a peer-to-peer portal and shut down the site in 2009, citing copyright infringement as the reasoning.

Protecting children as a sub-category included incidents where officials explicitly sited threats to children and minors as reasons for intervention. While many of these incidents related to pornographic material, only those cases that specifically included reference to child pornography were included under this sub-category. States often adopted Internet laws and policies to protect children; an illustration includes Brazil's adoption of policies that require ISPs to provide lists of the websites they host to a child protection agency and put a button on their website that says "Pedophilia is a crime, denounce it."

Lastly, only four, yet thematically distinct, cases represented the final sub-category under this theme: *protecting individuals' privacy*. This sub-category included incidences in which authorities determined that an individual's privacy was jeopardized by content posted on the Internet. Perhaps the most clear example of such a case was when a Tunisian official jailed and fined an individual for "causing harm by means of telecommunication networks" because he did not obtain an official permit or consent of the individuals he filmed for an online video.

There are certain types of cases that are difficult to categorize. These include reports of some incidents where there was not enough information to assert the reasons for the intervention. This includes cases in which officials simply did not cite a reason for intervention, or when our primary texts did not provide enough insight into why the intervention took place. These incidents categorized as *unknown/other*. Additionally, there were cases in which officials simply denied any responsibility for censorship or claimed it was a technical issue, thus we are unable to attribute reasons for the intervention. These cases are captured in the sub-categories, *censorship denied* and *alleged system failure*. While it is not surprising that authoritarian regimes invoke intervention policies to protect state authorities and institutions, Table I.2 reveals that democratic regimes exercise intervention efforts at nearly the same level for these same reasons, which severely limits civil society groups from participating in the foundational democratic practices of the regime.

The advantage of a comparative approach is that it allows us to avoid and move beyond organizational and technological determinism (Howard 2002). It does so by allowing us to build grounded typologies of real government responses to the development of new media, and particularly social media. The lasting impact of a temporary disconnection in Internet service may actually be a strengthening of weak ties between global and local civil society networks. When civil society disappears from the grid, it is noticed. What lasts are the ties between a nation's civic groups, and between international non-governmental organizations and like-minded, in-country organizations. Certainly not all of these virtual communities are about elections, but their existence is a political phenomenon particularly in countries where state and social elites have worked hard to police offline communities. Thus, even the bulletin boards and chat rooms dedicated to shopping for brand name watches are sites that practice free speech and where the defense of free speech can become a topic of conversation. The Internet allows oppositions movements that are based outside of a country to reach in and become part of the system of political communication within even the strictest authoritarian regimes. Today, banning political parties could simply mean that formal political opposition is now organized online, from outside the country. It could also means that civil society leaders turn to other organizational forms afforded by network technologies. When states disconnect particular social media services, student and civil society leaders develop creative workarounds and relearn traditional (offline) mobilization tactics. This almost always means that target sites, such as YouTube, Facebook, and Twitter, are accessible through other means.

The Causes and Consequences of Digital Interventions

When a political, military, or other security crisis is over, what remains is the lasting impact of a temporary outage in digital network connectivity. The Internet has become a crucial component of political communications during elections—even rigged ones. It has also become a crucial component of political communication during other kinds of regime transition, such as executive turnover, foreign military intervention, natural disasters, and social protests that challenge a regime's legitimacy. Information infrastructure is not simply part of the general context of contemporary social mobilization. Indeed, social computing is a defining feature of elections these days. Digital media such as mobile phones and the Internet now help incubate civic conversations, especially in countries that heavily censor the national print and broadcast media.

Internet access is often limited to wealthy social elites, but these elites have a key role in either accepting or rejecting the outcome of an election. The Internet has become a necessary infrastructure for the development of civil society and election season is often the time for civic groups to be most active. Most (though not all) of the regimes studied in this event catalogue are authoritarian, or were when the decision to disconnect from global information networks was taken. For authoritarian regimes, the single greatest threat to stability is often internal: elite defection. When the cohort of wealthy families, educated and urban elites, and government employees decide they no longer wish to back a regime, it is most likely to fail. In most of the countries studied here, only a small fraction of the population has Internet access through computers and mobile phones. However, this small population is the one that authoritarian regimes work hard to broker information for.

It is not Twitter, blogs, or YouTube that cause social unrest. But today, successful social movement organizing and civic engagement is difficult to imagine without them, even in countries like Iran and Egypt. Many people in these countries have no Internet or mobile phone access. Nevertheless, the people who do—urban dwellers, educated elites, and the young—are precisely the population with the capacity to enable regime change, or tacitly support electoral outcomes. These are the populations who support or defect from authoritarian rule, and for whom connections to family and friends have demonstrably changed with technology diffusion. Comparative analysis reveals the degree to which different regimes feel threatened by social media, whether such tools are actively used to organize dissent, or passively used for producing and consuming culture.

The political climax of uprising takes the form of state crackdowns or major concession to popular demands that can include executive turnover. Stalemates between protesters and ruling elites can result in protracted battles. But in each country, the political climax of uprising can also be marked by a clumsy attempt by the state to disconnect its own people from digital communications networks. Banning access to social media websites, powering down mobile phone towers, or disconnecting the Internet exchange points in major cities are an authoritarian government's desperate strategies for asserting control. And there are serious economic consequences to disconnecting a nation from global information infrastructures, even temporarily. Interrupting digital services cost Egypt's economy at least $90 million, and their reputation among technology firms as a stable place for investment. In Tunisia it was activist hackers—"hacktivists" as many call themselves—who did the most economic damage by taking down the stock exchange. But for the most part, it is recalcitrant authoritarian governments who make the decision to interfere with their country's digital networks.

When regimes disconnect from global information infrastructure, they employ a range of stop-gap measures that usually reinforces public expectations for global connectivity. But not all of these tactics are short-term innovations by the regime during moments of crisis. As the contributors of this collection detail, some regimes have an astoundingly long-range vision for understanding the political threats and opportunities that may arise from the diffusion of new communication technologies to civil society sectors. But state hegemony is by no means an absolute guarantee, and is more realistically determined by a regime's ability to anticipate and calculate new ways of dominating democratic outcomes and civic innovations by creative and brave political activists. This is why the following collection, *State Power 2.0: Authoritarian Entrenchment and Political Engagement Worldwide*, is divided in two parts including 12 original chapters.

Part I focuses on the advancement of authoritarian power through information infrastructure. Chapters 1 and 2 offer historical analyses of Tunisia and Iran's digital management and censorship strategies, while Chapter 3 offers a contemporary and comparative analysis of how these regimes' differences garnered both successes and failures in moments of political uncertainty. Chapter 4 further advances this perspective by investigating the strategic leveraging of information infrastructure to extend political control over Gaza's fragile regime. Finally, Chapter 5 examines the most destructive outcomes from a regime's inability to rein in the political capacity of digital networks: decision pathways that lead to state-sponsored violence against peaceful activists, particularly true for cases like Syria and Bahrain.

Part II of this collection draws on cases from around the world, including North Africa, the Middle East, Eastern Europe, Southeast Asia, and from the emerging presence of digitally-enabled and transnational political hackers, like Anonymous and Telecomix. This set of chapters (Part II) counterbalances the advancement of state power (Part I) with overwhelming evidence documenting the ways in which democratic activists are using these very technologies to outmaneuver dictators in brave and creative ways. Chapter 6 begins this with regional observations from Arab countries, while chapters 7, 8, and 9 investigate the cases of Egypt, Kuwait, and Morocco, respectively. All offer evidence for the ways in which digital media have come to overlap with existing media systems and communication norms to support *long-term* democratization. Finally, the last three chapters (10, 11, and 12), focusing on Vietnam, Russia, and the transnational hacktivist network "Anonymous," provide some of the best evidence of the creative civic and political innovations—innovations that have come as a consequence of activists repurposing existing technology infrastructure that their regimes have yet to fully comprehend and struggle to buffer against.

The political culture that we now see online during elections and political crises comes not just from political elites, but from citizens: using social media, documenting human rights abuses with their mobile phones, sharing spreadsheets to track state expenditures, and pooling information about official corruption. Perhaps the most lasting impact of digital media use during crises is that people get accustomed to being able to consume *and* produce political content. Most technology users in most countries do not have the sophistication to work around state firewalls or keep up anonymous and confidential communications online. But within each country (and increasingly transnationally) a handful of tech-savvy students and civil society leaders do have these skills, and used them well during the Arab Spring. Learning from other democracy activists in other countries, these information brokers used satellite phones, direct landline connections to ISPs in Israel and Europe, and a suite of anonymization tools to supply international journalists with pictures of events on the ground—even when desperate dictators attempted to shut down national ISPs. When digital networks are reactivated, personal networks that cross international boundaries also reactivate. Digital outages have become sensitive moments in which student leaders, journalists, and civil society groups experiment with digital technologies. Even if their favorite candidates are not elected and repressive regimes succeed in holding on to power, the process of experimentation with digital media is important because it results in infusing more information habits and news diets independent of the state into their daily engagement with public life. This is also why information infrastructure *is* politics—and because of its international organization, it is increasingly an important domain of international politics.

PART I
Information Infrastructure and Social Control

Chapter 1
Origins of the Tunisian Internet

Katherine Maher and Jillian C. York

In 1985, the government of Tunisia under President Habib Bourgiba received a $3 million (USD) Computer Technology Transfer Project Grant from the US Agency for International Development (USAID). This funding contributed towards the establishment of a national research body, the Institut Régional des Sciences Informatiques et des Télécommunications (IRSIT) in 1987, dedicated to the promotion of telecommunications and computer sciences in Tunisia (Kavanaugh 1998). IRSIT was the country's most prestigious technological research institution, and attracted some of the Tunisia's finest research and engineering talent, employing 45 full-time computer scientists on staff (Curtis 1996).

Many of IRSIT's engineers had conducted their graduate studies abroad in the 1980s, at institutions in Europe and the United States that were early adopters of packet-switching "internetworks" for academic information sharing, such as the Michigan State University (home to the Merit Network, one of the earliest "internetworks") (Silver 2011). The experience these engineers brought to IRSIT was at the cutting edge of computer internetworking. The TCP/IP protocol they used to connect discrete local networks was still relatively new; although in use by research and academic networks in the United States over the previous decade, its adoption in Europe was not widespread until the late 1980s.

IRSIT made Tunisia's first connection to the global network in April 1991, via IP connection to an Amsterdam EUNet node, becoming the first African country to connect to the Internet (Curtis 1996). This initial trans-Mediterranean link was later complemented by connection via BITNET to European research networks, and services such as the FidoNet bulletin board systems (BBS) (ASC 1994, NSRC 1995), putting Tunisia on par with comparable networks in the US and Europe. In 1992, on the basis of its advanced networking capacity, Tunisia was selected to participate in the UNESCO Regional Informatics Network for Africa (RINAF) initiative, intended to increase Internet connectivity across the African continent through increasing the density of regional networking exchanges (UNESCO 1993).

As Tunisia's first implementer of internetworking technology, IRSIT became the country's primary resource for expanding connectivity across the country. In 1993, IRSIT was awarded a mandate by the Government of Tunisia to connect the country's universities and research institutions through the Réseau National de Recherche de Tunisia, or RNRT (Kavanaugh 1998). In 1994, Tunisia initiated participation in the Sustainable Development Networking Program (SNDP), a United Nations Development Program (UNDP) program to support local development objectives; the SNDP awarded a contract to IRSIT to wire Tunisian non-governmental organizations (NGOs). Through these efforts, connectivity expanded; by 1995, Tunisia had roughly 1,000 Internet users utilizing services such as email and FTP; however limited bandwidth precluded the use of the World Wide Web (Kavanaugh 1998).

Creation of the ATI

In these early years, the Tunisian Internet mirrored the global Internet at large: a non-hierarchical, freewheeling network run by enthusiast engineers. Research institutions and telecommunications providers operated distributed, decentralized server clusters, with client servers running local email networks free of government oversight (Silver 2011). Access to the network was largely limited to those affiliated with universities or research institutions; and the network was used accordingly. However, in April 1996, this freewheeling national experiment came to an abrupt halt, with the government-ordered creation of the Agence Tunisienne d'Internet, popularly known as ATI.

The ATI was an unusual body from its inception. Established with a mandate to "catalyze Tunisia's 'Information Society'," it functionally allowed for consolidated state control over the country's burgeoning network. It quickly centralized oversight of the Internet under the executive branch and distributed preferential contracts and services to allies of the ruling regime. So close was ATI to the presidency that the agency was headed by a director close to the family of the dictator and located its offices in a whitewashed hillside villa belonging to Ben Ali, its director's office in the President's former sitting room.

Although established by the government, ATI is a limited liability private company, with its executive oversight managed by a board composed of its shareholders. However, a significant portion of its shares are held by firms with state interests, and those firms themselves are subject to further regulatory oversight by state agencies, enabling the Tunisian state to wield significant indirect power over ATI functions. At the ATI's founding, the national incumbent operator Tunisie Telecom held a 27 percent majority stake and IRSIT owned 10 percent. After the abolishment of IRSIT, Tunisie Telecom became the main shareholders with 37 percent and the now-defunct Agence Tunisienne de la Communication Extérieure (ATCE) held 13 percent, with the remaining 49 percent held by a mixture of semi-public Tunisian banks and technology firms (Market Access Database 2002). And despite its status as a nominally independent private firm, the ATI and its Executive Director were placed under the supervision of the Ministry of Communications.

ATI's first function was to assume responsibility from IRSIT for the national network, taking over administration of network services for the military and universities, and the provision of commercial and consumer Internet services (Kavanaugh 1998). Following the transfer, IRSIT was defunded and privatized, its assets sold to Tunisian technology and engineering firms, including the state-owned incumbent Tunisie Telecom, now majority-shareholder in ATI (Market Access Database 2002). IRSIT's employees were subsequently absorbed into the new private firm, as well as into state institutions, including the national regulator, the Ministry of Communications Technologies, as well as Tunisie Telecom.

Two years after ATI's founding, the agency had established itself as the sole national operator of the Tunisian Internet backbone. One of its earliest actions had been to outsource consumer Internet services to the country's first commercial ISP, Planet Tunisie, owned by Cyrine Ben Ali, daughter of the president; additional services were later added through ISP 3S Global Net (UNECA 2012). ATI also controlled registration for ".tn" top-level domains (ATI 1998), giving it effective censorial control over domain allocation. This consolidation of domain registration and authority over service provision in one organization gave ATI unprecedented control over the allocation of national network resources.

Although busily engaged in centralizing network oversight, the Government of Tunisia continued to actively encourage national adoption of the Internet as an economic development strategy. It launched its PubliNet initiative in 1998, aimed at increasing Internet access options through community centers, while in 1999 "Internet Caravans" were launched to travel the country providing mobile workshops about the Internet. In 2000, the ATI introduced an encrypted e-payment system, called E-Tijara, to support the development of the commercial web (Rao 2001). In 2004, seeking to encourage widespread computer use, the government lifted customs fees on computers, set a price ceiling for hardware, arranged low-interest loans, and offered Internet subscriptions with each computer purchase; however, costs remained stubbornly high, and the program was not particularly successful (Freedom House 2011).

The Tunisian government's efforts to expand usage of the Internet while consolidating its management and use foreshadowed its later struggles to maintain control over a network with growing civil and political importance. The tensions between the networked authority and the decentralized users would continue over the course of the next decade; with government movements toward consolidation met by vigilant, resilient, and increasingly technically sophisticated opposition. Initially organized as a counterforce against government encroachments on issues such as free speech and privacy, this opposition would ultimately appropriate the network itself for broader political resistance.

State Regulation and Ownership

Tunisia recognized the potential of the Internet as an economic and social development tool relatively early on; however it took some time before the ruling regime deliberately consolidated the network for its commercial and political ends. The first step in this process was the shifting of networking authority from IRSIT to ATI; the second part of the process was establishing legal frameworks that would guarantee government sovereignty over networks and obfuscate direct lines of accountability. The result was the creation of an Internet and telecommunications regulation framework that was often opaque, and at times intentionally byzantine.

At the time of ATI's creation in 1996, the cabinet-level Ministry of Communications was the primary authority for the planning, supervision, and regulation of the telecommunications industries in Tunisia. Through its General Directorate for Telecommunications, it managed the national regulatory and oversight functions for Internet, spectrum, broadcasting, digital certificates, and mobile communications; it was also responsible for attracting international investment and growing the domestic ICT sector. The Ministry also housed an office on open communications, headed by a Secretary for Internet, Computers, and Free Software, an office recognized and denounced by Internet activists as a government effort to co-opt the open source community.

In 1997, Tunisia signed an agreement with the WTO to reform its telecommunications sector (Kamoun 2010). Four years later, DL No. 2001-1 was passed, outlining the framework for a new telecommunications code. The Tunisian Telecommunications Code, or TTC, officially opened the sector to the private market, and authorized the creation of semi-independent national regulatory agencies, including the Instance Nationale des Telecommunications, or INT (Market Access Database 2002). However, the precise legal mandate of the INT was left undefined in the TTC, with the Ministry of Communications continuing to exercise significant budgetary and executive authority.

The clear allocation of responsibilities, as well as the organizational structure and relationships among national institutions, were often indistinct, even to government officials. Ministry staffers were often left in the dark about the precise rationale of policy decisions: senior officials were disinclined to provide justification, and civil servants were discouraged from inquiring. Competing and unclear mandates for oversight over the Internet (and mobile network operators) helped insure minimal accountability on the part of policymakers and the executive office, while enabling maximal governmental controls over resources, content, and use.

When the ATI issued a contract to the Ben Ali family-owned ISP Planet Tunisie as one of five providers of commercial Internet services, it was one among many instances of state contracts and network licensing granted to firms and operators owned or associated with allies of the ruling family. According to US State Department cables obtained by Wikileaks, the extent of corruption by the Tunisian ruling family was so pervasive that "whether it's cash, services, land, property, or yes, even your yacht, President Ben Ali's family is rumored to covet it and reportedly gets what it wants" (White 2011).

Following the 2001 TTC reforms, the state owned incumbent mobile network operator (MNO), Tunisie Telecom, was joined by Orascom Telecom Tunisie (d.b.a. as Tunisiana) in 2002, and Orange Tunisia in 2010. However, the reforms did not guarantee a more competitive marketplace: under Ben Ali, MNO licensing was described by bidders as uncompetitive (CWS 2012). Concessions were awarded to members of the extended ruling family; their stakes grew larger and their influence bolder over time.

Tunisiana, the country's largest telecom and second entrant to the market, was owned 25 percent by a holding company of Sakher El Materi, the son-in-law of Ben Ali. In 2002, Tunisiana was founded. In 2009, the country's third license was granted to Orange Tunisie; a joint venture between Orange France (49 percent) and Groupe Mabrouk (51 percent), the holding company of Marwan Mabrouk and Cyrine Ben Ali, daughter of the former president. Orange France has since been plagued by accusations that it paid bribes to acquire the operating license, paying less than full licensing fees to the state, and the remainder to Groupe Mabrouk. (Tesquet 2011) The Groupe Mabrouk majority stake has since been confiscated by the Tunisian government and is pending resale (Saigol 2011).

Tunisian State Controls on the Emergence of Censorship

As the Tunisian government promoted Internet connectivity, citizens went online, using the networks to find information and communicate. This early gradual adoption—going from .03 percent Internet penetration in 1996 at the time of ATI's creation to 5.25 percent by 2002 (ITU 2012)—coincided with the introduction of commercial online platforms for self-publishing. The launch of services such as Blogger and LiveJournal in 1999 enabled anyone with a computer and Internet access to share their thoughts with a global audience, and gave birth to the "blogopshere," an interconnected web of personal opinion and expression.

Much like the early Internet, these digital spaces had the allure of the unregulated: free of censorship and offering the appearance of anonymity. Tunisians took to blogging and other self-publishing forums to express dissidence on a broad range of sensitive cultural and political issues, countering official state narratives and offering a range of opinions rarely evident in the traditional press. As expression in these spaces grew increasingly critical of the Ben Ali regime, the government responded: Tunisia, the first Arab country to connect to the Internet also became the first to utilize the Internet for repression.

In 2002, security forces arrested the creator of a popular online forum and magazine, TUNeZINE. Zouhair Yahyaoui, then 33, had crossed Tunisia's unstated red lines, and subsequently arrested by security officers at the cybercafé he used to work at. Later charged and convicted of "intentionally publishing false information and using stolen communication lines," Yahyaoui served a reduced sentence of 24 months in prison, during which he was subjected to torture and kept in squalid conditions. He was released in 2003, but died two years later from complications related to his maltreatment while in detention (Watson-Boles 2004).

In its brief existence TUNeZINE became known for its bold treatment of Tunisian human rights issues, prompting the government to block access to the site within Tunisia. In censoring TUNeZINE, the government likely believed it would be able to deter future digital activism; however, TUNeZINE was soon joined by other dissident voices. In 2000, journalists Naziha Rejiba and Sihem Bensedrine launched the independent news site *Kalima* (kalima-tunisie.info). Like *TUNeZINE*, *Kalima* was quickly censored by the authorities; Rejiba found herself the target of sustained harassment, detention, and surveillance. In response, Rejiba and Bensedrine founded the Observatoire de la liberté de la presse de l'edition et de la création (OLPEC), a press freedom group, in 2001. OLPEC itself was quickly banned in Tunisia (CPJ 2009).

In 2004, another dissident blog launched, backed by technologists prepared to outfox and resist the official state censors. *Nawaat* was co-founded by Tunisian exiles, several of whom were to remain anonymous until after the ouster of Ben Ali. At the time of *Nawaat*'s launch, pseudonymous contributor "Astrubal" released a video that remixed the popular "1984" Apple Computer advertisement, replacing the advertisement's droning dictator with then-president Ben Ali (Zuckerman 2007). This innovative approach would set the stage for later interventions by Tunisian bloggers and activists, though *Nawaat* was soon blocked by government censors.

By 2005, online censorship of dissident opinion had become an established practice in Tunisia. That year, the World Summit on Information Society (WSIS) scheduled its meeting in Tunis, providing an opportunity to draw attention to the issue. At the time, the country had fewer than one million Internet users, but 2004 research by the independent OpenNet Initiative (ONI) found 72 "global" sites blocked out of 770 tested (ONI 2005). Censorship was concentrated in four main areas: "political opposition, criticism of the government's human rights record, methods of circumventing filtering, and pornography." ONI noted the blocking of 39 out of 110 "high-impact sites" containing topics known to be sensitive to the Tunisian government (2005); these sites included human rights information and political opposition.

Dissidence to Activism

Digital freedom advocates responded to the announcement that WSIS would be held in Tunisia with dismay. However, Tunisian activists—led by a group called the *Association Tunisienne pour la Promotion et la Défense du Cyberespace*—saw an opportunity to draw broader global attention to Ben Ali's stronghold on online information. They launched the *Yezzi Fock, Ben Ali* (*Enough is enough, Ben Ali*) and *Freedom of Expression in Mourning* campaigns, calling for virtual demonstrations and expressions of solidarity (ATPDC 2005). Though the campaigns were successful in raising awareness amongst WSIS participants, WSIS attendee and researcher Ethan Zuckerman (2005) later recounted meetings being interrupted by security forces, as well as local human rights activists being beaten by government thugs after meeting with summit attendees.

The success of the WSIS campaigns encouraged others to take similarly innovative approaches to digital activism. In 2006 and 2007, activist Sami Ben

Gharbia reported (2008) that Tunisian bloggers had organized "Blank Post Day," encouraging bloggers to publish an empty post in protest of censorship, and on July 1, 2008, bloggers around the country were encouraged to dedicate their blog posts to the topic of freedom of expression. A different 2007 campaign, created by *Nawaat* (Foreign Policy 2007) tracked the use of the Tunisian presidential plane for unofficial and unreported trips to European and Arab Gulf cities, presumably by the First Lady and her entourage.

By 2008, the Ben Ali government had established itself as willing to utilize all means to silence its online critics. In a report for *Global Voices Advocacy*, Sami Ben Gharbia (2008) wrote, "Blocking [websites] is the most obvious way of cracking down of the online free speech in Tunisia. It should be emphasized, however, that this is only one tool in the regime's hand. Tunisia has adapted to the web 2.0 revolution by developing a broader strategy [including the punishing and persecution of] outspoken online writers, bloggers and dissidents." According to Ben Gharbia's report (2008), more than 12 people were arrested and/or sentenced for a variety of crimes, from "visiting banned websites" to "violation of morality standards."

As Internet penetration grew, and use of circumvention tools spread among users, the Ben Ali government also sought to increase the sophistication of technological means of censorship. As Sami Ben Gharbia reported in 2010, this included the adoption of a four-pronged strategy that utilized DNS poisoning (redirecting a server request to a different destination); IP filtering (blocking access to sites based on the numerical address of the server or device, known as an IP address); keyword filtering (blocking access based on the presence of selected words in the requested content); anything not caught by these three methods was subject to selective blocking by URL. In addition, researcher Ben Wagner (2009) believed that it was likely "some forms of DPI technology for surveillance and filtering are currently in place," enabling the government access to most traffic transferred via standard web encryption protocols.

Between the time of the ONI's first report (2005) and its third (2009), Tunisian Internet usage increased dramatically, from 9.66 percent of the population in 2005 to a staggering 34.1 percent in 2009 (ITU 2012). So too did online censorship: it encompassed social networking and video-sharing websites; the sites of human rights organizations including Amnesty International, Freedom House, and Reporters Without Borders; a wealth of political opposition websites; and anonymizer and proxy tools used to bypass censorship (ONI 2009).

Users attempting to visit blocked websites were never informed explicitly that the site they were seeking had been censored; instead, queries returned a fake result for an HTTP 404 error. The misleading result, indicating a problem with the website rather than blocked content, was likely intended to provide plausible deniability about the extent of the government's expanding censorship apparatus. This clumsy effort earned the censorship apparatus its own identity—personified by the nickname "Ammar404."

Despite protest by activists against Ammar404, once a site was added to the "block list," it rarely was unlisted. However, in August 2008, government censors appeared to cross a line too far, blocking the immensely popular Facebook. Facebook had become increasingly popular with activists, who were using the platform's "Groups" feature to organize anti-government events. But the government had overreached, underestimating the popularity of the platform with ordinary users. Infuriated Tunisians took to the streets, and the censors relented, restoring access to the site.

In 2010, the government dramatically increased its efforts to stifle online discourse, blocking individual activist Twitter accounts and instituting a widespread ban on most social networking sites. By April of 2010 (Gharbia 2010), nearly every major video-sharing service was blocked, and the response time of censors to new websites had fallen to fewer than 24 hours. In July 2010 the ATI blocked the operating ports for the secure transmission protocol HTTPS, pushing Tunisian communications onto unencrypted plaintext channels. In certain cases, users attempting to login to Gmail, Yahoo, or Facebook were redirected to spoofed login pages, used to capture individual username and password details (Amamou 2010).

The increasingly heavy-handed and indiscriminate application of these techniques reached Tunisians far beyond a dedicated cadre of activists, stirring an ordinarily disinterested public. In response, a group of Tunisian activists launched a new campaign under the slogan *Sayeb Sala7*. On blogs and social networks, Tunisians protested "Sayeb Sala7, ya Ammar," local slang imploring the "Ammar404" censors to "let it go," or ease up on censorship. The message spread quickly, reaching beyond a traditional activist audience. On May 22, 2010, Tunisians organized "#manif22mai" protests against censorship in Tunis, Paris, and other centers of the Tunisian diaspora (Ben Gharbia 2010b).

Though the May 22 protests were large enough to force coverage by the local media, the government tried to prevent them from ever happening. According to blogger Nasser Weddady (2010), several of the organizing activists were arrested by internal security on May 21, a day before the protests. They were forced to record a video calling off the May 22 protest, and sign a document testifying their understanding that "calling for a demonstration is wrong." To mitigate the effects of the video (Gharbia 2010b), friends of the detained activists signed a communiqué calling for a "Plan B": a march down the main boulevard of Tunis, dressed in white, followed by a temporary occupation of the avenue's many cafés: a symbolic act protesting censorship.

The Internet in Revolution

By late 2010, efforts by the state to stifle communications had given rise to an established and experienced online activist community. When Mohamed Bouazizi self-immolation in the town of Sidi Bouzid sparked protests across Tunisia in

December of 2010, the online activist community had the networks, skills, and agility to respond. As ordinary Tunisians shared videos and images of quickly spreading protests, the online community was critical to sharing and confirming information. International media outlets like *Al Jazeera*, long-banned from Tunisia, used these networks to source first-hand reports of unrest and state response (Morozov 2011). With an estimated 36.6 percent of the Tunisian population online (World Bank 2010) social media became the primary tool for circumventing official state narratives.

The rapid spread of these stories and images was facilitated by market forces: only one year previously the country's largest mobile network operator, Tunisiana, with roughly 70 percent market share and quarter-owned by the extended ruling family, had introduced data packages that enabled Tunisians to access Facebook for very low rates. This data package drove adoption of smart phones and the social network itself, offering channels for simple one-to-many sharing of updates, video, and images. Facebook's ability to share rich-media was of particular importance, given Tunisia's blocking of video- and image-sharing platforms.

As inflammatory images of protests and state violence spread the government responded aggressively. Utilizing techniques such as phishing, spoofing, and brute-force hacking, it worked to obtain user login credentials to social networks, infiltrate activist communications networks, and freeze user social media accounts. According to a report by the Committee to Protect Journalists (O'Brien 2011), Tunisian authorities "[modified] web pages on the fly to steal usernames and passwords for sites such as Facebook, Google and Yahoo." Tunisians logging into those sites would find their login credentials stolen and used by unknown parties which, in some cases, deleted the stolen Facebook accounts and affiliated groups and pages.

Furthermore, nominally "independent" ISPs were reported to throttle consumer bandwidth and instituted caps on large file transfers (Reinhard 2010). Users across the country reported unconfirmed outages of mobile network and data service in areas near protests, though it is possible that outages may have been the result of network load failures rather than deliberate service shutdowns.

As demonstrations multiplied and conflict between citizens and the regime escalated, bloggers inside and outside of Tunisia were harassed and detained. Two weeks into the protests, prominent blogger and government critic Slim Amamou was detained at the Ministry of the Interior. Others, including the well-known citizen journalists Lina Ben Mhenni and Sofiane Chourabi, found their email and Facebook accounts hacked, while exile activist and regime abuse cataloguer Sami Ben Gharbia documented and published intrusions into his personal webmail account (Maher 2011).

As the battle escalated online, Tunisians found themselves beneficiaries of foreign attention from sympathetic "hacktivists," including the distributed global movement known as "Anonymous" (Ragan 2011). The majority of efforts were of limited technical sophistication; including distributed denial of service (DDOS) attacks aimed at Tunisian government websites from "Low Orbit Ion Cannon"

(LOIC), an Anonymous botnet. However, the collective also ran a campaign encouraging Internet users to set up relays and bridges of the Tor anonymization network for use by Tunisians, and offered Tunisians struggling with malicious script injections on their email and social network accounts help with instructions on overriding forced-login phishing attacks (Maher 2011).

Despite the use of aggressive tactics by the Tunisian government, attempts to disrupt information networks were largely ineffectual, and diminished in relevance as protest momentum grew offline. Efforts to target individual users proved insufficient as discontent spread beyond traditional activist communities, and targeted interventions were unable to sufficiently scale to all Tunisian Internet users. Unlike the Egyptian and Libyan governments in their subsequent popular uprisings, the Tunisian government never resorted to whole-scale network shutdown, perhaps fearing the potential damages to the economy or underestimating the severity of the unrest it faced.

Protests continued to multiply in force and intensity across Tunisia. On January 13, 2011, following unprecedented crowds on the main boulevard of downtown Tunis, President Ben Ali appeared on television for a third time, in what would become his final speech to the nation. In the seven-minute speech, the dictator promised "full freedom for all means of information, no more blocking of the Internet, and rejection of all forms of censorship while respecting our ethics and the principles of the journalistic profession." Within hours of Ben Ali's appearance, Tunisians reported most known blockages to have been lifted. The following day Ben Ali and his family fled the country for Saudi Arabia, ending the president's 23-year rule.

Dismantling the Digital Deep State

Following Ben Ali's abrupt flight from the country, Tunisians waited for the country's censors to similarly abandon post. Within hours, an easing of censorship was reported (Wagner 2012); one week later, on January 22, the Secretariat of State for Information Technologies released a statement asserting the restoration of full, unfiltered access, with the exception of sites "with indecent content, comprising violent elements or inciting hatred." Although the statement gave little definition of the exceptions, it marked the beginning of the end of censorship in Tunisia.

When Ben Ali fled Tunisia for Saudi Arabia, Kamel Saadaoui was in his third year as director of the ATI. Saadaoui was among the original IRSIT engineers who had remained with the government following the establishment of ATI and was familiar with the operations of the regime. He soon granted interviews with the Western press, such as *Wired* magazine, providing insight into the details of the country's censorship and surveillance apparatus (Elkin 2011). Shortly after the revolution, Saadaoui was made head of the INT, and was replaced at the ATI by Dr Moez Chakchouk, a former ministerial advisor in the Ministry of Communications Technologies.

While Saadaoui oversaw the suspension of Tunisia's filtering regime, it was under Chakchouk's leadership that the ATI began the process of dismantling the structures of censorship and surveillance. As Chakchouk reported (Abrougui 2011b), one of the first actions of the ATI post-revolution was to cancel contracts with Western surveillance technology suppliers. The systems of control were revealed to be so extensive that Chakchouk quipped to *Wall Street Journal* reporter Paul Sonne (2011) that a group of visiting security researchers had suggested to him that "[the] Chinese could come here and learn from you."

The details of these contracts, including the identities of specific providers of software, hardware, and support services, remain unknown due to contractual confidentiality stipulations. Research by the OpenNet Initiative (2011) identified SmartFilter, from US-based MacAfee as in use in Tunisia since 2002, an assertion Chakchouk later confirmed (Ryan 2011). *Bloomberg News* (Silver 2011) identified Tunisia's mobile phone interception and logging systems to have been provided by ETI A/S, a Danish firm now wholly owned by UK-based BAE Systems, and Trovicor GmbH, a German firm recently divested from Nokia Siemens Networks. Utimaco Safeware AG, a subsidiary of UK-based cybersecurity firm Sophos, provided further support systems. All of these firms have deferred questions or denied direct sales arrangements with the Tunisian government.

Former ATI head Saadaoui further acknowledged that the Tunisian government was known to procure vendor services from corporations represented at the ISS World conference, more commonly known as the "Wiretappers Ball," an infamous trade show for surveillance frequented by intelligence and national security agencies from around the globe (Silver 2011). In October 2011, Chakchouk revealed that companies offered Tunisian authorities significantly discounted prices in exchange for software testing and bug-tracking, asserting that "the Internet Agency has extracted itself from these partnerships and thus can no longer afford to censor, even if they wished to" (Messieh 2011).

According to Saadaoui, Internet traffic under the Ben Ali regime was routed through surveillance equipment maintained and operated by ATI, monitored by the INT, and evaluated for content by the Ministry of the Interior. Under ATI's oversight, the surveillance equipment and software was (and allegedly remains) physically hosted in three separate Tunis-area facilities of the state telecommunications carrier, Tunisie Telecom. Monitoring reportedly occurred separately in a closed facility, operated by the INT, in which staffers would review traffic and forward "suspect" communications to the Ministry of the Interior for further investigation (Silver 2011).

Saadaoui also confirmed the capacity of the three Tunisian mobile network operators for monitoring mobile traffic, including voice and data. Traffic was reportedly monitored by specialized teams at undisclosed sites within the Ministry of the Interior, with additional capacity at the presidential palace complex (Silver 2011). While "lawful interception" systems for mobile traffic are a common feature of mobile networks worldwide, there is no evidence that the use of interception technology under the Ben Ali regime was subject to due process, placing such surveillance in the realm of "mass interception."

Since the revolution, Chakchouk has claimed that ATI was only the technical executor for censorship and surveillance, and that the agency did not play a role in deciding what content to filter or which citizens to monitor (Ryan 2011). Chakchouk stated that orders would have likely come from the ministries or the presidential palace and that, following the revolution, ATI did not have records of these instructions. While acknowledging its role in implementing censoring and filtration, the ATI has further denied its involvement in surveillance of Tunisian citizens, and stated that it has no access to any surveillance files. Bloggers have given some credence to this narrative, placing blame with unknown "cyberpolice"; however no records of this function have been made public (Ryan 2011).

In the period since the fall of the Ben Ali regime, there is little confirmed information about the continued use of surveillance. It is widely assumed by Tunisian activists and Internet observers alike that the Tunisian government maintains surveillance capacity and continues to use it at will (Silver 2011). The new government has not made public statements about the role of surveillance, nor is there publicly available information about the use of surveillance on mobile networks, whether by government or compliant mobile network operators. ATI has stated that although it continues to host Tunisia's known surveillance equipment, it no longer plays an active role in mass surveillance (Ryan 2011).

Testing the Limits of Openness

Although the Tunisian Internet is more open and free than at any point since its introduction in 1999, these gains remain fragile. Operating conditions in late 2012 are the result of a patchwork of elective and unofficial policies instituted and maintained by key leadership in select institutions, many drawn from the former ranks of IRSIT. Among Tunisian citizens, no coherent norms have emerged; while there are many vocal proponents of the open Internet, many others continue to call for the blocking of "offensive," "harmful," or "insulting" content.

The first test of the Tunisian Internet's openness occurred in May 2011, four months after the revolution, when the Ministry of National Defense received an order from the Magistrate of the Permanent Military Tribunal ordering the ATI to block five Facebook pages accused of insulting the military and promoting violence (Abrougui 2011). On its official website, the Ministry of National Defense stated, "some citizens have deliberately created personal pages on the World Wide Web in an attempt to damage the reputation of the military institution and its leaders by the publishing of video clips, the circulation of comments, and articles that aim to destabilize the trust of citizens in the national army and spread disorder in the country."

ATI resumed filtering, and those attempting to access the pages over an unencrypted Facebook session received the following message: "Cette page web a *été* filtrée en application d'une réquisition *émanant* du Juge d'instruction auprès du Tribunal Militaire Permanent de Tunis." ("This webpage is filtered under requisition from the Judge for the Permanent Military Tribunal of Tunis.") In parallel ATI launched filtrage.ati.tn, listing all blocked sites with the official or legal justification for their censorship. Despite this attempt at transparency on the part of ATI, Internet activists condemned the resumption of filtering, noting with concern the application of censorship without due judicial process. A short time later, the ATI quietly discontinued filtering these five sites, claiming insufficient capacity (Abrougui 2011b).

On May 19, 2011, three lawyers lodged a complaint against the ATI, seeking the institution of a ban on pornographic websites. Citing negative 'psychological, physiological, social, and educational effects' on children and Muslim society, they secured a court order directing ATI to resume filtration of pornographic sites (Al Arabiya 2011). On 26 May 2011, in Case No. 2011/99325, the presiding judge of the Court of Appeals of Tunis issued an execution order for ATI to resume filtration on the basis of the plaintiffs' arguments. ATI submitted a petition to the Court of Appeal of Tunis, citing technical incapability due to diminished capacity.

On June 13, 2011, the presiding judge denied the ATI's request for a stay of the order, and on June 14, the agency resumed filtration of "offensive content," but limited filtering to national ISPs for government agencies, military, and universities. On August 15, following a series of hearings, the appellate court judge found in favor of the 26 May decision against ATI. As a final effort, ATI announced its intent to appeal the case at the Court of Cassation, Tunisia's highest court. Following a series of deferred decisions, the Court of Cassation found in favor of ATI, returning the case to the Tunis appellate court for reconsideration. At time of publication, the case had not been decided.

Since the fall of the Ben Ali regime, the interim government of Tunisia has passed a series of laws intended to reform the country's restrictive press and media laws. Notably, none of the relevant new legislation (DL Nos 2011-10/41/115/116) explicitly address digital communications, whether Internet or mobile. Areas that remain unclear include what protections are afforded to bloggers and citizen journalists, the creation of a framework for digital publishing liability (intermediary or otherwise), mobile and Internet subscriber data privacy, minimum legal standards for government requests to service providers for subscriber data, and provisions for lawful interception.

On November 2, 2011, the Constituent Assembly passed DL Nos 2011-115/116 regarding media and the press. This legislation represented long-overdue reforms of the 1975 Press Code (updated in 2006), which contained key articles prohibiting the press from publishing government legal documents, publishing "false news," or publishing content deemed to be in breach of "public order." These articles, along with a 1997 presidential decree granting the Ministry of Communications the authority to monitor for "compliance" and establishing harsh punishments for visiting "dangerous" websites, were often used to justify crackdowns on bloggers.

However, the legislation did not explicitly define its scope in relation to the Internet, raising concerns among digital activists.

On September 6, 2012, at the annual meeting of the Freedom Online Coalition—a conference of governments committed to Internet freedom as a matter of policy—Dr Moez Chakchouk announced that Tunisia would join as the first Middle Eastern country in the coalition. This announcement marked the first official shift in Tunisian government policy; in the year and a half since the revolution, Tunisia had not seen any introduction of new legislation, revised regulatory statute, or judicial precedent that would institutionalize Internet freedom as a matter of national law and practice. However, despite these changes, many Internet activists in Tunisia remain skeptical, believing past monitoring practices remain in practice (Samti 2011).

The protests that began in December 2010 and culminated with the January 14, 2011 ouster of President Zine El Abidine Ben Ali revealed the prevalence and sophistication of state systems of control over Tunisia's communications infrastructure. The oversight of the Internet by the Ministry of Communications Technologies was literal, and the ATI, keeper of the country's Internet backbone, was among the most loathed, feared, and corrupt government institutions. With technical support from the West, Tunisia blocked great swaths of the Internet and spied on its citizens. The Tunisian Internet, born at the hands of the country's elite engineers and promoted throughout the country as a tool for economic empowerment, became a battleground between activists seeking greater freedoms and their government oppressors.

If the actions of the state to control and dictate the content of the Tunisian Internet were an effort to assert network-making power—the ability to program the network for its assigned goals—then the emergence of a coordinated and resilient cadre of Tunisian online activists was the ultimate assertion of active reprogramming of that goal, or counterpower. As activists responded to the Tunisian government's imposition of filtration and coercive social controls on the Internet by eroding and circumventing those controls, they subverted the network for an altogether different purpose. The efforts of the Tunisian state to forcefully narrow the purpose of the network to a tool for economic growth and personal enrichment was met by a response that sought to reinforce the network as a tool for countering regime hegemony.

Chapter 2

The State of Digital Exception: Censorship and Dissent in Post-Revolutionary Iran

Babak Rahimi

Integral to authoritarian regimes is the multifaceted employments of various measures to manage, control and reshape the public sphere, as spaces of association identified with contentious activities. Inclusive of these measures are the regulative mode of performances to limit contention, including expressions and interactions of civic associations in the public deemed subversive by the state, and also proactive modes of performance that set frames of action for limited dissent to be freely expressed only within the defined frames parameters of discourse or practices sanctioned by the state. The second type of measures characterize deliberative practices that direct discussions or debates and construct new public forums that set defined frames for public discourse that ultimately stabilize authoritarian rule. Known as "authoritarian deliberation," such measures, at times subtle and indirect, are popular among states such as China where there is a strong claim for populism of revolutionary brand as a way to legitimize state power (He 2006; Perry 2007). Yet behind the façade of popular sovereignty associated with democracy is an authoritarian structure that governs through a complex regulative and surveillance regime.

There are also exceptional cases in the delicate balance between regulative and proactive measures that requires other, extraordinary measures for control. How can order and legitimacy be preserved at sensitive moments when the state maintains the least control over its population or its territories? Carl Schmitt, the German political theorist and the ideologue of the Nazi state, described the use of alternative measures in the legal terms of "state of exception," as the moment when the sovereign authority can decide when to transcend the legal boundaries to reconstitute order in the name of common good. Violence in its extra-juridical, unregulated form can enable a sovereign to suspend all laws in order to ultimately restore them (Schmitt 1985, 13).[1] But more important than the power to decide is

1 The suspension of law does not mean a state of lawlessness, but a special claim to legal authority by the state. Schmitt explains "What characterizes an exception is principally unlimited authority, which means the suspension of the entire existing order. In such a situation it is clear that the state remains, whereas law recedes. Because the exception is different from anarchy and chaos, order in the juristic sense still prevails even if it is not of the ordinary kind" (Schmitt 1985, 13).

the moment of suspension when the state with the claim over organized violence can exert authority with extraordinary force. Networks of communication serve as powerful sources of organization and mobilization for both state and non-state actors, and historically during critical times various media outlets have been entirely shutoff as a way to restore power back to the state.[2] Now there is a tantalizing puzzle here and that is when and why states, in particular modern authoritarian types that increasingly depend on information communication technologies, disconnect digital communication. And do such operations in what can be called states of digital exception strengthen state power?

This chapter investigates the Iranian state's patterns of media censorship, in particular the exercise of specific measures of blocking Internet access and disabling digital networks. As a case study, it examines the 2009 post-election unrest in Iran and studies specific incidents when and why the government interfered to disable digital network, particularly the Internet, satellite and phone networks. It also examines the shared perceptions of activists who used digital media and online social networking for mobilizing street protests in the weeks following the June 12, 2009 elections. The main argument here is that the Iranian state preemptively and selectively disabled a range of significant interactive means of communication (e.g. online social media) and land-base and mobile technologies on the day and, sporadically on the day of protests, weeks after the elections. This was done as a means to prevent the activists of dissident actors, particularly the bridge-makers or digitally savvy activists (mainly students and civil society activists), who heavily relied on digital network connectivity for offline mobilization during and after the elections. Amid the shutting off operations, there were also a number of selective surveillance digital operations that enabled the intelligence services to identify protesters and monitor information online.

The 2009 election protests represent one of the most wired of all political events in the history of the Islamic Republic. With the Iranian security apparatus fully aware of state-led communication infrastructural developments, together with demographic and urban transformations, since early 2000s, the preemptive move to shut off the flow of information on the day of elections, and the days that followed, involved the direct involvement of the intelligence units of the Iranian Revolutionary Guard Corps (IRGC) and other security agencies to interrupt a range of social media communication, excluding national information such as radio broadcast and TV. But the temporal and selective patterns of intervention were only based on a short-term tactical move, as the street protests were unfolding amid crackdowns on street protesters. As the social media lines, including mobile

2 Such practices are not exclusive to authoritarian states, as democracies too employ shutdown measures, as in the cases of British government contemplating shutting off mobile services during the summer 2011 riots. The case of the Patriot Act under the Bush administration also carried the potential for disabling the flow of information in case of an act of terrorism. For the case of democracies shutdown of digital networks, see Howard and Hussain 2013.

texting, came back to operation in the weeks after the June elections, the long-term strategic was aimed as a way to gather, share and circulate information about the protesters and offline centers of dissident activities. The combined use of measures from hard (i.e. shutting down information technologies) to soft (i.e. surveillance practices) highlights the capacity of the Iranian state that is increasingly dependent on information technologies to consolidate control over the social media sphere. Even with the implementation of various regulative and proactive measures, including the capacity to disable Internet access and digital networks, the Islamic Republic faces major challenges with the expansion of social media networks as a socio-cultural phenomenon of irreversible trajectory.

Evolution of Iran's Digital Censorship Regime

The 1979 revolution that brought to power the first theocracy in modern times marked a utopian project with immense social and political consequences. The Islamist imaginary of the Shia brand saw the Islamic Republic, based on the ideology of *Velayat-e Faqih* (Guardianship of the Jurist), as a radical expression of an Iranian political modernity that would fuse religion and a modern polity with nativist ideals of autonomy and freedom from Western dependency, in particular scientific knowledge and technological advancement. Iran's military conflict with Iraq during the 1980s prevented the coherent institutionalization of such (Shia) Islamist utopian project. The emerging factional politics of the early revolutionary period, largely a result of the "hybrid" democratic and authoritarian institutions of the state, also marked a period of political instability. Nevertheless, the developmentalist policies of the Pahlavi regime continued to expand along with the growth of the cities and industrialization and spread of educational institutions in the provinces, entailing a significant social transformation in the postwar period (Ehsani 2009).

With the reconstruction (*baz-sazi*) and construction policy (*jihad sazandegi*) phase under the presidency of Hashemi Rafsanjani (1989–1997), new state-building patterns and institution buildings emerged with an emphasis on empowering the middle class in developments of education, consumerism and strengthening of the urban policy. Certain social restrictions were relaxed, in comparison to the war period, as the government and the growing private sector heavily invested in the higher education, giving rise to Islamic Open universities which opened up new opportunities to a growing young generation as a result of changing demography. The training of a new technocratic and scientific community emerged during this period, as new technological advancements in industrial, medical and especially computer sciences began to change the way government would manage the post-revolutionary Iranian society. The manufacturing and research with computer technology, as the most important symbol of scientific modernity, had already been in use at highly specialized institutions such as the College of Computer Programming and Application and Institute for Research in

Communications in the early half of the 1980s (Mohammadifar 1992). However, the marketization of computer technology was initiated under the auspices of the Rafsanjani administration, as the first Persian-text software was developed in 1991 (Mohammadifar 1992). Along with Israel and Turkey, Iran was one of the earliest countries to incorporate computer technology into its developing economy.

The combined privatization of universities, together with the demand for advanced technologies and scientific studies, in particular computer-mediated research, matched the structural transformation of the Iranian economy. Rafsanjani's economic policies had wide-ranging consequences that included domestic growth of the private sector and significant urban developments, along with the devolution of administrative centers to the provinces (Ehsani 1999). The liberalization policy in particular generated greater demands for the global market and the strengthening of consumerist culture, which defined the decade prior to the 1979 revolution. In correlation with the rise of consumerist society, by the 1990s an emerging market for digital technology ushered a new age of information communication in Iran, as it did in the United States and Europe.

The Internet first appeared within the higher educational sphere in the postwar period. Between 1992 and 1993, Iran's first Internet connection was initiated by the Institute for Studies in Theoretical Physics and Mathematics and later in the expanded in the educational and business centers (Farivar 2012; Rahimi 2008). By the early 1990s other ICTs like facsimile and mobile technologies also made their way into the Iranian domestic market, albeit some were deemed as potentially dangerous by the state. Satellite TV in particular was the most problematic in this expanding digital environment. Like the underground market of VCR cassettes in the 1980s, satellite presented a new challenge to the regime, as a stream of oppositional channels aired from outside of the country (Khosravi 2008). Satellite was first banned in 1995 just four years after satellite dishes began to appear on the rooftops of northern Tehran. But the ban did not inhibit the popularity of emerging communication technologies like mobile phones, which served as both a useful means of everyday communication, especially text messaging, and a symbol of social status for a youth culture that increasingly demanded participation in the consumerist global market. By the late 1990s the rise in the number of mobile users, similar to Internet, had dramatically increased to millions (Sreberny and Khiabany 2010).

The economic and social transformations of the Rafsanjani period however entailed a political side as well. With the government relaxing social spaces, new critical political discourses emerged from the growing Iranian middle-class with daring demands for reforms. The presidential election of 1997 that marked the victory of the reformist cleric, Mohammad Khatami, was a result of cross-section of civic associations, activists, students and workers who sought to overturn the overwhelming influence of the conservative leadership. With the reformist victory, post-revolutionary Iran saw the production of alternative newspapers, books and video recordings of dissident intellectuals and reformists who bolstered an unofficial public sphere, one that was not sanctioned by the state nevertheless operative as a dissident digital public. With new communication technologies rapidly entrenched in everyday life of younger Iranians, the new activists also began to use Internet and other digital technologies to express views that would be normally prohibited in the face-to-face public life.

In reaction to suppression of the print media by the conservative faction based in the judiciary and security forces, political reform entered a new stage of opposition in that it increasingly took refuge in new media outlets as a way to circumvent censorship. Internet became the most popular forum of communication, as a way to express critical views or make accountable state activities in its previous treatments of opposition and management of economic and social change. Online news sites provided the first instances of a post-print media culture that circumvented print media restrictions imposed by the judiciary.

The state reaction to regulate the new technology was gradual and not necessarily effective—and also marked with key learning moments. Four stages may be underlined in the case of Internet. The first stage, from 1999 to 2004–5, focused on regulative practices such as blocking, filtering and Internet service governance that targeted Internet Service Providers as a way to outsource control over content and interaction online (Gheytanchi and Rahimi 2008; Rahimi 2008; Sreberny and Khiabany 2010). In what Guobin Yang calls the "mediaziation of the Internet" many regulative practices that were implemented over the Internet revolved around previous laws applied to mass media (Yang 2009).[3] This could be perhaps explained in light of the state's initial inability to define the Internet, as it first began to be used in the educational sphere, and hence perceived as "scientific," rather than the media domain with potential political implications. Since the early reformist period under Khatami's presidency, Iranian Internet users have experienced several mediaziation initiatives. The most important one was the comprehensive set of decrees ratified by the Supreme Council of the Cultural Revolution (SCRC) in 2001 that imposed a more centralized system of regulative frameworks through the employment of filter systems by the ISPs (Deibert, Palfrey, Rohozinski and Zittrain 2010). The implementation of other regulative measures also involved the 2006 reduction of Internet speed to 128 kilobits per second as a reaction to the emerging social media sites that enabled users to download and forward photos and videos online.

The second stage, from 2004/5 to 2008, identified the digitization of governance and rise of e-commerce in the Iranian economy. Electronic governance identifies the first instances of proactive measures to promote and legitimize the state through effective governance and shape the online landscape with its presence. By mid-2005 Iranian e-governance became widespread involving the creation of new public-administrative provisions that ranges from embassy, library to passport and tourist services (Beygijanian and Richardson 2008). E-commerce too, in particular

3 The Press Law of 1986 served as the principle legal source for the early regulation of the Internet, followed by the 2000 amendment to the Press Law, a reaction to the growing dissident activism in the print media.

in the banking sector, has served as a way to both provide financial efficiency and also legitimacy for the state, seeking to keep pace with the burgeoning public sector and the consumerist society in the late Khatami period.

The third and fourth stages, from 2008/9 to present, coincide with the growing clout of the Iranian Revolutionary Guard Corps (IRGC) over the political sphere and the security apparatus of the state, which began with the conservative consolidation over the legislative and executive office between 2004 and 2005. The 51 percent takeover of the Telecommunication Company of Iran by Mobin, an IRGC-dominated private company, and the establishment of "Cyber-crimes" units in 2009, set the stage for a new regulative framework. Toward the end of Mahmoud Ahmadinejad's first term in 2008 and with the 2009 elections and the social upheaval that erupted in reaction to the allegedly rigged elections, the Islamic Republic underwent in what Farideh Farhi has called a "securitization" phase, an elevated security-conscious system of governance with the aim of establishing a complex network of surveillance and intelligence-gathering for control over the public sphere (Farhi 2010). IRGC, responsible for national security and the ideals of the revolution, has been the leading state organ, using various surveillance technologies for identifying dissidents on the Internet and mobile phone. As I have argued elsewhere, securitization however should be viewed as an aspect of a new kind of militarization dynamic within the regime apparatus, which heavily relies on a network of intelligence and informational sharing with an emphasis on "soft power" to tackle various threats, especially domestic ones (Rahimi 2012).

The rhetoric of "soft war" emerged just months after the June 2009 elections and its focus was to create new cultural and public institutions that would implement diverse disruptive, coordinated and co-optive efforts through, in words of Price, "information-related measures" to undermine the foreign-directed media initiatives and seek to disintegrate the "value" system of the country, the moral order, from within. (Adelkhah 2010; Price 2012; Akhavan 2014). The strategy of soft war aimed to reframe the regulative media policies into an aggressive "psychological operation" and, in terms of new cultural practices, promote perception of soft revolution from the outside and the need to safeguard the native culture through creative media practices. Reflecting the multifaceted media environment in the post-election era, Iran's digital-control regime showed how it can change with the political situation. In light of new securitized measures, the discourse of soft war emerged as the most intriguing deliberative strategy to stifle dissent in the emerging communication media such as mobile and Internet, where the state continues to have difficulty maintaining full control, in contrast to broadcast media such as radio or the national TV.

Finally, the launch of the "Fifth Five Development Plan of the Islamic Republic of Iran (2010–2015)" marks the fourth stage in the regulative process over cyberspace. The creation of a "national information network" with the official aim of promoting e-governance and increase in productivity in economic and cultural programs primarily serves as a security strategy to form a closed network and isolate Iran's Internet users from the global Internet sphere (Anderson

2012). Such closed national computer network should be viewed in light of the increasing securitization of the Islamic Republic to protect online governance from hackactivism and establish a more effective online surveillance regime. Yet the creation of a closed national Net could also reflects the need to maintain a stable Internet service for government and business sector when the state decides to shutdown the regular Internet that is connected to the world, as a way to implement greater control over cyberspace, especially in the way it could shape street protests.

The Shutdown under a Crisis State

The June 2009 elections changed the Islamic Republic into what Howard has called a "crisis state"—a destabilizing political experience of transition or turmoil caused by internal or external conflict (Ansari 2010; Howard 2010: 74). Though certainly not Iraq or Somalia, the election chaos caused by a popular perception of malpractice over the voting results that favored the incumbent president, Ahmadinejad, pushed the theocratic regime closer to the edge of a major crisis of political legitimacy with the breakdown of governance over civic life and state management over the public sphere. The Iranian Green movement, a socio-political opposition current described as a "civil rights" movement by Hamid Dabashi compromises a new generation of activists who integrated new communication technologies in their contentious activities (Dabashi 2010). While the Internet, in particular popular sites like Facebook, Balatarin, a popular Persian-language social site, and Twitter, together with mobile phone, were already in use during the election campaign season, the new media served as a distinguishing aspect of the post-election street protesters, as the activists recorded, circulated, spread and aesthetically exposed state corruption, deception, brutality and by and large the authoritarian character of the regime in digital space (Gheytanchi 2010; Rahimi 2011). For nearly two months after the elections, the streets of Tehran and other major Iranian cities were in a state of strife, bringing the state to apply a combined set of hard and soft measures to stifle growing dissent with the blessing of the Supreme Leader, Ayatollah Khamenei, who had publically supported Ahmadinejad during the elections and later ordered the arrest of Mir-Hussain Mousavi and Mehdi Karoubi, the two opposing candidates.

Despite warnings of a "Velvet Revolution" of eastern European style by the IRGC weeks prior to the elections (Peterson 2010), the regime's security apparatus were taken off-guard by the sheer size of the crowd and, more importantly, the new tactics used by the activists. Footages of the street demonstrations and scenes of security forces brutality against the unarmed demonstrators first appeared on social media sites, and eventually (and rather quickly) found their way to satellite TV news channels like Al-Jazeera and CNN International. They served as a major threat to the official image that the state wanted to portray about the elections, as a popular and the most uncontested aspect of Iranian political life. BBC Persia, launched on January 2009, played a critical role in bringing "i-reports," produced by the activists on the ground, from the streets back to Iranian homes, as millions watched the protests unfold after the elections through non-state televised media. When Neda Agha Soltan was killed on June 20, the video footage was first posted on Facebook, then immediately posted on YouTube and in hours picked up by Al-Jazeera and CNN International (Rahimi 2011b).

In light of major transformations over censoring and the policing regime, designed over the years since 2001, various security agencies within different branches of government led by IRGC engaged in a combination of measures to push back dissident activities in the digital domain. The most obvious to the pro-Mousavi supporters was the outage of mobile services, in particular text messaging services, and the Internet hours before the day of elections, June 12, which continued to the morning (Enayat, Smith, Wojcieszk 2012; Mackinnon 2012).[4] On the day of elections Internet access was so slow that it made it almost impossible to check or send email. In the weeks following the elections, during the days when Mousavi would call out his supporters to storm the streets to demonstrate, Yahoo messenger and other chat-room like services would be shutdown, while regular online news sites, permitted by the state, would be available.[5] Facebook, though unblocked in February of that year, was blocked from the day of elections onwards. Landlines were operational, but mobile services were severely limited during day times and late into the night, when the assumption was that next day organizations by activists would take place. At night, especially during the crucial hours when protesters chant anti-government slogans on rooftops, most Internet services would be either shutdown or considerably slowed down. During the critical days of protests, major satellite channels, in particular BBC, CNN International and VOA Persian, would experience electronic signal jamming. During the critical days of protests, major satellite channels, in particular BBC, CNN International and VOA Persian, would experience electronic signal jamming. This was the case when there would be a report on the Iranian turmoil. In many ways, the jamming practice was selective and hardly comprehensive in scope, as number of state-funded channels like Press TV and Al-Alam are also aired on satellite TV.

Along with physical attacks on Mousavi campaign offices, other measures were also used (Yahyanejad and Gheytanchi 2012). Based on field observations, and as Howard has noted, later in the afternoon on the day of elections, as reports of protests in central Tehran began to emerge, Internet access was completely disabled for nearly an hour by the Data Communication to begin the process of "deep packet" inspection system, which pushed off Iran from the global communication channels for nearly a day (Howard 2010: 6). The surveillance regime was mostly

4 The shut off was not however comprehensive as universities and many businesses continued to have access to service. Also, mobile services were down mostly around specific geographical areas where Karoubi and Mousavi's campaign centers had a major concentration.

5 Field work observation, Tehran, Iran June, 2009.

effective over mobile communication, as reports of arrest bespeak of prisoners describing transcribe copies of their conversations over the cell. The surveillance of Facebook activism is also noteworthy, as the social networking site saw a rise of Iranian users in the pre-election period. The most creative measure was the propaganda mechanism of overtly guiding the direction of debate by spreading rumors and conspiratorial theories in favor of the government helped slow down the momentum of the movement (Rahimi 2011a). In what can be called the camouflaging tactic, members of IRGC, which also include the Basij, while pretending to be Mousavi supporters, would engage with social media sites to change the directions of street protests, relying on the decentralized organizational aspect of the new media to inject rumors or new discourses, sometimes of highly violent nature in order to confuse the discussions or norms of actions over how best to tackle brutality by the security forces.

This last feature also brought to full view a new measure already in use by the Chinese state. The 2008 call by the IRGC to recruit Basiji militias to populate the blogosphere resembles the Chinese "Internet commentators," as an online community on the government's pay role and first used in 2004 (Sreberny and Khiabany 2010; Rahimi 2011a; Yang 2009). The idea behind the pre-election project was to offer alternative, "Islamic" social media sites to blogs and popular networking sites such as Facebook and Balatarin. The launch of the Velayatmadaran social site provides the best example of such initiative, which was perceived as part of the state's attempt to manage the virtual domain of interaction. The hacking and defacing of opposition websites also appeared in correlation with the state's growing use of the discourse of "soft war" in late summer of 2009. To the IRGC, in charge of protecting the Islamic Republic, the state now faces a new threat and that is the new media as the West's most covert attempt to initiate a color coup. In response, the Iranian government reframed the crisis in terms of a foreign-led coup and emphasized the idea of soft power as the best way to challenge the West's psychological warfare.

As the censorship regime managed to limit, at least on a short-term basis, the momentum of the Green Movement, and in some respects hinder its street influence by imprisoning key activists in the movement, the opposition also found ways to evade restrictions. One central problem was the diverse ways dissidents would use alternative ways to have access to digital media, and subsequently challenge the state's propaganda machinery. For instance, in the case of Internet, some users with access to business accounts with higher speed of connection would post short video clips on YouTube, or hand over USB flash drive with recorded footages or photos to friends or family members travelling to United Arab Emirates and Turkey, where large Iranian Diaspora communities reside. Many students activists, realizing university online services would be took risky, would particularly use the business outlet to have better access to the Internet. Proxy servers and RSS services also played a role, as activists would hack or engage in distributed denial of service attacks (DDoS) to disrupt government's websites including Ahmadinejad official website (Rahimi 2011a). There was also the problem of effectively creating alternative social media sites to tackle Facebook and YouTube. Velayatmadaran was shut down months after it was launched primarily because the pro-government users were too busy using Facebook for social interaction. Also, total shutdowns of online services would cause major problems for governance, as the economy by 2009 had become considerably dependent on digital transactions, especially in the banking sector. Though several attempts were made during critical political events, there were no total shutoff moments, only selective ones that mostly revolved around consumer rather than business services. This played a critical role for the dissidents to break through the rare states of exception and make digital communication possible on both local and global scales.

Conclusion

This chapter has examined the current censorship trends in the Iranian digital media environment, with a focus on the Internet for the management of the public sphere and contentious politics. While ICTs necessarily undermine authoritarian power, as the case of Green Movement in post-election shows, they also do not necessarily empower them either. The advantage of ICTs is in the capacity to provide a forum for the circulation of information, new discourses and social imaginaries that would ultimately legitimize and bolster state power and in a socio-political context out of which various forms of governance are maintained. The disadvantage, however, is primarily about the inability of a networked state, increasingly governing through digital communication, to entirely undermine the digital networks that operate, interact and communicate in the public domains of social media environments. The appropriation of technology for power is especially ineffective when the state's faction-ridden political process, as in the case of Iran, is enhanced, mostly as a result of changing elite realignments, or as its power center(s) develop toward an unanticipated direction in shifting spheres of intra-state contestation. Iran represents another example of digital state that has failed to entirely set the parameters of governance over digital media and the information infrastructure.

Technologies can fail and so do authoritarian spheres of influence to exert power, especially during states of exception when a polity undergoes a crisis of legitimacy. As the case of Hallal Internet shows, the formation of a national network as a form of governance over the Internet may carry numerous challenges, including mundane technical ones. Equally important is the role of infrastructural conditions and, more importantly, shifting contexts of global and local networks through which social movements become possible. The degree of transnational ties and technological diffusion in a country, such as Iran, always carries the element of surprise in dissident mobilization. In this sense, the level of digital and network organization and how entrenched ICTs are in everyday life determines the failure or success of authoritarian power and resistance to it. In this regard, it is in the unforeseen opportunities in the broader landscape of political contention that enable authoritarianism to either succeed in its efforts to control or succumb to the opposition's demands for reform or total change.

With the presence of a vibrant dissident political culture since 2009 elections, especially pervasive in the new media sphere, the evolving Iranian state, with its distinct securitization trajectories since the 2005 election of Ahmadinejad, has largely succeeded to curtail oppositional activism on the street level, but failed to prevent the growth of dissent within digital networks. In this sense, the Iranian state recognizes the significance of network technologies and overall information infrastructure that enable activists to organize and mobilize contentious performances at opportune moments. During the 2013 presidential election, the state was more prepared in the implementation of several shutoff strategies ahead of the election day. While weeks before elections the state slowed down the speed of Internet, the afternoon before and on the election day most websites, especially email servers like Yahoo and Gmail, were either considerably slowed down or shutoff.[6] On June 16, just minutes after the Iranian football team won a critical game in order to qualify for the World Cup, the Internet was again shut down, as Iranians took to the streets and celebrated the victory of the national team.[7] While there were no anti-government street protests in 2013 elections, the strategic move to disable the Internet ahead of elections and the football match shows how the government security apparatus views digital media as a potential threat and treats it as an integral part of Iran's oppositional politics. Digital connectivity and diffusion of networks of communication remains a threat to authoritarian states. Increasing interconnectivity between social media, (smart) mobile communication and satellite TV programs enable civic activists or ordinary citizens to organize, mobilize and creatively express discontent or claim transparency in a complex media environment to defy easy control over the content and form of communication in everyday life. Perhaps what is most problematic for the authoritarian states is not why or when ICTs can be used for dissident activities, but the complex socio-cultural processes through which they can construct new mental environments, daily/nightly practices and civic engagements that on a long-term can undermine the social context of authoritarian power. At the heart of Iran's communication revolution is a social revolution of everyday subversive force of which no state of exception can manage to restrain it.

6 Fieldwork observation, Tehran, Iran, June 8–14, 2013.

7 The Internet came back on to normal speed at midnight. Fieldwork observation, Tehran, Iran, June 16, 2013.

Chapter 3
Information Infrastructure and Anti-Regime Protests in Iran and Tunisia

Matthew Carrieri, Ronald J. Deibert, and Saad Omar Khan

The 2009 Iranian election protests and the Tunisian uprising of 2011 are contemporary and salient examples of anti-authoritarian movements in the Middle East and North Africa (MENA). International news media have reported at length on the role of information and communication technologies (ICTs) in facilitating organized protests against authoritarian regimes across the region, referring to these and similar displays of dissent as "Twitter Revolutions" (*Washington Times* 2009). "Web 2.0" applications like Twitter, Facebook, and YouTube allowed dissidents and activists to bypass state media controls and broadcast steady streams of news updates, photos, and video clips to local and international audiences. Social media platforms also served as forums through which activists could rally disparate individuals to collectively mobilize in the streets.

Iran and Tunisia also stifled dissent online with highly developed telecommunications infrastructures of remarkably similar architecture. From the mid 1990s onwards, the two countries channeled Internet bandwidth through a single point of connection, creating a bottleneck through which online content could be extensively filtered and opponents easily monitored. Legal frameworks and regulatory bodies supplemented technical tools by providing governments with the pretexts and institutions necessary to physically suppress dissidents. The Open Net Initiative (ONI) has provided extensive coverage of Iran and Tunisia's heavy censorship regimes up to 2009, including pervasive filtering and legal controls on content (ONI Iran 2009; ONI Tunisia 2009). The two governments' ICT policies attracted considerable attention from human rights activists, who awarded them a number of dubious honors. Reporters without Borders, for example, named Iran and Tunisia "Enemies of the Internet" in 2005 (RSF 2005), and the Committee to Protect Journalists listed them among the most dangerous places from which to blog in 2009 (CPJ 2009).

Iran and Tunisia used their information infrastructures to quell unrest in response to the 2009 "Green Movement" and the 2011 "Jasmine Revolution." Yet Mahmoud Ahmadinejad survived to preside over another term, while Zine el-Abidine Ben Ali fled the country. Do these divergent outcomes invalidate the importance that many have accorded to ICTs in precipitating unrest? Assuming Iran anticipated its post-election turmoil, is the successful exercise of state power over information infrastructure simply a matter of preemptive preparation? While we make no argument that the dissemination and use of ICTs is a necessary causal variable for democratization in modern authoritarian societies, this chapter adopts the position that communications technologies and social media can play a role in precipitating regime overthrow. It treats ICTs as tools that provide opportunities for organization and popular mobilization that may not otherwise exist in contexts of regime repression. As such, state-level responses to digital expressions of dissent help us understand the conditions that contribute to the relative success or failure of social movements.

Despite their similarities, Iran and Tunisia responded to their respective episodes of unrest in different ways. In contrast to Tunisia, Iran was considerably more proactive in implementing filtering and consistently maintained its extensive grip on information infrastructure in the face of popular demands. These factors proved vital in containing telecommunications-aided mass mobilization and preventing regime overthrow.

Internet as Threat or Opportunity in Iran and Tunisia

Tunisia's approach to information technology prior to the 2011 revolution was rooted in the imperative of economic development. Almost immediately after the introduction of the Internet, the government invested some 1.5 billion USD to promote access among businesses and individuals (Abdulla 2007). Ben Ali himself publicly made the association between information technology and a robust, competitive economy, bragging that his government had "[laid] the foundations of the information society and the knowledge-based economy" for Tunisia (Jelassi 2010: 162). As a key facet of its tenth and eleventh development plans (2002–2006 and 2007–2011 respectively), Tunisia nearly tripled the number of domestic Internet users between 2006 and 2009 from 1.3 million to 3.4 million users (Jelassi 2010). The ICT sector's share of the economy rose dramatically in the years prior to the revolution, from 2.6 percent in 1997 to 10 percent in 2008 (Jelassi 2010). The regime's Internet strategy under Ben Ali revolved around information technology as a driver of economic growth and an opportunity that should be exploited and encouraged, if also carefully controlled.

Like Tunisia, Iran at first welcomed the Internet as a tool for economic growth and academic progress (Rahimi 2003). The government promoted its development and expansion among commercial and educational sectors and, consequently, Internet use among the general public expanded dramatically from its inception in 1993. But as Sreberny and Khiabany (2010) note, Iran's ICT development was "constrained by confusion in government policies, varied institutional interests and above all the dialectical tension between the imperative of the market and 'revolutionary' claims of the state" (11). Long-standing US sanctions on Iran have also made the acquisition of information technology hardware and software difficult, if not impossible (Sreberny and Khiabany 2010).

More importantly, the Islamic state has aimed to root out and destroy Western cultural imperialism in order to replace its vestiges with an indigenous "Muslim" culture as defined by the religio-political establishment (Sreberny and Khiabany 2010). In the 2000s, the state began to view the private sector's control of ICT infrastructure and the market's role in dictating accessible content as an arena of contestation and a threat to its cultural and political hegemony. While the third five-year plan (2000–2005) outlined privatization and liberalization of the telecommunications industry as a main objective in the effort to build a "knowledge-based economy," these initiatives were only haphazardly implemented. The state proved reluctant to release its grip over ICTs and deepened its control over the sector to such an extent that it became the leading provider of Internet access and services (Sreberny and Khiabany 2010).

Since 2005, Iran has also allegedly been developing its own "National Information Network": a domestic intranet that limits users' access to content hosted on the World Wide Web and facilitates surveillance of those who continue to use the Internet (Nouri 2010). The "National Information Network," which was initially slated to launch in 2009 but has since been delayed, represents the culmination of the Iranian regime's plans to promote its ideological vision of an indigenous Islamic society via the Internet. By creating a system in which Iranian users' traffic need no longer be routed through external (often US-based) servers, the government can more easily create a climate in which all content complies with its overarching cultural vision and minimize ideological threats to its political legitimacy. The Iranian state's philosophy of the Internet thus differs significantly from Tunisia's. While Ben Ali enthusiastically sought to develop Tunisia's ICT industry, concerns over political hegemony and cultural integrity trumped economic and social development in Iran.

ICT Infrastructures and Filtering

Tunisia's emphasis in creating a "wired" country coincided with the state's development of its information infrastructure in a way that created a centralized system of control. Wagner has described Tunisia's cyberspace landscape as one in which "control of telecommunications infrastructure and Internet infrastructure are closely linked" (2012: 485). When the Internet was introduced in 1991 and public access was still limited, state controls were nonexistent. The Internet's opening to the public in 1996 coincided with the creation of the Agence Tunisienne d'Internet (ATI), which was tasked with regulating Tunisia's Internet backbone and domain name system (DNS), and providing connectivity to government agencies (ONI 2007; Wagner 2012). The ATI also possessed a monopoly on the country's bandwidth, which it leased to all Internet service providers (ISPs), many of which were government-owned. Its central position in regulating and maintaining Tunisia's Internet infrastructure greatly facilitated the installation of government control mechanisms. Because all bandwidth needed to pass through the ATI's gateway servers on its way to ISPs, the government could conveniently filter content at a single bottleneck. The state also had significant control over domestic Internet service providers. The country's main ISP and single provider of international connectivity, Tunisie Telecom, was believed to have close links to government figures even after its supposed "privatization" in 2006 (Wagner 2012). Even if the government did not officially own Tunisie Telecom, it was understood that all ISPs in Tunisia were state controlled. In a personal interview with Moez Chakchouk, current CEO of the ATI, Chakchouk explained that ISPs during the Ben Ali era were all "somehow linked to the regime" (April 25, 2012).

From the ATI's inception, the government installed several layers of content controls (Wagner 2012). Until 2003, the ATI used Secure Computing's SmartFilter to consistently block content across all ISPs and NetApp's NetCache proxy solution to display a generic "Error 404" blockpage. According to Chakchouk, the government listed four website categories of concern to censors, including pornography, sites related to the political opposition, sites relating to Ben Ali's family, and sites seen as encouraging violence and "terrorism" (interview, April 25, 2012). By 2003, dissidents had begun distributing censored content via email, and the government consequently supplemented its website censorship with manual email filtering. The ATI collected suspect emails and handed them over to the Ministry of Interior, where employees read, deleted, and modified their contents. Deep packet inspection technology was added in 2007, as the introduction of broadband overwhelmed monitoring efforts via earlier mechanisms of control.

Despite the ATI's centralized control over censorship, decisions about what sites should be censored came from outside of the agency. Statements by Kamel Saadaoui, former ATI director (Elkin 2011) and Chakchouk indicate that the regime itself had sole discretion over what sites were blocked. As Chakchouk explained, "ATI does not decide which site to be filtered or not. The ATI is just responsible to maintain equipment and to set up new equipment in the centers … the demand to do censorship came from Ben Ali himself" (interview, April 25, 2012). The list of blocked sites was unknown to the ATI, which often received knowledge of filtering only when citizens inquired why a particular site was inaccessible (Elkin 2011). While the ATI as an Internet exchange point provided the functionality and the technical expertise to filter, it lacked the authority to make decisions about which sites should or should not have been banned. In this sense, Tunisia's infrastructure of control prior to the revolution was considerably "top-down," with little deliberation outside the confines of a select coterie of officials.

On the surface, Iran's telecommunications infrastructure and filtering practices were remarkably similar to those of Tunisia. During the 1990s, freedom of speech on the Internet was relatively unregulated. The Iranian regime viewed the Internet as a potential opportunity to export its "cultural revolution" through state-affiliated media outfits and to legitimize its rule by appearing "modernized" (Rahimi 2003). However, hardline factions began to crack down on expressions of liberalism in the mainstream media following the election of Mohamed Khatami to the presidency, pushing political writers to the Internet as a vehicle of free expression (Amnesty International 2010; Yahyanejad and Gheytanchi 2012). Even as the Internet became a platform for Iranians to publish opinions critical of the regime or to expose controversial topics, authorities sought to monopolize the telecommunications industry and control online content.

Like Tunisia, Iran has "centralized [its] Internet infrastructure so that all traffic must pass through a limited number of gateways or service providers" (Karlekar and Cook 2009: 7). The Ministry of Information and Communications Technology oversees two subsidiaries: the Telecommunications Infrastructure Company (TIC) and the Telecommunications Company of Iran. The TIC provides Internet bandwidth to ISPs, acts as the sole purchaser of international gateways, and maintains data traffic for the public and private sectors (TCI website). Like Tunisia's ATI, all Internet traffic from commercial ISPs must connect via the TCI; it is therefore easy for the government to implement filtering technology at a single point of connection (ONI Iran 2009). The TCI was established as a government organization in 1971, but was supposed to be privatized beginning in 2007. Upon its initial public offering, however, the Iranian Revolutionary Guard Corps (IRGC) purchased over 50 percent of the TCI's shares through one of its affiliated companies—the Mobin Trust Consortium (BBC Persian 2010). Similarly, the second largest mobile-phone operator in the country, Iran Cell, is owned by a number of commercial entities said to be "proxy companies" controlled by the IRGC (Freedom House 2011a: 190). For a long time the Iranian government employed SmartFilter—the same software used in Tunisia—to limit access to foreign content, while manually shutting down undesirable local sites (ONI 2007). The regime gradually developed its own domestic tools to search for and filter objectionable content (ONI Iran 2009). Finally, the TCI uses proxy servers and deep packet inspection tools provided by Nokia-Siemens Networks to facilitate government surveillance by logging all unencrypted traffic that passes through the data bottleneck (Rahimi 2011). Effective January 2012, however, Nokia-Siemens pledged to reduce ties with Iran (Stecklow 2011).

However, noticeable differences exist between the two countries' approaches to Internet and telecommunications management. While no filtering regime is completely transparent, Iran's infrastructure of control appears to be relatively more direct from a user's perspective. Tunisia's "blockpage" appeared as a nondescript 404 "File Not Found" error message, obfuscating the fact that the government was actively blocking the site (ONI Tunisia 2009). Iran makes the filtration process transparent, explicitly telling users that a site is forbidden and providing users with suggestions for more acceptable websites (ONI Iran 2009). More stakeholders are involved in the process of creating and maintaining Iran's digital firewall, and the surrounding bureaucracy of the telecommunication sector is larger and more horizontally structured than Tunisia's. An interagency committee, the Committee in Charge of Determining Unauthorized Sites (CCDUS), was established in 2002 to set criteria for censoring websites based on guidelines provided by the Supreme Council of the Cultural Revolution (ONI Iran 2009). No equivalent organization existed under Ben Ali as part of Tunisia's filtration regime.

Recently, the process of governmental control over the Internet in Iran has become even more organized with the creation of the Supreme Council of Cyberspace. In contrast to the relatively more opaque style of Tunisia's Internet filtering decision makers, the Supreme Council's existence as a policy-making committee comprised of high-ranking officials from several government bodies is openly publicized (Press TV 2012). A number of organizations have also been established and charged with policing Iran's Internet infrastructure since 2009, including: the IRGC (through its Cyber Defense Command); the Passive Defense Organization; the Information Communication Technology Section of Iran's Police Forces (FAVA/ICT Police) (Yeganeh 2010); and the "Cyber Police" (FETA) established in April 2011 (Moqaddem and Naja 2011). Iran's multiple stakeholders provide it with a more comprehensive grip on Internet governance than that of Tunisia at the height of its censorship policies.

Legal and Regulatory Controls

Beyond technical filtering, both Tunisia and Iran have used legal means to stifle dissent as part of their infrastructures of control. Prior to the revolution, Tunisia's Press Code made "defamation" punishable through fines or imprisonment (Freedom House 2012). These measures were only selectively implemented: criticizing the presidency or government was illegal, but pro-government reporters were given free rein to attack and discredit independent reporters (Campagna 2008).

Commercial telecommunications entities under Ben Ali were similarly subject to specific legal mechanisms and regulations. In 1997, two laws were enacted to hold ISPs directly responsible for online content: the "Telecommunications Decree" and the "Internet Decree." The former mandated that the press code applied to online content. All ISPs directors were made responsible for ensuring that information trafficked across the provider's network complied with the press code and for submitting their subscribers' names to the ATI on a monthly basis (Freedom House 2011b). The Internet Decree obliged ISPs to remove content deemed contrary to "public order or good morals" and to collect hard copies of offensive material for court proceedings. Although there is no evidence that any of these laws have actually been applied in Tunisia since their adoption (Article 19 2012: 29), ISPs were legally complicit in implementing cyberspace controls that the Tunisian regime had created.

Despite Tunisia's regulatory complexity, Iran's legal regime is far more extensive due to a number of Internet-specific laws that have no equivalent in Tunisia. As in Tunisia, Iran has used existing press laws to stifle dissent online and offline. Article 6 of Iran's 1986 press law restricts content considered un-Islamic, "atheistic," or that instigates "individuals and groups to act against the security, dignity and interests of the Islamic Republic of Iran." It also forbids content that can be considered libelous against state officials, institutions, and organizations (*Pars Times*). In keeping with conservative factions' increasing concern over the Internet during Khatami's presidency, the law was amended to include all electronic publications in 2000 (al-Aamri 2012).

Iran has, however, developed legal doctrines specific to cyberspace. The 2009 Iranian Cyber Crimes Act gives detailed punitive measures against those committing crimes such as: illegally accessing data and information systems protected by "security measures" (Article 1); concealing data in a way that would provide "authorized individuals" from accessing to data, such as through basic encryption (Article 10); sending obscene material through computers and other devices (Article 14); using computers and other telecommunications technology to "disseminate lies" (Article 18); and neglecting to filter out objectionable sites as an ISP, thus making service providers complicit in censorship (Article 21: Article 19 2012: 23–43). This cyberspace-specific law indicates the increasing concern of Iranian authorities about curtailing dissident voices and molding Iranian cyberspace according to the state's ideological vision. Rather than simply attack journalists, bloggers, and dissidents using an ambiguous press law, Iran has tailored legislation to protect the Islamic Republic against perceived domestic and geopolitical threats.

Iran's regulatory regime bears certain similarities to Tunisia's legal mechanisms for controlling cyberspace. Both used press laws to punish journalists and activists and developed telecommunications laws specifically for ISPs. Arguably, however, Iran's legal regime more directly addresses Internet-related transgressions. The ideological differences between the secular Ben Ali regime and the religiously oriented Iranian government are reflected in their legal contexts. Iran's press law explicitly mentions the unacceptability of "un-Islamic" and "atheistic" content. Tunisian penal codes forbid acts that upset "public morals," but say nothing about content considered offensive to religious morals.

Information Controls in During Political Unrest

Iran in 2009 and Tunisia in 2011 both responded to widespread unrest by engaging in physical repression—often legally sanctioned under the laws described—and tightening ICT controls. Given that social media websites and cellular telephones played a key role in organizing protests and broadcasting human rights abuses, cyberspace formed a highly contested sphere in the conflicts between state and civil society (Howard and Hussain 2012; Zuckerman 2011). Arguably, the two regimes' well-developed technical and legal infrastructures were tailor-made to shut down popular mobilization and to pinpoint and prosecute those responsible. Iran largely succeeded in this endeavor, but events in Tunisia resulted in the end of Ben Ali's 23-year rule and precipitated calls for representation across North Africa and the Middle East. A number of factors contributed to these different outcomes.

Tunisian information controls during the Jasmine revolution were multifaceted. Reports indicate that the ATI was responsible for harvesting protesters' Gmail, Yahoo, and Facebook login credentials (Ragan 2011). As the revolution ran its course, websites were blocked, particularly Facebook pages about the unrest and foreign online articles (including *France24*, *Al-Jazeera*, *BBC*, *Deutsche Welle*) covering the events (RSF 2012). In an interview, ATI CEO Moez Chakchouk claimed that part of the reason for not blocking Facebook itself was its use by the Ben Ali regime for pro-regime propaganda (interview, April 25, 2012). Despite all of these efforts to control the revolution online, the protests continued. Howard and colleagues (2011) explain how the lack of centralized leadership in the revolutionary movement actually made efforts to stamp out the protest movement more difficult. By contrast, the Green Movement coalesced around the figure of Mir-Hossein Mousavi and, to a lesser extent, Mehdi Karroubi, both of whom were reformist politicians by profession and recently defeated electoral candidates. Centralized infrastructures of control like those in Iran and Tunisia may be better suited to targeting websites and individuals specifically aligned to political movements (as in Iran) than to dealing with decentralized opposition movements (as in Tunisia).

Others have argued that the Tunisian regime was either ill-prepared to crack down effectively on new media, which provided vital information during the blackout of traditional media (Bounenni 2011), or simply underestimated its efficacy (Al-Saqaf 2012). The former head of the ATI, Kamel Saadaoui, said that the regime had "signed a deal to add monitoring of social networks," but "hadn't yet delivered the solution when the Facebook revolution" crested in January (Silver 2011). As a result, the Tunisian regime's approach to social media filtration and monitoring was reactive rather than proactive (Wagner 2012). The widespread use of social media and mobile phones to transmit messages and images of the protests continued without significant government intervention or effective prevention. Facebook, which remained unblocked and saw a huge spike in use beginning in December 2010, became the primary source of breaking news for many in an otherwise bleak media landscape.

The Tunisian regime's reactive policies ultimately proved ineffective, and, in a token show of reform, Ben Ali removed all Internet restrictions on January 14, 2011. The new freedoms accorded to Tunisian Internet users came within hours; Ben Ali fled the country shortly thereafter. The speed at which he was able to lift online controls has been attributed to the centralized role of the ATI in enforcing filtering in Tunisia. Once a decision was made to lift restrictions, all the ruling authorities had to do was push a metaphorical button at the ATI (Wagner 2012) to stop filtering. The speed at which filtering ended thus illustrates how centralized and narrow the Tunisian information infrastructure had become under Ben Ali.

Iran's information controls during the 2009 election protests were comparatively more far reaching. The Iranian regime ramped up its filtration, surveillance, and cyber-attack activities as early as January 25 (Yahyanejad and Gheytanchi 2012). Facebook and Twitter, both of which were previously censored, were unblocked in January 2009 either in a token display of tolerance or in an effort to monitor dissidents. However, the government banned them shortly ahead of the June elections as an anticipatory move, possibly in an effort to block users from disseminating information in support of Mousavi (Sheikholeslami 2009). Compared to Ben Ali's weak concessions, Facebook and similar social media sites remained unequivocally banned throughout the protests. On the day of the election, the Iranian government disabled the country's short message service (SMS) system when protests against Ahmedinejad's re-election started (RSF 2009). While officials claimed that the disruption aimed to prevent illegal campaigning on election day, Mousavi supporters argued that it prevented them from monitoring the election results. On days that protests were anticipated, the Iranian government effectively blocked 60 to 70 percent of Internet traffic and closed off ports commonly used by circumvention tools; on quieter days, it engaged in deep packet inspection (Dutton et al. 2010).

Months prior to the election protests, the IRGC announced its support for the pro-government paramilitary Basij in a project to launch 10,000 blogs as a way of promoting Iran's "revolutionary ideas" (Tehrani 2009). Even prior to the protests, then, the military vanguard of the Iranian state felt the need to compete with the voices of the opposition in cyberspace. The so-called Iranian Cyber Army also emerged as a cyberspace actor directly in the wake of the protests. Cyber army attacks are numerous, some of the more notable ones being those against Twitter (Finkle and Bartz 2009). Twitter's role in the Iranian protests made it an obvious target for pro-regime forces after the election protests. In Tunisia, despite the widespread acknowledgement of Twitter's role in supporting the protest movement, there is no evidence that the site was wholly blocked; protesters used the platform to inform, organize, and galvanize Tunisians against the regime. The links between the cyber army and the Iranian regime are tenuous, although there have been some reports that they receive direct support from the IRGC (Payvand 2012).

Tunisians' and Iranians' discontent in 2011 and 2009 respectively took two very different trajectories. Despite the hopes of many dissident Iranians, the "Green Movement" did not lead to the same end as Tunisia's "Jasmine Revolution." Both movements uses information and communication technologies for organizational purposes, and as a tool to promote the revolution at home and abroad. Conversely, the 2009 and 2011 protests also showed how ICTs could facilitate the process of state repression. As much as Tunisia tried to control online content, their controls seemed relatively lax in contrast to Iran's hyper-vigilant approach to cyber security and censorship during the election protests.

Conclusion

Though the technologies were similar—both governments, for example, used SmartFilter—the political and bureaucratic contexts in Iran and Tunisia differed. From the beginning, Tunisia invested heavily in its ICT infrastructure as a vehicle of economic growth. In Iran, the state's political ideology and a religiously inspired animosity toward the Internet hampered the development of a telecommunications sector, while international sanctions prevented the importation of hardware and software that helps facilitate digital communication. Both countries retained a degree of control over Internet content by ensuring that ISPs funneled traffic through state-affiliated enterprises that essentially served as bottleneck points for filtration. But where Tunisia's decision-making structure was vertical, with power ultimately held in the person of Ben Ali and a small group of his supporters, Iran's infrastructure of control consisted of multiple stakeholders with overlapping responsibilities. Moreover, Iran was relatively more open about its filtration policies and justifications for them than was Tunisia, as exemplified by their respective blockpages. This relative transparency is apparent at the legal level as well. Iran and pre-revolution Tunisia had extensive press laws to suppress dissent. Only Iran, however, developed legislation to specifically punish crimes committed using digital technology and established government institutions to determine the limits of permissible online activity. Iran's legal environment also specifically targets un-Islamic content, a regulatory concern without equal in secular pre-revolution Tunisia and a convenient pretext for censorship. Philosophically, the Iranian regime's willingness to separate itself from the World Wide Web both as a policy and as a *de facto* consequence of its cyberspace controls also contrasts with the Ben Ali government's relative openness and desire to instrumentalize the Internet as a tool for economic growth.

Iran in 2009 proved more effective at blocking content it found threatening than did Tunisia throughout its revolution. The lack of an overarching social media blackout at the time of the Tunisian protests stands in contrast to Iran's blocking of Facebook, Twitter, and foreign media in 2009. As was evident in Ben Ali's speech and his subsequent removal of all online censorship, the Tunisian government clearly had the capability to extensively and expeditiously censor content, but perhaps lacked the bureaucratic structure to deliberate effectively. The importance of preemptive preparation must also be noted. The "Green Movement" emerged in response to a foreseeable event, the planning for which began well in advance of its occurrence. Iran's multi-stakeholder control regime anticipated a negative response to the 2009 election results; it thus took preliminary steps to limit free speech online and responded forcefully to displays of disaffection. By contrast, Ben Ali's regime could not have predicted Mohamed Bouazizi's actions and their strong resonance among the Tunisian people. The government was forced to improvise by implementing piecemeal measures but was neither well organized nor quick enough to combat opposition online. In the struggle between regimes and dissidents over control of communication technologies, a government's opportunity to prepare its infrastructure of control for a coming shock is a clear, though by no means decisive, advantage.

Following their respective periods of civil conflict, Iran and Tunisia's telecommunications infrastructures and policies developed in divergent ways. In Tunisia, the state's role in censorship and surveillance disappeared, as the ATI sought to reinvent itself as a neutral, semi-governmental Internet exchange point (Chakchouk interview, April 25, 2012). In Iran, however, state control of the country's ICT infrastructure deepened after June 2009. The establishment of the Supreme Council on Cyberspace in March 2012 and the expanding roster of regulatory bodies responsible for policing the Internet reflect the Iranian authorities' increasing concern with cyberspace as a sphere of domestic and geopolitical conflict. The government's plan to launch the "National Information Network"—essentially an intranet closed off to international traffic—threatens to establish an environment in which all content serves to propagate an official message and legitimize state power. These developments were predictable: Tunisian civil society made use of its newly representative political system to demand a free flow of information, while the victorious but shaken Iranian regime doubled down on defending its interests.

The Iranian and Tunisian case studies show that authoritarian power need not necessarily be undermined by ICTs as long as the flow of information can be extensively and consistently controlled by the regime, especially in times of crisis. As Deibert and Rohozinski (2010) argue, communications technologies are tools that in different contexts may be used for either "liberation" or "control" (44). While ICTs were certainly not the cause of the uprisings or the sole manifestation of civil conflict, they undoubtedly provide civil society with a space to grow in otherwise repressive political environments. However, our analysis suggests that regimes that fully leverage the control and surveillance capabilities of their information infrastructures can successfully curtail movements that seek to upend the political order. Keeping in mind specific contexts, other states in similar situations of political instability might learn a lesson or two from this comparison. Regimes that adequately prepare, adopt an offensive stance, and "stick to their guns"—as in the Iranian case—can deal a devastating blow to social movements by using ICTs to their own advantage. As of this writing, such "regime learning" could be evident in Syria, where the ruling party has displayed a consistent willingness to combat opposition at all levels, including by using ICTs to aggressively monitor dissidents and promote an "official narrative" counter to its opponents' criticisms. Assuming that ruling powers do look to Iran as an example of regime resistance, social movements seeking to use information infrastructures for their own ends will face governments that are more prepared, more technologically empowered, and more willing to leverage the same tools as their opponents.

Chapter 4
Digital Occupation in Gaza's High-Tech Enclosure

Helga Tawil-Souri[1]

Since the Israeli regime's disengagement from the Gaza Strip in Summer 2005, Gaza has become an "airborne-occupied enclave" (Hanafi 2009: 118), an open-air prison, and a testing-ground for the latest military technologies. Israel's approach towards Gaza has been a balancing act "of maximum control and minimum responsibility" (Li 2006: 39) which has resulted in a form of occupation—and state power—that has become increasingly technologized. Unmanned aerial reconnaissance and attack drones, remote-controlled machine guns, closed-circuit television, sonic imagery, gamma-radiation detectors, remote-controlled bulldozers and boats, electrified fences, among many other examples, are increasingly used for control and surveillance (e.g. "Israeli Arsenal Deployed against Gaza" 2009 and "Agreed Documents on Movement and Access" 2005). Disengagement, in other words, did not mark the end of colonial occupation and control, but a move from a traditional military occupation towards a high-tech one. Rooted in Israel's increasingly globalized security-military-high-tech industry, the technological sealing of Gaza is part of the transformation of the mechanics of Israeli occupation that began with the first intifada (1987) and the ensuing "peace process" (1993) (e.g. Gordon 2008).

The Israeli regime—by which I mean the apparatus of ministries, military powers, corporations, individuals, and practices as they act with and towards the Palestinians—is not a classically authoritarian one. (My concern here is not so much Israeli policies within what one may call "Israel proper," but rather in the Palestinian Territories.) Nor is the Palestinian Authority (PA), which became the official political representative of Palestinians in the West Bank and Gaza in 1993, an authoritarian regime, even if it exhibits authoritarian-like behaviors. The PA remains at best a pseudo-government, attempting to balance a largely impossible situation of being responsible to 'govern' the Palestinian Territories, yet having very little autonomy to do so because of Israel's strangle-hold. The relationship between them is fundamentally one of settler-colonialism. There are however variegated manifestations, most notably the difference in approach towards

1 A longer version of this article was originally published as Tawil-Souri, Helga. 2012. "Digital Occupation: Gaza's High-Tech Enclosure." *Journal of Palestine Studies* 41(2): 27–43.

Gaza and the West Bank: Israel's attempt to completely segregate and control the first; and Israel's infiltration, envelopment, and discombobulation of the latter. Sometimes Israeli policies exhibit apartheid-like similarities, other times, they bear morose similarity to authoritarian practices. In the uneven power matrix between Israel and Gaza (and Palestinians more generally), information technologies play a significant role in strengthening and expanding the power of the Israeli regime, as will be described below. It is important to recognize that high-tech is one of the means through which Israeli occupation continues, but also that the occupation has been a critical component in Israeli high-tech. Somewhat ironically, for the PA as well, power over its "citizens" is consolidated through the realm of information technologies, most obviously in the economic realm.

My focus in what follows is to unveil the ways in which high-tech infrastructure in the Gaza Strip—that which is used by Palestinians as opposed to the Israeli regime—is also a space of control. Technology infrastructures form part of the apparatus of Israeli control over Gazans. A telephone call made on a landline, even between Gaza City and Khan Younis, is physically routed through Israel. Internet traffic is routed through switches located outside the Gaza Strip. Even on the ubiquitous cellular phones, calls must touch the Israeli backbone at some point. Like much else about the Gaza Strip, telecommunication infrastructures are limited by Israeli policies. Geographic mobility, economic growth, political mobilization, and territory are contained, but so are digital flows: Gazans live under a regime of digital occupation.

The phrase "digital occupation" highlights a dynamic process. First, it suggests that Israeli territorial control over Gaza continues, but increasingly also includes the high-tech realm. Second, digital occupation articulates the ways in which Palestinian and multinational corporations, the PA, international NGOs, and international capital networks combine to lead the development of telecommunications to follow a neo-liberal economic agenda. A core contradiction arises against which to understand technology infrastructures: the confinement of Gazans in a narrowing and disconnected space occurs at the same time that high-tech globalization is posited as the route to openness and to overcoming confinement. Third, Gazans themselves "occupy" digital spaces, even if with constraints and sometimes illegally: they reach out to friends and family, report abuses, and escape physical confinement in virtual ways. It is an on-going dialectic. Thus, the issue to consider is not whether there is a net gain or a net loss to authoritarian rule, for there exists a constant tension between information technologies' intended inventions, applied controls, actual uses, and outcomes.

In what follows, I focus on the telecommunications infrastructure—telephone landlines, cellular telephony, and Internet access—as a space of control. I analyze how high-tech spaces are subject to control—a control necessary to Israel's strategy to contain Gaza and accompanied by the capital controls of neo-liberal globalization that the PA has embraced. My interest here is not the ways Gazans negotiate living under such a regime (what Gazans do on the Internet and the uses to which they put their mobile phones, while important, are beyond the scope of this chapter but the *structure* of digital occupation. "Digital occupation" here highlights the relationship between territorial and technological enclosure.

Many scholars and politicians suggest that while Gazans may be territorially locked up, if they have mobile phones and the Internet they are not just plugged into the world but can—at least virtually—overcome their territorial confinement (e.g. Lunat 2009; World Bank 2008). The liberatory aspects ascribed to information technologies acquired increased salience with the Arab uprisings: if Tunisians and Egyptians managed to shake off their overlords in part thanks to Facebook, Twitter, and mobile phones, it is argued, perhaps Palestinians can too. These are tensions that I challenge: it is impossible to speak of a Gaza that is territorially sealed and digitally boundless; there are "material" limitations to high-tech spaces—in terms of physicality *and* in the Marxist sense of economic. Particularly in the Palestinian case, one must consider Israel's continued demand that any future Palestinian state—to say nothing of the current configurations of enclaves such as Gaza—not only be demilitarized and without control over borders, but also, in the words of Israeli Prime Minister Binyamin Netanyahu, "without control over its … electro-magnetic field" (Wikileaks 2009). This is significant, not only in assessing whether a "new media revolution" is possible for/in Gaza, but in understanding the relationship between technology, political freedoms, power, and occupation.

Enclosure

Digital networks have their own forms of controls, their own "checkpoints" and nodes that serve to limit and contain flows (e.g. Deibert 2009; Galloway 2004). Gaza is enclosed both by concrete and high-tech "walls" through a complex set of inclusions and exclusions operating through a variety of practices that render Gaza *both* a physical and a digital enclave. A useful way to look at Gaza and to assess the implications of digital occupation is through the concept of "enclosure," drawn from the disciplines of economics, history, geography, and digital media studies.

"Enclosure" is a historically, geographically, and economically specific process that evolved as part of the industrial revolution in eighteenth-century Great Britain, which actively transformed a territorial space's social economy, demography, and culture. Hegemonic groups asserted control over territory both through law and architecture. The legal element redefined property rights and, by reorganizing systems of ownership, use, and circulation, imposed different structures of sovereignty and access. The architectural element, meanwhile, recast the land's contours through the building of hedges, walls, fences, and gates. This combination of legal and architectural articulations resulted in new "enclosed" spaces that enforced a different system of circulation, flow, and trespass. Parts of social and economic life that were formerly common, non-commodified, and largely outside the realm of control and surveillance were turned into private and surveillable possessions under a new property regime limiting free (meaning both sovereign and not paid for) mobility. This pattern can be seen in Gaza, where the

Oslo Accords would be the legal element, and the spatial mechanisms that enclose it (walls, checkpoints, control towers, permits and identification cards, aerial drones, etc.)—poignant examples of land enclosure—would be the architectural element.

The enclosure of Gaza is also to be understood as the production of a particular kind of economic space. Marxist analyses by scholars such as Henri Lefebvre and David Harvey and cultural theorists ranging from members of the Frankfurt School to Raymond Williams have shown how the spread of neo-liberal capitalism and dispossession has been a dynamic that exists throughout the circuits of capital, resulting in uneven spatial and economic development. Gaza's economic landscape is not simply unevenly developed, but entirely de-developed: drowning in poverty, besieged by Israel, and almost entirely dependent on external aid (except for the tunnel economy). Sara Roy's (1987) argument of the de-development of Gaza is as relevant today as it was more than 20 years ago. Gaza is certainly not enjoying the "economic peace" that (parts of) the West Bank enjoys today. As for Hamas, since its take-over of the Strip in 2007, it has neither tried nor been given room to counter the neo-liberal approach initially subscribed to by the PA (see Khalidi and Samour 2011 for a critique of PA neoliberal policies with a particular focus on the West Bank).

The process of enclosure is omnivorous in its drive for total assimilation: all kinds of spaces become inscribed and appropriated within its logic. Various scholars have expanded enclosure to geopolitical and economic analyses beyond industrial-age Great Britain, including to analyses of information networks. For example, Dan Schiller (1999) argues that what began as telecommunications networks capable of becoming "common" and public instead became leading edges in trans-national capitalism. That telephone and Internet access in most parts of the world are now privately held and have become largely commercial "spaces" is due to the legal, political, economic, and social decisions that rendered them such. This process of "digital enclosure" traces the relationship between a material, spatial process—the construction of networked, interactive environments—and the private expropriation of previously non-proprietary information (see Boyle 2002, 2003). It results in the construction of an increasingly restrictive legal regime that extends and enforces property rights over a growing range of information and practices. Thus, digital enclosure is two-fold: the network and/or access to the network is privatized, and the data produced on high-tech networks becomes the property of the networks' owner-operators.

I propose the term "digital occupation" to describe the multi-faceted process that combines the territorial and economic dynamics of land and digital enclosures (alongside other limitations). In Gaza, we witness the privatization of networks and information flows: a large corporation (Paltel) manages the telecommunications infrastructure and structures, with the terms of access driven by legal and economic modalities instituted by the PA and continued by Hamas. (Since 2007 Hamas has established its own Ministry for Information and Telecommunications in Gaza. But Hamas inherited the telecommunications infrastructure as was originally allowed to be developed by the PA and has not changed ownership, economic, or legal policies.) But the allocation of bandwidth; the placement, number, and strength of Internet routers or telephone exchanges; the range of cellular signals and the equipment used are all limited by Israeli restrictions. Israel actively structures both the spaces of (high-tech) flows and the spaces of control in order to enclose, border, and surveil Gazans.

Segregated but Dependent

"Digital occupation" manifests itself on multiple levels, notably the PA's economic and legal decisions, and second, Israel's "legal" and "architectural" decisions. In the "legal" realm, I mean policies imposing limitations on kinds of equipment permitted and limiting the kind of infrastructure, often according to the Oslo Accords. By "architectural," I mean within the physical equipment itself, in that all networks have software and hardware architectures, and territorial decisions such as where equipment is permitted.

The Israeli–Palestinian technological relationship, like their political and economic relationship, has been one of Israeli control and restrictions and Palestinian dependence. From the outset of occupation in 1967, Israel controlled and maintained telecommunications systems in the occupied territories and imposed legal and military restrictions on them. What little was done with regard to telecommunications in Palestinian areas rendered the network subservient to Israeli infrastructure. For example, all telephone switching nodes were built *outside* areas that might eventually have to be handed over to Palestinian control. The Israeli government (and after industry liberalization in 1985, the state telecommunications provider Bezeq) was in charge of telecommunications throughout Palestine-Israel. Despite the fact that Palestinians paid income, value-added, and other taxes to the Israeli government, Bezeq was neither quick nor efficient in servicing Palestinian users. Telephonically, Palestinians were enclavized and largely disconnected from the network, living under a regime that restricted both their mobility and their access to the outside world.

Oslo II, signed in September 1995, reversed many of these restrictions. Palestinians were promised direct domestic and international telephone and Internet access. Oslo II stated: "Israel recognizes that the Palestinian side has the right to build and operate a separate and independent communication systems and infrastructures including telecommunication networks" (Oslo 2, Annex III, Article 36). It then went on to stipulate the conditions within which an "independent" Palestinian telecommunications system would be constrained, as follows:

> the Palestinian side shall be permitted to import and use any and all kinds of telephones, fax machines, answering machines, modems and data terminals … Israel recognizes and understands that for the purpose of building a separate network, the Palestinian side has the right to adopt its own standards and to

> import equipment which meets these standards ... The equipment will be used only when the independent Palestinian network is operational. (Ibid., D.2)

The point that the network would become independent only when the system became operational is crucial, because the Palestinian network to this day is not independently operational and continues to rely on Israel's. As with other infrastructures (broadcasting, sewage, population registries, water, transportation, etc.), Palestinians were subjected to Israeli constraints that countered their "right" to build separate and independent systems.

The PA proceeded as if the limitations set forth in Oslo would eventually be lifted, and after Israel handed over responsibility for the infrastructure in 1995, the PA established a simulacrum of an "independent" telecommunications system. Reflective of the neo-liberal agenda of the PA and its foreign donors, the only options posited for a successful "state" were private-sector growth, liberalization, and privatization, and the PA passed responsibility for telecommunications to the private sector. Paltel (the Palestine Telecommunications Company) was awarded a license to build, operate, and own landlines, a GSM cellular network (global system mobile communications), data communications, paging services, and public phones. Paltel's largest investors were the economic powerhouses of Palestine. As in much of the rest of the world, investment in and profit from large-scale infrastructure projects benefited those who already wielded substantial economic power. By 2010, Paltel's market capitalization represented more than half the value traded on the Palestinian stock exchange, contributed over a third of the PA's tax income, and its revenues accounted for approximately 10 percent of the Palestinian GDP.

The PA's privatization of telecommunications bespeaks the supremacy of market logic; in fact, from the day that it was handed over, Palestinian telecommunications privatization was a *fait accompli*. Between September 1995 and January 1997, the PA contracted with the Canadian firm Nortel to build and maintain the telecommunications network. Thereafter, the Palestinian telecommunications infrastructure continued to be "enclosed" in that the network was privately owned and users had to accept whatever forms of access and fees Paltel instituted. The PA, in keeping with its approach to state-building more generally, treated telecommunications infrastructure neither as a public good nor considered the benefits of universal access. Paltel was celebrated as one of the first functional national institutions, but in fact it was only symbolically "national," its services available only to those who could afford them. Thus the process of enclosure was not sanctioned simply by Israel, but *doubly* state-sanctioned insofar as the proto-state PA apparatus instituted neo-liberal infrastructure-development policies.

These policies did not challenge Israel's ultimate control over telecommunications. Reliance on Bezeq for most domestic connections and all international connections, for example, continued under Paltel. As Bezeq spokesman Roni Mandelbaum remarked in 1996, Palestinians "are not entitled to any signs of sovereignty

... They have to rely on the infrastructure we supply them" (quoted in Prusher 1996). This has yet fundamentally to change. The only "sovereignty" gained since Oslo resulted from the liberalization of the *Israeli* market, which allowed Paltel to choose between different Israeli providers. In late 2009, after much political difficulty, a second cellular provider, Wataniya, began operating, but to date it has not been given Israeli permission to provide service in the Gaza Strip.

In summer 1999, the first call on Paltel's cellular subsidiary, Jawwal, was made in Gaza (in the West Bank, Jawwal service began in October of the same year). As in the rest of the developing world, cellular telephony is more widespread than landline service, since it is cheaper and relatively easier to install. Thus tensions over the development and control of cellular telephony have been even more controversial and important. The four Israeli cellular providers at the time continued to sell services to Palestinians (illegally according to the Oslo Accords and PA regulations), without any economic, social, or political accountability to the PA. Since 1999, Jawwal has garnered a larger market share, but an estimated 20 to 40 percent of Palestinian cellular users today still use Israeli cellular service, which is cheaper. It is also generally available throughout the occupied territories because Israeli providers build and install infrastructure not only throughout Israel but also in the West Bank, usually on and along bypass roads, on hilltops, in settlements, outposts, and military installations. While there is no Israeli-owned infrastructure inside post-2005 disengagement Gaza, cellular signals from Israeli towers along the perimeter reach well within the narrow sliver of the Strip. Moreover, since cellular spectrum all over Palestine-Israel is under the management of the Israeli Communications Ministry, the four Israeli cellular providers collectively boast signals more than 2,000 times stronger than Jawwal's. And, as with landline telephones, much cellular traffic on Jawwal (and Wataniya in the West Bank) depends on the Israeli backbone.

Both landline and cellular telephony are mostly creations of the Oslo era; what little landline infrastructure existed before 1995 was handed over to the PA, all Palestinian cellular infrastructure had to be built from scratch. The politics of the two technologies ought not to be understood as different, even though landlines are integrated into the Israeli system and cellular telephones are not. Both are forced to be segregated from yet dependent on Israeli networks. While landline and cellular technologies require different mechanisms to operate, the entire underlying structure of Palestinian telecommunications is occupied.

The infrastructure needed to connect to the Internet is much the same as that for telephony, and as such the possibility and limitations of "independent" Internet connection parallel those of landlines. Until 2005, Internet service in the occupied Palestinian territories was "competitive" in that there existed about a dozen Internet Service Providers (ISPs) in the West Bank and a handful in the Gaza Strip. All were resellers of Israeli bandwidth because no international gateway switches were allowed within the Palestinian territories. In January 2005, Paltel began purchasing all existing Palestinian ISPs through its Internet subsidiary,

Hadara, and by that summer had a monopoly on the market, further demonstrating the privatization of access and the enclosure of high technology.

Although the Oslo Accords stated that Israel would release more bandwidth "as soon as any need arises," the entirety of Palestinian telecommunications functions of sub-par infrastructure. Jawwal continues operating on the same narrow frequency allocation it was first awarded and is largely retarded in its upgrading to new platforms. In the West Bank, Wataniya also operates with less bandwidth than needed to adequately serve its subscribers. The maximum transfer rate Hadara provides any one subscriber is 2Mbps, and that bandwidth often has to be shared among numerous subscribers, effectively slowing down Internet traffic. But it is not the Palestinian providers that are to blame for limited bandwidth. As with cellular telephony, it is Israel's Communication Ministry that determines how much bandwidth Hadara is permitted in the first place. Above and beyond the privatization of high-tech space by Palestinian actors (Paltel/Hadara and PA decisions), there remain controls determined by Israeli legal and architectural limitations.

Boundaries on Telecommunications

Hadara is mandated by Israeli authorities to provide limited bandwidth for Palestinian Internet use, making it invariably slower to surf the Internet in the territories than in Israel. Israeli providers sell bandwidth to Hadara at substantially higher rates than to providers in Israel, making Internet access relatively more expensive for Palestinian users. Moreover, the Israeli government has enforced strict limitations on the kinds of equipment permitted. In the case of the Gaza Strip, all switching routers for Internet traffic are located in Israel. The combination of higher costs, slower speeds, and limited technologies results in a bondage of bandwidth, meaning that Gazan Internet flows are limited, thus also limiting Gazans' integration into the network.

Internet users in the Gaza Strip can surf the Internet—assuming the electricity works—but are forced to do so at a high price and slow rate, effectively limiting their virtual connections and flows. Furthermore, as is the case across the telecommunications sector, limitations imposed by the Israeli state force Internet traffic through Israel. The Internet is enclosed due to the privatization of the network, high costs, and the limitations of bandwidth, and territorially confined as well.

Boundaries have been erected on several layers of the telecommunications infrastructure. For example, Article 36 of Oslo II stipulated that "Israel recognizes the right of the Palestinian side to establish telecommunications links (microwave and physical) to connect the West Bank and the Gaza Strip through Israel" (Oslo 2, Annex III, Article 36, D.3d). A microwave link was installed in 1995 to connect the West Bank and Gaza Strip but was quickly saturated (because of the Israeli Communication Ministry's refusal to provide more bandwidth) so that the majority of traffic had to be re-routed back through Bezeq's network. Paltel was forbidden to import equipment—telephone exchanges, broadcasting towers, etc.—that could have allowed it to build an actually independent network that could connect across all Palestinian territories.

These kinds of "territorial" limitations are combined with "legal" and military measures that further contain Gazan telecommunications infrastructure. These include confiscating and forbidding the import of equipment, illegal competition by Israeli providers, limited bandwidth, limitations on what equipment can be installed where, delay of approvals, and purposeful destruction of machinery and infrastructure. There are ample examples: Jawwal's limited spectrum means that its more than two million subscribers are paying for poor service because the network was built to support only its initial 120,000 subscribers. Hadara is still waiting for permission for an Internet trunk-switch to allow Internet traffic to circumvent Israel. Gaza's telecommunications networks are continually shut down for various reasons, including Paltel's failure or delay in paying its Israeli providers (often because cash flow is itself controlled by Israel) and for Israeli-defined "security" issues. Telephone and broadcast signals are jammed and hacked into by the IDF. During the 2008–9 war, for example, the Israeli military sent text messages and voice mails to cellular and landline users in the Gaza Strip. Eyal Weizman (2009) argues that these are "technologies of warning" that provide the IDF the ability to warn Gazans of impending bombings and thus "legally" render their recipients into "legitimate targets." From the perspective of the Palestinian user, however, these technologies of warning are also technologies of enclosure and occupation. Moreover, the mechanisms of digital occupation are exercised through the disruption of everyday life, not simply during exceptional moments of violence. On any "normal" day, a Gazan's phone call is routed through Israel, his signals are jammed whenever a drone passes overhead (sometimes as often as every 15 minutes), his phone service may be shut down or tapped, and his Internet connection surveilled. And for these interruptions and intrusions the Gazan user must pay nearly twice as much as his Israeli counterpart.

It is not just the end-user but also the telecommunications infrastructures themselves that are subject to the occupation's logic. Although former Israeli Prime Minister Ariel Sharon's Gaza disengagement plan stated that Israel would hand over the landline infrastructure in Palestinian areas intact, the IDF severed the main north-south connection in the Strip and buried the line's remnants under the rubble of the Kfar Darom settlement. In some cases, the destruction has been widespread and debilitating, most obviously during the 2008–9 assault on Gaza, when damage to Paltel's network in Gaza was estimated at more than US$10 million ("Interview with Saa'd" 2009). Both the purposeful destruction of equipment and the prevention of its importation and installation limit the development of high-tech infrastructure. As is with all infrastructural limits imposed on Gaza—from electricity to sewage—impeding a "normal" infrastructure occurs on a daily basis, not only during military operations. In August 2011, for example, international landline, mobile phone, and Internet connections within Gaza were shut down when an Israeli military bulldozer severed connection lines near the Nahal Oz crossing, and Paltel had to request Israeli permission to repair the line. On the rare occasion that Paltel is permitted to upgrade its infrastructure, such as in October 2012, it must coordinate such efforts with the Israeli military; as one Israeli officer explained, the "operation [for high speed Internet cables along parts of the 'wall' surrounding the Gaza Strip] was treated and run like a military operation" (quoted in Sheinman 2012).

Paltel and its subsidiaries say they are pushing for complete "separation" from Israel, including ending their reliance on Israeli providers and equipment. Nevertheless, Israel has made it easier for Paltel, Jawwal, and Hadara to acquire equipment from Israeli suppliers than from foreign ones. "They [the Israeli authorities] make us prefer suppliers from Israel. There have always been limitations on our technology," explained a Paltel executive in 2005 (personal interview, July 5, 2005). Another Paltel executive raises an additional concern, widespread among Palestinians: "How do we know that the equipment that comes from Israel is not tampered with? … maybe they make it weaker, maybe they put surveillance mechanisms in there" (personal interview, July 7, 2005). Such claims could seem outrageous, but there have been enough occasions when Palestinians have been killed while using high-tech products. Most famously, bomb-maker Yahya Ayyash was killed in Gaza when a cellular phone given him by a Shin Bet informer exploded in his ear, while an Israeli airstrike killed Hamas political leader Abdel Aziz Rantissi, believed to have been pinpointed through the GPS-locator inside a cell phone (Katz 2002). There have also been widespread rumors of Paltel public phones blowing up in the Gaza Strip.

The measures of control outlined above reinforce territorial barriers on high-tech flows, inhibit the development of Palestinian infrastructure, and perpetuate Gazans' economic dependence and de-development (and hence the uneven economic relationship). Paltel and its subsidiaries have no choice but to purchase telecommunications capacity from the Israeli market. That Gazan infrastructure is made to rely on the Israeli backbone and suppliers means that Israeli firms financially benefit from Palestinian telecommunications uses. Israeli operators surcharge calls between Jawwal phones and Israeli land and cellular numbers. Since all international calls, all calls to the West Bank, and many intra-Gaza calls are routed through Israel, Israeli operators also collect "termination charges." As one Paltel executive lamented in 2006, "Paltel is one of Bezeq's biggest customers."

Telecommunications highlights the PA's and Paltel's roles as dependent agents of Israeli control that have nonetheless been able to profit from the situation economically. When one adds to the mix Israel's "securitization" of all forms of borders, the high-tech realm becomes a microcosm of Palestinian/Israeli power imbalances. There is room to maneuver, to modernize, and of course room for hegemonic interests to accumulate capital, but only if Israeli-imposed limitations allow for such room. Inevitably, this not only prevents the full and independent development of telecommunications infrastructure, but also serves as a high-tech bordering mechanism to prevent or hinder territorial, communicative, and symbolic connections.

The Power of Digital Occupation

Limitations imposed on high-tech flows have important repercussions because of growing importance of these flows in our globalized world. It is no exaggeration to posit, as do Varnelis and Friedberg (2008), that in globalization's new space of flows "areas and populations outside of this logic are subject to the tunnel effect: they virtually don't exist as far as the networks, and hence, the dominant world economy is concerned." Certainly, Gazans' economic relations—among themselves and to the outside world—are largely determined by Israel, but the "tunnel effect" also indicates how Gaza is both subsumed into the global network and excluded from it—or at best marginalized within it. Either way, it is an ominous example of capital's uneven development.

As being plugged into the global network becomes more pervasive and necessary, it is access to the network and the flows this network affords that are important. What matters are the points of contact, the junctures, the on-ramps and off-ramps, the lines and cables underground and the towers and spectrum above ground, and, most of all, the control and ownership of all these. Here, it is the Israeli regime and its apparatus (the government, the police force, the military, the intelligence services, the high-tech industry, all with incestuous ties to each other) that is the site of power; the PA, Paltel, Paltel's subsidiaries, and other Palestinian high-tech firms are secondary. It is the Israeli state apparatus that decides whether, when, and where Palestinians may install, manage, and maintain infrastructure, just as it is the Israeli apparatus that limits and destroys that infrastructure.

Israel's occupation of Gaza has not so much ended as been modified to include the digital spectrum. Bordering Gazans is achieved through "hard" conventional borders even as it is simultaneously diffused and concentrated in the ethereal and "soft" realm of digital infrastructure. Similar to the process of land enclosure, an active landscaping process produces new forms of property rights and different systems of circulation, trespass, and exclusion. Gaza for all intents and purposes is a "real" territorial penitentiary, but also a high-tech one.

The Israeli "space of power" has become one of indistinction: there is a wall, there are unmanned drones flying around, there is a limited telecommunications infrastructure, and Internet traffic must pass through the Israeli backbone. These are all interconnected so as to create a space of control. Israeli production of and control over Gaza's borders are conventional and new, real and abstract, physical and cyber. Control over both land and high technology defines Israel's spatial containment of Gaza.

Digital occupation characterizes the pernicious confluence between neo-liberal capitalism and colonialism in actively transforming Gaza's social economy, demography, and culture towards increasing privatization, surveillance, and control.

On the one hand, both the PA and the Israeli regime benefit from information infrastructure: capital accumulation and profit, the semblance of being part of the "global network age," and, certainly from the perspective of the Israeli regime a possibility to surveil and control Gaza with as little man-power as possible. On the other hand, digital occupation also demonstrates the ways in which information technologies are used to strengthen and extend forms of repressive power. Ultimately, the relationship between state power and information infrastructure remains a historically specific, political, economic, and territorial process that cannot be separated from realities on the ground. As this case demonstrates, digital networks are designed processes integral in the production of space.

Chapter 5
Leveraged Affordances and the Specter of Structural Violence

David Karpf and Steven Livingston

As autocratic regimes across North Africa and the Middle East fell in the spring of 2011, an intense debate erupted concerning the role of digital technology. What explained the dramatic and largely unexpected political upheaval that had erupted in Tunisia, Egypt, Libya, and elsewhere? Several observers pointed to the catalytic effect of digital technologies. Wael Ghonim, the former Google engineer who helped launch an important digital platform of protest in Egypt said, "This is the revolution of the youth of the Internet, which became the revolution of the youth of Egypt, then the revolution of Egypt itself" (BBC News 2011). Not everyone agreed. If digital media led to the overthrow of autocrats in Tunisia, Egypt, and Libya, why did several similar periods of unrest in Bahrain, Saudi Arabia, Yemen, and—as of this writing—Syria fail? What explained the variation in outcomes?

This chapter seeks to formulate an intellectually elegant and balanced framework for understanding *when* and *how* digital technology plays a role in revolutionary political change—and when it does not. Our goal is to replace either/or debates about the role of technology in revolutionary change with an analytical framework that offers conditional statements about technology's role in revolutionary change. We are interested in boundary conditions—specifying the conditions that lead to successful revolutionary change in some cases, and failure in others. In this endeavor we will limit our focus on only the most extreme kinds of political activism—revolutionary change. To do so, we rely on a *leveraged affordance* model of political change (Earl and Kimport 2011). Following a discussion of leveraged affordances we will illustrate our points with a review of some of the Arab Spring revolts. In such a limited space, we cannot hope to do justice to the complexity of any one of them, much less several. The model we develop is not meant to help situate the role of digital tools within discussions of revolutionary protests.

In sum, our framework contends that the leveraged affordances of new ICTs augment revolutionary mobilization, contingent on three overarching factors: (1) the degree to which central actors use ICTs to "supersize" traditional protest activities; (2) the degree to which national or international media institutions make use of the digital traces left by "theory 2.0"-style protest efforts; and (3) the willingness of authoritarian security forces to adopt violent counter-strategies.

Leveraged Affordances

An *affordance* is a quality of an object or environment that allows individuals to perform an action (Gibson 1977). A well-designed doorknob, for example, has the quality of an object that allows one to open a door. A jet aircraft contributes to a quality of an environment that is conducive to high-speed travel over long distances. These qualities do not *cause* actions—you could alternatively use a doorknob as a convenient place to hang a jacket—but they make some actions more likely than others. An affordance is a key enabler, allowing the possibility of actions that would, in the absence of the affordance, be improbable, if not impossible. Originating in design studies, the term has been adapted to the field of computer-mediated communication. It has recently been used as a conceptual device for understanding the effects of digital technology (an affordance) on political actions. Jennifer Earl and Katrina Kimport, for example, rely on the concept in their efforts to build a new model of protest actions.

One of the principal benefits of their approach is its move away from a key assumption about protest organizations. Traditional models of contentious politics assume that protest movements face uniformly high and fixed collaboration costs. Collaboration costs are the costs associated with collective actions, such as organizing, communicating, and sustaining social movement organizations. The larger and more complex the action, the greater the costs, as Mancur Olson (1971: 48) made clear in his landmark work, *The Logic of Collective Action:*

> As group size increases, so, too, do the costs of communication and collaboration. (T)he larger the number of members in the group the greater the organization costs … For these reasons, the larger the group the farther it will fall short of providing an optimal supply of a collective good, and very large groups normally will not, in the absence of coercion or separate, outside incentives, provide themselves with even minimal amounts of a collective good.

Fixed high costs can be overcome only by one of several means, each emphasized by different research traditions. One possible solution is found in the expected ideological zeal of oppressed classes, either according to the realizations of class-consciousness or at the direction of a vanguard class of revolutionary leaders. Literacy, urbanization, working conditions, and the presence of charismatic leaders are a few of the conditions that are thought to be important in determining the effectiveness of a mobilization (Burks 1961; Street and Leggett 1961). Effective communication is also a key determinant. "If communication is more or less effective, the group is more likely to take some concerted action to rectify the grievances" (McCarthy and Zald 1973: 17). Yet communication is often costly. In describing the classic model, John D. McCarthy and Mayer N. Zald noted, "financial resources are needed to support the propaganda apparatus of the movement, to support organizers and leaders, and to procure equipment—from mimeograph machines to arms."

McCarthy and Zald offer an alternative to the classical model, one that focuses on factors that are internal to an organization, such as the professionalization of social movements that occurred in the mid twentieth century. Tarrow (1998) offers yet another school of thought, one that focuses on exogenous resources and opportunities. His political opportunity theory contends that increased political pluralism, a decline in repression, and a lack of elite consensus all constitute opportunities for political change. He describes these political opportunities as "consistent—but not necessarily formal or permanent—dimensions of the political struggle that encourage people to engage in contentious politics."

The success or failure of actions undertaken by activists depends on these external factors, and not just the resources a professional organization can muster (Meyer 2004). It also calls for the adroit use of "repertoire of contention" (Tilly 1978) by movement leaders. Such repertoires consist of various protest-related tools and actions available to a movement in a given time frame. Other social actors often mimic repertoires. Standard modern repertoires of contention include rallies and demonstrations, sit-ins, petition drives, media campaigns, boycotts, strikes, and innovative combinations.

All of these approaches share an assumption that collaboration costs are *high* and *invariable*. Those costs must be met by either ideological fervor, organizational prowess in resource mobilization, or political acumen in taking advantage of political opportunities. It is in exactly this area that we suspect the affordances of the Internet to play an important role. In Olson's time, communication and collaboration costs were indeed high and invariable. ICT's have radically reduced these costs, *but only under certain conditions*. Following Earl and Kimport, among others (Bimber 2003; Bimber, Flanagin and Stohl 2005; Lev-On and Hardin 2008; Lupia and Sin 2003), we postulate that contemporary collaboration costs are variable from high to vanishingly low, depending on circumstantial and strategic contexts. In particular, *we consider the role of violence and intimidation as a countervailing factor to technological affordances*. What digital technology affords, violence and the credible threat of violence and intimidation can negate. To understand our point it is important to begin with a clear understanding of the leveraged affordance model

Some kinds of protest can be fully contained online, what Earl and Kimport call a *theory 2.0* protest, while other protest actions take only limited advantage of technology, what they call *supersizing*. Theory 2.0 protest actions include online petitions or digital sit-ins. They are based upon the novel affordances and reduced transaction costs of the online environment, and as such do not face the classical Olsonian limitations on large-group collective action. Such protest actions have the benefit of leaving digital traces—tweets, social media postings, YouTube videos, and emails—that can be picked up by the hybrid media system. These protest actions can be limited in their scope, however. If one's strategic objective involves exercising influence in the physical world, offline actions will remain a necessary component of the repertoire of contention. Supersizing takes advantage of common features of ICT to more efficiently organize traditional protest actions, such as street demonstrations and marches. The challenges inherent in organizing a large march in 2012 are very similar to the challenges faced by Civil Rights activists in the 1963 March on Washington. Yet new ICTs simplify the work of large-group coordination. "Supersized" protest events involve a difference in degree, while "Theory 2.0" protest events involve a difference in kind.

Both types of Internet-enabled protest can yield results. In the United States, the online petition site Change.org has demonstrated a remarkable capacity for converting user-generated online petitions into massive pressure campaigns with real-world results. Change.org has opened multiple international offices and, like the United Kingdom's Downing Street petition site, allows for a type of effectively organization-less organizing that can rapidly grow to encompass millions of online voices.

Yet the limits of theory 2.0-style, organization-less collective action become apparent when the goals and targets of the campaign rest within well-formed institutional boundaries. In the United States, Change.org has avoided targeting members of Congress, because those members have well-formed practices responsive to electoral incentives. Likewise, Twitter-based activity cannot alone topple a dictatorship. Rather, theory 2.0-style activism in contentious politics often yields a second-order impact. Activity through social media channels affects international media coverage, providing images and content to international news organizations. Much as Amnesty International's letter-writing campaigns have succeeded by convincing autocratic regimes that "the whole world is watching," the digital traces of online activity pressure affect the decisions of media and political institutions, in turn creating pressure on target governments. Simultaneously, revolutionary objectives call for supersized protest efforts, in which new ICTs enable strong ties and weak ties alike.

What matters most then is not the technology, but rather how people leverage technological affordances. The social impacts of technologies "depend on the extent to which people notice and then skillfully (or less skillfully) try to leverage key affordances" (Earl and Kimport 2011: 33). This position is tied to theories of contentious politics championed by Charles Tilly, Douglas McAdam, and Sidney Tarrow (2001). As noted above, this position focuses on exogenous factors in shaping political opportunity structures while relying on the skills and political acumen of movement leaders in their use of repertoires of contention. Earl and Kimport claim that the increasing availability of outlets for online participation, lead to a new "digital repertoire of contention" (Earl and Kimport 2011: 16).

Extending across Theoretical and Geographic Borders

The literature on the Internet and collective action has focused almost entirely on the domestic context in the US (Bimber, Flanagin and Stohl 2012; Karpf 2012). The United States represents something of an easy case, however. It has a robust civil society sector, an independent media, and a stable government. We contend that in addition to variation in activist skills, one must also consider the effects of government counterstrategy, particularly when that counterstrategy may include intimidation and violence. Variability in collaboration costs are not only affected by technologically enabled affordances and the varying skills of protest organizers; they are also affected by the ability and willingness of a state or other elites to use intimidation and violence to coerce protesters into submission.

Joyce (2011) has noted the US-centric limitation of Earl and Kimport's formulation, which draws upon an implicit qualitative hierarchy of tactical skill, placing theory 2.0 actions above supersized actions. Skillful use of digital technology is equated with leveraged affordances while unskillful capacities are equated with a failure to leverage. This overlooks the possibility that movement leaders might choose to not fully leverage digital affordances. Leaders of this sort "have noticed the affordance and understand it, but skillfully realize that a digital tactic will not be effective in their particular context. That is, they make a *skillful* decision *not* to maximally leverage digital affordances." This would seem to be the case when revolutionary change is the ultimate objective of the protest action. Online action alone is not likely to bring down an autocratic state. But leveraged affordances nonetheless prove useful in coordinating resistance movements (Meier 2012). Similarly, Howard (2011) has found that new ICTs are a necessary, but not a sufficient condition for democratization in the Middle East. The affordances of new ICTs influence the range of activities chosen by activists, but the causal relationship is quite complicated.

Another criticism of existing leveraged affordance theory targets underlying assumptions about the nature of the protest actions and the political environment in which they take place. In some important instances, collaboration costs remain prohibitively high, even when technologically enabled affordances are present, such as when technologically coordinated street protests face the threat of extreme physical or psychological hardships. Put another way, Earl and Kimport assume an open political space (a political opportunity structure) where protest actions are relatively free to select from a menu of repertoires of contention. This may be true in some democratic states, but not in most autocratic states. Being arrested in most Western democracies is a much different experience than being arrested in a non-democratic regime. Protesting in the face of teargas and rubber bullets can be harmful, even occasionally deadly. Yet protesting in the face of live ammunition and even artillery and tank rounds is altogether different. In other words, variability in collaboration costs involves more than the presence of technological affordances. It also involves the presence or threatened presence of willingly used repressive violence. Even where ICT-enabled collaboration is possible, regimes may be able to marshal forces that are willing to use extreme and sustained violence against domestic populations, such as when external forces are invited in to a country to quell an uprising. Even when the digital traces of online action attract international coverage, regimes may remain undeterred when selecting a violent response. The result of this is, centrally, the re-imposition of (a different set of) high collaboration costs. The affordance created by ICT cannot be leveraged for fear of the consequences of doing do.

Whether this is the case does not turn on technology, but rather on the will of people to put themselves in the path of a regime bent on staying in power—leveraged affordances enhance the *tactics and strategies* of social movements. But the end goal of social movement participants involves changes to the power structure. That power structure learns and responds as well—a process Tarrow (1998) terms "innovation and counter innovation." Leveraged affordances are conditioned by the willingness of a regime to use force and intimidation at a level sufficient to collapse the opportunities created by new technologies. This opens up new and important questions. They do not involve the overly simplistic question of whether digital media "caused" the Arab Spring. Rather, the questions involve contingent conditions: When and under what circumstances can technologies be used to leverage revolutionary change and when can they not?

For example, what factors influence the willingness or ability of a regime to use extreme violence against its own civilian population? Why do some armies (e.g. Bahrain) shoot while others (e.g. Egypt) refuse? Barry R. Weingast (1997) argues that whether the state transgresses or respects citizens' wellbeing and rights depends on the depth and degree of citizen cohesion. Perceived ethnic, racial, or religious schisms can be leveraged by the state to its advantage. Protestors can be made a vilified out-group, facilitating brutality and repression. In the cases presented below, this dynamic is quite evident. In other cases one might well imagine (and see) the effects of other exogenous factors, such as powerful allies, technical assistance and inspiration to protest movements from other groups or countries, and even the outsourcing of repressive forces.

There is also a regime learning dynamic. Having watched and learned from neighboring states, regimes may develop a counter-strategy. They may choose to become brutal at the first signs of unrest. They may engage in deep-packet inspection or create fake social media accounts to identify dissident activities in their nascent stages. If regime opponents learn and adapt based upon peer efforts in neighboring states, we ought to expect that oppressive regimes learn and adapt as well. Where social, religious, or ethnic schemes do not exist, or when the regime is reluctant to leverage them to its advantage, outside forces can be brought in to do the job. As such, successful leveraging of technological affordances in one time and place may make the leveraging of those same affordances in another time and place more perilous. Revolutionary events in Tahrir Square inspired global activists while also serving as a warning to neighboring regimes and their allies.

Within these competing dynamics, we see a framework for an expansion of the leveraged affordance model. The success of digitally enabled social movement activism in one country does not directly imply its success in others. All protests throughout history have featured the use of the dominant ICTs of the day. What makes contemporary ICTs particularly valuable is their capacity for lowering traditionally high costs of collective action.

In the following illustrations, we argue that three boundary conditions determine success. First is the degree to which protest movements can utilize ICT to expand the strength and size of their actions. This varies based both upon technical infrastructure and population dynamics. In keeping with longstanding findings of the social movement literature, some revolutionary movements have access to greater resources or stronger political opportunities than others. Second is the degree to which media institutions make use of the digital traces left by online protest activity. Twitter cannot bring down a political regime, but it can play the intermediary role of attracting mass international attention. Third is the willingness of the ruling regime to adopt violent counter-strategies. New ICTs lower *some* of the high costs of collective action, but regime reactions can raise other collaboration costs. What's more, this third variable evolves over time, as oppressive regimes in one nation adapt to the digitally mediated experiences of other regimes. The following vignettes further demonstrate the importance of these variables.

Illustrating Cases

On January 28, as hundreds-of-thousands of demonstrators demanded the immediate resignation of President Hosni Mubarak, Egyptian authorities ordered communications and Internet services shut down. Even the country's mobile-phone carriers (Vodafone, Mobinil, and Etisalat) terminated operations, plunging Egypt back into an earlier technological era, a rapid reversal of an impressive growth in capacity.

By 2011, fast Internet-based ICTs had become relatively accessible in Egypt. According to the Egyptian Ministry of Communications and Information Technology (MCIT), at the beginning of 2010 the country had over 17 million Internet users, a 3,691 percent increase from 450,000 users at the beginning of 2001. Four million of these users had a Facebook account. One hundred and sixty thousand were bloggers. These figures constitute the basis for underscoring the importance of the leveraged affordance model for understanding the Egyptian revolution in 2011.

Shutting off access to digital services was met with the disapproval of business elites and common Egyptians who needed the Internet and cell phones as much as the protesters (El Gazar 2011). The inability and effectiveness of this blocking effort is one key factor in understanding the role of ICT in the Egyptian revolt against the Mubarak regime. Another important factor is found in what *didn't* happen. Government security forces refused to use the full weight of force against the anti-Mubarak demonstrators. As a result, the leveraged affordance created by ICT remained intact while the imposition of higher collaboration costs through violence and intimidation never fully developed.

There is no question that police and security forces in Egypt were often brutal and repressive in the weeks leading up to President Hosni Mubarak's resignation on February 11, 2011. Indeed, security forces in Egypt had the reputation for brutality well before the demonstrations. It was, after all, the police beating death of 28-year-old Khalid Said that sparked the revolt in the first place (BBC 2010). Though the exact tally is impossible to determine, the Egyptian Ministry of Health said 846 persons died during the protests in January and February (Human Rights Watch 2012).

Many of the deaths occurred on January 28, the "Friday of Rage" when protesters confronted security forces in cities across the country. Late in the day, as police withdrew from the streets, the military was ordered to assist in controlling the growing revolt. Despite the growing presence of the military on the streets and a curfew, protests continued throughout the night. Yet, crucially, the military refused to obey orders to use live ammunition and tanks to crush the rebellion (BBC 2011). Correspondent Robert Fisk described the moment.

Last night, a military officer guarding the tens of thousands celebrating in Cairo threw down his rifle and joined the demonstrators, yet another sign of the ordinary Egyptian soldier's growing sympathy for the democracy demonstrators. We had witnessed many similar sentiments from the army over the past two weeks. But the critical moment came on the evening of January 30 when, it is now clear, Mubarak ordered the Egyptian Third Army to crush the demonstrators in Tahrir Square with their tanks after flying F-16 fighter bombers at low level over the protesters. Many of the senior tank commanders could be seen tearing off their headsets—over which they had received the fatal orders—to use their mobile phones. They were, it now transpires, calling their own military families for advice. Fathers who had spent their lives serving the Egyptian army told their sons to disobey, that they must never kill their own people (Fisk 2011).

On February 11, Mubarak's resigned. In the limited space available, we cannot fully address the deeper underlying question at the heart of these events: Why did the Egyptian military refuse to attack anti-Mubarak demonstrators? For the point of our analysis, the central fact is that they didn't. Part of the answer has to do with the culture and structure of the Egyptian military. There is no inner circle of specially chosen forces, unlike Bashar Hafez al-Assad's Syria or Saddam Hussein's Iraq. The officer corps is professional and largely independent, having attended the Egyptian Military Academy, as well as college or professional schools in Europe or the United States. And while the beating and murder of Khalid Said happened under the cloak of anonymity, Tahrir square had drawn the eyes of the international media.

Furthermore, calling Weingast's analysis to mind, there were no significant sectarian splits that could be used to encourage violence against protests. The vast majority of Muslims in Egypt are Sunni. Of the total population, 10–20 percent is Coptic Christian. Again, the point here is that when the Egyptian military looked at the protesters, they had greater reason to see their brothers and sisters and co-religionists.

A similar dynamic had already played out in Tunisia. By 2011, Tunisia had one of the most developed and broadly affordable ICT infrastructures in North Africa.

In March 2010, for example, there were 3,600,000 Internet users, or about 34 percent of the population (Internet World Stats). There were also about 2,603,000 Facebook users in June 2011. Like Egyptians, Tunisians had a foundation in place to take advantage of digital affordances. The much discussed and central role that was played by social media sites like Facebook and Twitter underscore this point.

On January 13, 2011, as mass demonstrations escalated, Tunisian dictator Zine el-Abidine Ben Ali attempted to save his rule by ordering the internal security services—the police and the National Guard—to respond with force. As the demonstrations continued, despite the police crackdown, Ben Ali promised a number of concessions while, at the same time, ordering the military to buttress the internal security forces. On January 14 he also declared a state of emergency that prohibited gatherings of more than three people while authorizing deadly force against those who did not comply (Hanlon 2012).

The army refused to enforce Ben Ali's orders. The head of Tunisia's armed forces, Gen. Rachid Ammar, told more than 1,000 demonstrators in a square near his office, "Our revolution is your revolution. The army will protect the revolution." It was General Ammar's refusal to follow orders to fire on civilians that led to Ben Ali's fall from power. In the days following Ben Ali's departure, the military stepped in to control both civilian looters and repeatedly intervened to protect civilian protesters from violence at the hands of the police (Kirkpatrick 2011). As a special report of the United States Institute of Peace noted, the Tunisian army's inaction makes them stand out in comparison with their counterparts in other MENA (Middle East North Africa) nations. They are unique in the region for other reasons as well. The Tunisian military, unlike the armed forces of other MENA countries, is subordinated to the government and controlled by it. Consequently, the Tunisian armed forces never played a political role, nor did they legitimize the former regime (Hanlon 2012).

A fairly cohesive national identity and a decision by military commanders to not use force against protesters preserved the revolution. Beginning in 1994, Tunisia has been one of the top 20 recipients of US International Military Education and Training (IMET) Funding. Indeed, since 2003 Tunisia has been ranked tenth in overall funding and is the top IMET recipient in Africa. Over 4,600 Tunisian military personnel have trained in US institutions since its independence. Tunisia is also one of the few countries in the world that has cadets in all United States military academies, plus the Coast Guard academy (US Embassy Fact Sheet). Tunisia, like Egypt, has a professional and historically apolitical military that was not directly under the control of President Ben Ali's regime.

We turn next to an alternative case where leveraged affordance was effectively mitigated by the imposition of higher collaboration costs by use of force and intimidation. The number of Bahraini Internet users rose from 40,000 (out of a population of about 700,000) in 2000 to about 650,000 (out of a population of 738,000) by 2010. Put another way, in a decade Internet users rose from 5.7 percent of the population to 88 percent of the population. By 2010, there were over 250,000 Facebook users (Internet World Stats-Bahrian). Overall, the number of users jumped by 30 percent, compared with 18 percent growth during the same period in 2010. Usage in Bahrain grew 15 percent in the first three months of 2011, compared with 6 percent over the same period in 2010 year (Huang 2011).

Yet, despite these impressive numbers, even before the start of the Arab Spring, Bahrain had one of the most severe Internet surveillance and censorship systems in the world (Reporters Without Borders 2008). After a January 2009 government decree ordering ISPs to implement an official filtering system, an analysis by Harvard University's Open Net Initiative found that the filtering of political and social content had become what it called pervasive (on a spectrum of X, Y, Z, and Pervasive) (Open Net Initiative 2009). The capacity of the state's censorship system to contain civil society organizations was decisive during the protest period. At the start of demonstrations in Bahrain in mid February 2011, Internet traffic dropped by 20 percent due to aggressive government filtering (Glanz 2011).

But the repression goes well beyond software filter systems. Ali Abdulemam, the founder of Bahrainonline.org, a popular alternative news and information website, was arrested by Bahrain's National Security Agency in August 2010. He disappeared after his release from prison in late February 2011. He and 20 other opposition leaders were then tried in absentia in a military court and sentenced to 15 years in prison for what the Bahraini authorities described as plotting to overthrow the government (Desmukh 2012). Besides Abduleman's arrest, authorities imposed a gag order on the media in Bahrain and arrested over 200 other activists (Toumi 2010). It also suspended Bahrain's main human rights organizations (Human Rights Watch 2010).

The political tensions between the Shia majority and the Sunni minority center mostly on the policies of the ruling al-Khalifa family. The ruling Sunni monarchy has marginalized the Shia majority, justifying the discrimination by claiming Shia loyalties rest with Iran. Still, Shia animosity toward the al-Khalifa royal family has more to do with domestic politics and economics. Ironically, some part of the explanation rests with the fact that the Shia, who make up 80 percent of the labor force, are usually prevented from employment with the security forces, the largest source of employment in Bahrain. Prior to 1979 and the Iranian revolution, the Shia had staffed the majority of the non-officer positions in the security services. The monarchy has also exacerbated tensions by extending citizenship to as many as 100,000 Sunnis from Yemen, Syria, Jordan and Pakistan and offering them employment in the security services. The regime has also welcomed puritanical Salafis into government offices. "These Salafis are Muslims who abhor the Shia and often advocate violence against them—as has been the case in Iraq and Pakistan" (Sotloff 2010). It seems evident that Bahraini society is rife with serious sectarian divides. Located on the western side of the Persian Gulf, its strategic significance cannot be overstated. Not only is it home to the United States Navy's Fifth Fleet, its conservative Sunni ruling family in a majority Shia population is a bulwark for Saudi Arabia against Iran.

As Shia demonstrations in Bahrain escalated in March 2011, advertisements started appearing in Pakistani newspapers. "Urgent requirement—manpower for

Bahrain National Guard." Another advertisement said, "For service in Bahrain National Guard, the following categories of people with previous army and police experience are urgently needed." "Previous experience" and "urgent need" were emphasized. The overwhelming majority of Muslims in Pakistan are Sunni. At least 2,500 former servicemen were recruited by Bahrainis and brought to Manama, the capital of Bahrain. This move increased the size of the National Guard and riot police by as much as 50 percent. "Our own Shia cannot join the security forces, but the government recruits from abroad," said Nabeel Rajab, president of the Bahrain Center for Human Rights (Mashal 2011).

The protests in Bahrain were largely peaceful until a pre-dawn raid by police on February 17 to remove protestors from a major protest site in Manama. The police crackdown also included night raids in Shia neighborhoods, beatings at checkpoints, and denial of medical care. Approximately 3,000 people were arrested in the initial confrontation. At least five people died due to torture while in police custody.

Then, on March 14th, Saudi-led forces entered the country (Bronner and Slackman 2011). As *The New York Times* put it, "Saudi Arabia's military intrusion last year into the micro-sheikdom of Bahrain has effectively made the tiny island the 14th Saudi province" (Jacobs and Khanna 2012). The House of Saud, the anchor of Sunni Arabia, could not afford to allow a Shia revolt on its doorstep. Bahrain's protest movement was crushed. The affordance created by Bahrain's flourishing was negated by the brutality of the police and security forces. Bahraini blogger Zakariya Rashid Hassan al-Ashiri ran a website covering news in his village of al-Dair. He was arrested on April 2 and charged with "disseminating false news and inciting hatred." He died on April 9 while still in police custody. Photos of a brutally beaten body thought to be al-Ashir indicate he was beaten to death (Committee for the Protection of Journalists, 2011).

A similar story can be told of other revolts across North Africa and the Middle East that failed to leverage the affordance created by ICT. The presence of security forces willing to use extreme violence undermines ICT-based leveraged affordance. ICTs make it easier to "supersize" offline protest events, and can help draw the attention of international media. But these strategic benefits crumble against violent counter-strategy. Whether soldiers and police were willing to pull the trigger was itself often the product of other factors: professionalization of the officer corps, ethnic alignments, and external actors all play a part in determining the use of force against civilian protesters.

Conclusion

We have argued that the debate between cyber-pessimists and cyber optimists misses the point. ICT does indeed create the sort of leveraged affordance described by Earl and Kimport. Offline protest actions can indeed be "supersized" on the back of technological affordances. Social media activity can affect international intermediaries. But because people in supersized protest actions must still endure hardships, the nature of the hardships encountered in protest actions remains relevant. In their analysis of leveraged affordances, Earl and Kimport assume a rather unvaried level of physical hardship, as one might expect when considering a protest action in the United States or Europe. One might be arrested and endure the hardships involved with the experience. Of course, during certain periods of US history, the hardships of the Civil Rights Movement or the Labor Movement were sometimes much more serious than a night in jail. On the other hand, the hardships experienced by those participating in the Arab Spring have been sometimes quite extreme. Yet there is variability. In Egypt and Tunisia, the military refused to unleash the full weight of force against fellow Egyptians and Tunisians. In Bahrain, the ruling regime turned to co-religious in other countries to do the dirty work of repression for them. In Syria, we see the same general dynamic of repression. President Assad's inner circle of security forces is drawn from the ranks of fellow Alawites, whereas much of the opposition movement comes from the majority Sunni population.

> During its decades of rule … the Assad family developed a strong political safety net by firmly integrating the military into the regime. In 1970, Hafez al-Assad, Bashar's father, seized power after rising through the ranks of the Syrian armed forces, during which time he established a network of loyal Alawites by installing them in key posts. In fact, the military, ruling elite, and ruthless secret police are so intertwined that it is now impossible to separate the Assad regime from the security establishment … So … the regime and its loyal forces have been able to deter all but the most resolute and fearless oppositional activists. In this respect, the situation in Syria is to a certain degree comparable to Saddam Hussein's strong Sunni minority rule in Iraq (Bröning 2011).

The leveraged affordance model is useful for the study of revolutionary protest movements, but only once refined to account for these features of strategy and counterstrategy. Digital tools are useful to protestors. They help movements to grow in size and attract international attention. Presumably, regimes are less willing to turn violent against larger crowds while risking international condemnation. Yet the internal calculus of governing regimes is a complicated phenomenon. And the more eager the regime is to respond violently, the less useful new ICTs prove to be. We believe there is compelling evidence in support of the framework, though obviously the interplay of strategy and counter-strategy is a subject for much further and deeper analysis.

PART II
Digital Media and Political Engagement

Chapter 6
Technology-Induced Innovation in the Making and Consolidation of Arab Democracy

Imad Salamey

Persistent post-colonial Middle East and North African authoritarianism has long appeared to be the exception of the 'Third Democratic Wave' that ended many autocratic regimes in East Europe and South American countries in the 1980s (Huntington 1991). In notable contrast, monarchic, theocratic and autocratic Middle Eastern regimes, buoyed by sustaining oil revenues and foreign military and economic assistance, have consolidated their respective grips on power while their mass constituencies signaled little or no interest in joining the global trend. In the relative rare events that uprisings occurred, as in Syria during 1982 and Iran in 2009, regimes were generally swift to crush them at least for extended periods.

Explanations for the Middle Eastern and North African authoritarian regimes' robustness to the democratic wave have been offered by various oriental perspectives. Cultural views attribute Islamic authoritarian norms and practice as the primary reason behind 'submissive' publics under repressive regimes (Huntington 1993). Economic views focus on the notions of "rentierism" in oil rich countries where government revenues have been able to buy public support (Luciani 2009). Other economic views have associated the widespread informal economies of non-oil producing countries with a weakened middle class and reigning autocracy. International economic perspectives link faulty international economic policies to the undermining of reform movements. Strategic and international security perspectives highlight Western interests in Middle Eastern and North African stability at the cost of potentially unstable democracies (Bellin 2005). Western support to oil-rich monarchies and autocracies underline such views (Salamey 2009). The consequence of these various interpretations is an assumption of strong Middle Eastern and North African authoritarian states ready to use unrestrained coercive force against a weak civil society incapable of achieving collective action or democratic transition (Ulfelder 2005). And there is reason to heed some of these arguments—the dominance of authoritarian ruling elites was manifested in the military and secret services' control over all aspects of civil life and institutions in many cases (Posusney and Angrist 2005; Richards and Waterbury 2008).

In light of the 2011–12 uprisings and the subsequent collapse of various Middle Eastern and North African authoritarian regimes, such fearful institutions have been seriously challenged by public protest and armed rebellions. Mass movements have broken the silence, successfully galvanizing dramatic changes through collective action to bring down the long-entrenched regimes in Egypt, Libya, and Tunisia; significantly modifying the regime in Yemen, shaking the foundations in Bahrain before Saudi intervention helped stem the tide, and significantly destabilizing Syria. This begs the question of whether Middle Eastern exceptionalism has been finally deconstructed in favor of a "Fourth Democratic Wave" sweeping the Arab world. What other interpretations are necessary to explain the shortcomings of exceptionalist assumptions and provide grounds for an alternative explanatory discourse to political transition in the Middle East and North Africa (MENA) region? We should be careful not to jump to popular conclusions, or easy to reject existing frameworks—but to more fully understand the changes effecting political liberalization in the Arab Middle East we must be willing to consider new sources and spaces of power and contention.

Causes of the Arab Spring

At least three major political discourses have offered newer interpretations. Political economy views have attributed various causal interpretations to explain weakening Middle Eastern authoritarianism. Most associate political grievances and popular uprisings with autocratic mismanagement and widespread economic corruption (Corm 2012). Evidence is drawn from the corrupt rule and consequent economic disasters brought about by the regime of President Ben Ali in Tunisia, Mubarak in Egypt, Assad in Syria, Ali Saleh in Yemen, and Qaddafi in Libya (Anderson 2011; Wilson 2011). Liberal perspectives, on the other hand, have advocated global democratic values as an overriding cultural system driving the mobilization of youth in demanding the end to dictatorship. Calls for freedom, rule of law, accountability, free and fair election, human rights were among the popular outcry of protesters (Bormann, Manuel Vogt, and Cederman 2012; Gause III 2011; Paust 2012). Liberal values have overwhelmed traditional Islamist views in favor of democratic cultures prioritizing freedom, plurality, and human rights. In addition to political economy and democratic cultural proposals, realism has provided a third international relations perspective. Realism's views have proclaimed an underlying regional power struggle among rival states. Turkey and Gulf states, on one side, confronting, on the other side, an expanded Iranian influence in Bahrain, Iraq, Lebanon, Palestine, and Syria (Salamey 2009). The EU and NATO have found in Turkey and the Gulf States a common purpose to drive Russia and China out of Libya and North Africa and deter growing Iranian military and nuclear capacities. Along this line of argument is an overemphasis of the role of the military and security apparatuses and an external intervention option in forcing regime change.

Yet, protesters attributed different motives for their revolts that varied according to countries. Evidence of these differences has been revealed by a phone survey conducted by the Lebanese American University (LAU) on January and February 2012. The survey asked 40 key Arab activists from various political backgrounds in Egypt, Libya, Syria, and Yemen a series of questions regarding their views about the causes, demands, and mobilization factors that have helped the protesters confront their governments. Responses were analyzed and tabulated as to reveal common denominators as well as differences. The results identify a strong and common liberal orientation of the various movements as reflected in their common demands for freedom and fight against corruption. Media and ICTs appear to have played a significant and common role in the mobilization and organization of protests. Still, however, different country contexts have shaped the protest movements differently. Yemeni respondents for example stressed economic causes and demands and relied less on ICT in their mobilizations than other activists (see Table I.1).

The modes of revolutionary transformations have also varied between mild confrontations in countries where the military has taken a passive role, such as in Tunisia and Egypt, to extreme confrontation, such as the case in Libya and Syria. International interventions and active involvements have also varied between one country and another. The claimed causes did not contribute to similar outcomes in Jordan, Algeria, Morocco or most Gulf States. Still and critically important to this analysis is the question of timing. Why did the events in Tunisia, stir-up such a widespread public discontent and snowballing revolutions? For decades the same public stood passive under poverty and repression. Events in some countries remained nationally isolated without implicating another region or country. So why did the impact of repression and grievances become suddenly and widely intolerable? Addressing this question may shed light on the new forces driving postmodern protest movements, in consolidation with the reasons that have always stirred political change in the past.

When the 27-year-old Tunisian street vendor, Mohamed Bouazizi, set himself on fire to protest having his push-cart confiscated by local authorities in January 2011, this news spread rapidly via public media and Internet communication throughout Tunisia and the Arab region. The Bouazizi incident was fast to ignite massive protests throughout Tunisia, and soon after, in most Arab states against standing regimes. This sparking event stands as a close reminder of the 1991 Rodney King incident in the United States, which instigated massive protest and rioting in several African American populated cities. King, a black resident of Los Angeles, was brutally beaten by four white police officers after being arrested for a traffic violation. The incident would have passed unnoticed if not for the presence of a resident in the area who witnessed and videotaped the beating. A few hours later, footage of the arrest was simultaneously transmitted on almost every American TV and media outlet. The instant and massive transmission of brutal images of the beating was sufficient to exacerbate deep feelings of racial injustice that had long incubated with poor and marginalized African American residents of

Los Angeles. The city was swiftly engulfed in massive and violent protests that lasted several days without the ability of local authorities to control the situation. Both the Bouazizi and Rodney King incidents provide similar lessons. At a critical historic juncture, where resentment against the existing order has been deepened and ripened, the capitulation of the public with a shocking reminder can serve as a rallying call for collective action. In both events, the sensational and wide coverage of news were instrumental in the awakening of deeply held public bitterness. In the case of the Arab revolutions, however, the public's ability to utilize new information technologies in communication to organize public action was an added and important new factor.

To more fully appreciate why, we must understand the modern information infrastructure, including various technologies such as satellite media, Internet, and mobile technologies that have entrenched widely into Arab societies. After all, the role of innovations has long captured the imagination of political theorists in the explanation of historic transitions that went beyond traditional interpretations (Khun 1962). Developments in weaponry (cannons and dynamites) in the Middle Ages, for example, undermined the castle-based feudal system. Similar innovations in the print machine, textile industry, and steam-powered engine, among others were fundamental aspects in the nineteenth century industrial revolution and the political transformation toward a capitalist economy. Thus, in light of the Arab revolutions, it is worth investigating what roles modern innovations in communication technology have played in the transformation of society away from an outdated state control system.

ICTs and the Changing State-society Relations in the Arab World

Past revolutions and political transformations occurred without relying on advanced information infrastructures. Even during this Arab Spring, the revolution in Yemen against autocratic President Ali Abdallah Saleh erupted without the presence of a sophisticated information infrastructure similar to that that in other Arab spring countries. The point here is to reject reductionism in the making of political transformations (Howard 2011). Advancements in ICTs are not sufficient causes for revolution (Al-Yahyawi 2012; Howard 2010). Many scholars have identified structural drivers and prerequisites for democratic revolutions other than those related to communication technologies (Huntington 1991; Lipset 1959). Traditional means of communication such as local TVs, radios, newspapers, and religious centers have historically served the interests of authoritarian regimes and were only inclusive in the analysis of regime consolidation of power. State-controlled media provided authoritarianism with the ability to monopolize and manipulate access to information, thus preventing the public from having a free voice in communicating its collective grievances. Syrian state-run media outlets under Syria's President Bashar Al-Assad continued to deny existing problems in the country a year after public unrests have claimed over 10,000 lives. Two decades earlier, the same mouthpieces of the Syrian regime made no mention of the crackdown against the rebellious cities of Hamma and Homs, which are estimated to have claimed more than 20,000 lives.

Innovations in modern communication technology, however, have fundamentally altered the relationships between state and society. This can be attributed to the development of globally interconnected communication infrastructures that has provided publics with affordable, accessible, mobile, and interactive connections. In 2010, nearly two billion people worldwide used the Internet (Dutton, Dopatka, Hills, Law, and Nash 2011). The rapid transmission of information, its diversity, and comprehensiveness have helped destabilize traditional structures of control. The interconnectivity of the Internet network with other aspects of information transmission related to diverse economic activities such as banking and commerce synthesized the decentralization of both economic and political activism (Howard, Agarwal, and Hussain 2011). Arab states, such as Egypt, failed to shut down the Internet networks during public protests due to the dependency of global businesses on its operation. Satellite technology similarly undermined state's monopolies and provided the public with multiple and instant sources of coverage. The regional and powerful role of the Qatari Al-Jazeera network in live broadcasting of Arab protests was crucial in public mobilization and reactions. In almost every Arab Spring country, states resorted to shutting down Al-Jazeera offices and blocking its transmission (Egypt, Lebanon, Libya, Morocco, Syria, Yemen, etc.). The station, however, quickly retaliated by having coverage transmitted by activists through their mobile phones and cameras. In vain, Arab autocracies in Egypt, Yemen, Libya, and Syria tried to win the media war but lost in most encounters.

Even more significant to this strain of communication innovations is the introduction of social media and participatory technologies. The ability for the public to instantly interact on a massive level through mobile phones and away from the watchful eyes or control of the state using twitter, Facebook, Skype, Viber, YouTube, text messaging, etc., hammered the last nail in the coffin of a centralized information regime. Not only did the social media announce the liberalization of information from state centralization, it has also empowered a new generation of "users" who became the young active reporters and organizers of collective action. Mobilized through social networks, they required neither elaborate skills nor extensive resources to carry out their live broadcasts. Users were easily transformed to public informants when they transmitted the news and became public leaders when they called for protests (Chatfield, Akbari, Mirzayi and Scholl 2011). The net result is a paradigm shift in the traditional state-society relationship, where revolution in information infrastructure has significantly undermined state control over society and paved the way for the radical transformation of politics.

The establishment of social media had also facilitated the rise of new and free cyber-based deliberation forums (Kaplan and Haenlein 2011). They soon became occupied by a young, critical and cosmopolitan Internet generation. It is estimated that the number of Facebook users in the MENA region doubled from 11.9 million to 21.3 million in 2010 and to 45 million in 2012 (Arab Social Media Report 2012). The prevalence of bloggers, Twitter feeds and Facebook pages among Middle Eastern and North African youth helped open the discussion about traditionally sensitive topics such as sex, gender rights, political freedom, human rights and religion, among others. This moved intellectual and political discussions away from the watchful eye of the state and religious authorities, effectively dismantling the state's traditional monopoly on information. Ahlam Mosteghanami, an Algerian feminist and critical intellectual, gathered 193,059 likes on her Facebook and her daily statuses invited the critical discussions of thousands, with even more visiting her official website frequently. YouTube videos were also easily and quickly produced, downloaded and distributed to hundreds of thousands around the globe. As a result, youth empowerment reached unprecedented levels of intellectual maturity in defiance of the authoritarian parapet. Unconsciously, the divinity of the ruling elites began to break down in the Arab world's largest and most central state, with public consciousness growing firm in the direction of realizing a modern and transparent elected civil state (Salamey and Pearson 2012).

Innovations in information infrastructure have, therefore, provided crucial affordances in expediting the deconstruction of Arab authoritarianism. The emergences of new information regimes that favor diverse, affordable, accessible and interactive systems of communication have made political transformation possible in previously unimaginable ways. However, the ability of authoritarianism to cope with the antithetical information regime system is yet to be unraveled. Many Arab monarchies have already begun to reconstruct their national information infrastructure. Their efforts aim to introduce alternative and sophisticated centralization mechanisms to control and filter information and search engines. A virtual defense wall prevents 'unfriendly' exchanges in many countries with sophisticated filtering and blocking software. The Iranian theocracy has established Internet control units to analyze and track users' activities (Stepanova 2011). Other regimes' efforts have been made to orchestrate state-sponsored counter-Internet propaganda campaigns and wage cyber-attacks against dissidents' blogs and websites. In July 2012 Russia passed a law to create a blacklist of websites deemed as "extremists." The British government has attempted to draft a communications bill that would produce a system of blanket collection and retention of all online data (Kampfner 2012). China has succeeded in imposing many restrictions on Google and forced the company to comply with the government constrains. Most recently, Islamists have been mobilizing support to censor and ban Google and YouTube after an immature movie depicted Prophet Mohammad in offensive roles was shared globally on the Internet.

Yet, despite continued efforts to reformulate conservatives' and states' control of the information infrastructure, and consequently over society, their ability to do so has been significantly eroded. New innovations are destined to emerge and new generations of users will continue to overcome obstacles and restrictions. Howard (2011) observes that "in this global, digital media environment, it is going to be increasingly difficult for the strong men of North Africa and the Middle East to rig elections. It will also be increasingly difficult to suspend democratic constitutions and pass power to family members." This is not only because new innovations have strengthened public oversight, but also due to new information infrastructure that has decentralized political leadership and ruled out requirements for charismatic populist politicians (Chatfield, Akbari, Mirzayi and Scholl 2011; Salamey and Tabar 2012). Thus it is contingent for newly emerging democracies to protect the right to freedom of information as well as to consolidate a newly established decentralized information regime. They need to examine new ICT policies backed by constitutional amendments that can guarantee users' digital rights to free electronic networking, protect the rights to surf and exchange information, preserve web privacy, and provide for data protection. Important developments in this domain are visible in cases like Tunisia and Lebanon, but are also fraught with counter-movements even within these regimes.

ICT Policies in Arab Democracies

Dutton et al. have identified several policy dimensions essential for countries seeking to comply with digital rights. They include: access, freedom of connection, freedom of expression, equality, freedom of information (FOI), privacy, and data protection (Dutton, Dopatka, Hills, Law and Nash 2011). Several states have been quick to adopt new laws and regulations pertaining to freedom of expression on the Internet and the foundation of a new liberal information regime. In 2000, Estonia was among the pioneering countries that stipulated legal state obligations to provide access to electronic information and services. In 2008 it passed personal data protection legislation, and in June 2009, the French Constitutional Council followed by ruling that the freedom to access 'public online communication services' was a basic human right. In July 2010, Finland similarly pronounced broadband Internet as a fundamental human right (Finnish Ministry of Transport and Communications 2010). Most recently, Latin American countries show movement in similar ways: in September 2010 Costa Rica's constitutional court announced that the Internet was also a fundamental right and mandated the government to provide universal access for all (Argüero 2010), while the Argentinean province of San Luis passed a law guaranteeing all citizens the right to free Internet access.

There are also encouraging policy steps being taken to advance freedom and access to information in the MENA region. There have been partial reforms introduced in Tunisia and Morocco that provide citizens with greater access to information (Almadhoun 2012). Yet, Arab governments have remained slow to introduce relevant legislations particularly those pertaining to ICT infrastructure. Policy reforms in this area have remained exclusively confined to Northern and Western democratic states. A particular challenge in Arab states is a traditional legal framework that views laws as a means for the preservation of rule and order rather than that of serving the interests of the people. This historical and structural deficiency continues to antagonize the public and economic interests with that of the ruling autocracy. While the former seek laws that liberalize and decentralize the information infrastructure, the latter strives for the opposite.

Admittedly, the complexity of MENA states and societies, and the powerful coercive apparatus of authoritarian regimes were significant factors in delaying democratic transformations for many years (Posusney and Angrist 2005). Yet the Arab Spring has called for a dramatic political transformation in Arab states and societies. Understanding the causes and dynamic of contemporary protest movements is critical in the deconstruction of the Middle Eastern exceptionalism hypotheses. Among the lessons learned from the Arab spring is that revolutionary outbreaks cannot be understood in terms of incidental or sudden eruptions, but as an accumulation of structural causes and instrumental developments (Salamey and Pearson 2012). Revolutionary expressions can only fully blossom when both the structure and means for change are simultaneously established. The Arab Spring demonstrates how structural economic and political crises along instrumental innovations in media and the ICT have converged to spark protests and accelerate the downfall of outdated authoritarian regimes.

Beyond their role in accelerating the revolutionary outbreaks, innovations in global communication technology have turned economic, political, and cultural liberalization of state-society relations into an imperative outcome. Economic development, for example, has come to be linked to the formulation of a decentralized communication and information regime. One of the historic revelations of the Arab Spring, perhaps, is that regimes defying such a trend are destined to fall. Military strength and international balance of power emerged as insufficient requisites for state survival. A state's capacity to cope with the globally liberalized and decentralized ICT trends became an important determinant of political power. It seems no longer the case that states' military, economic, social, or international policy agendas can be formulated irrespective from that of its communication and information infrastructure. A new epoch in political discourse appears to have been unleashed where communication and information infrastructure innovations have extended the various existential requirements of the state.

Emerging democracies and transitional states have many challenges to confront, including the task to replace the dysfunctional political and legal frameworks with alternative transparent and representative political institutions. The decentralization of power and control is emerging as an essence for world politics where globally interactive and informed citizens along an integrated economy determine to a large extent the fate of the state. For the Arab world, the establishment of a new ICT infrastructure that preserves access, freedom of connection, freedom of expression, equality, freedom of information, privacy and data protection will be among the main policy challenges. A partnership of stakeholders consisting of civil societies, economic interests, and those of the state may represent a suitable forum to advance a liberal and decentralized ICT policy platform.

Chapter 7
Al-Masry Al-Youm and Egypt's New Media Ecology

David M. Faris

This chapter presents a case study of the Egyptian media system to explore the nature of the digital ecosystem and its implications for authoritarian media systems more generally. Despite the success of authoritarian regimes like Iran and China in tightly controlling digital space and closing down spaces for repression, digital media often contribute to long-term movements toward democratization in seemingly unpredictable ways. In the Middle East and the broader Muslim world, research supports the idea that the diffusion of digital media has strengthened democratic movements and practice, notably through improvements in civil society and citizen journalism (Howard 2011). The idea that technology diffusion strengthens democratic movements was supported by the events of the Arab Spring, in which Internet-based organizing tools played significant roles in the uprisings. Tufecki and Wilson (2012), find that those who attended the first day of the Tahrir Square protests in Egypt on January 25th were overwhelmingly likely to have Internet access at home, and that a significant share of protestors heard about the events through social media first, primarily Facebook and Twitter (Tufecki and Wilson 2012).

Others have argued that citizen journalism played a decisive role in transforming media environments (Khamis and Vaughn 2011) or that in both the Egyptian and Tunisian uprisings, a decade of digital activism laid the groundwork for successful campaigns (Hussain and Howard 2011; Faris 2012). Studies asserting a limited role for digital media in these uprisings are in an observable minority (e.g., Aday et al. 2012). Some of the campaigns during the Arab Spring were successful in changing regimes, while others were not; the exact trajectories do not concern us here because they concern other architectures of political control and civil-military relations. The aim of this chapter is not to determine the circumstances such movements might succeed, but rather to ask how digital media change repressive media environments even when the regimes take significant steps to interfere, control, or co-opt digital spaces. I use the case of Egypt to examine how social media can broaden and deepen democratic discourses even in cases where journalists themselves are threatened. This study was inspired and informed by ethnographic fieldwork with the Egyptian independent daily newspaper *Al-Masry Al-Youm*, 18 months prior to the Arab uprisings.

Prior to the January 2011 uprising, journalists at *Al-Masry Al-Youm* and other independent journalists operated in environments that international observers considered at most "partly free" (on a scale of free, partly free, to not free). Other observers maintained an even more conservative view of the Egyptian digital environment. Mohamed Abdel Dayem, coordinator of the Committee to Protect Journalists Middle East and North Africa Program, wrote in 2010 that, "Judging by what's transpired in recent weeks, press freedom in Egypt is in a deplorable state" (Dayem 2010). The Committee to Protect Journalists, and numerous other NGOs, condemned the 2010 sentencing of Wael Abbas, a popular and international-renowned blogger, critical for his work in breaking stories of torture and police abuse in Egypt, to six months in prison in March 2010. Other abuses of press freedom in Egypt include the ongoing imprisonment of blogger Abdul Kareem Nabeel Suleiman Amer, and the repeated and persistent arrests of bloggers as well as digital activists organizing through Facebook.

The Egyptian context was not as dangerous to journalists as more repressive contexts, perhaps because state power can sometimes be checked by a willing judiciary (Waisbord 2002). But pre-2011 Egypt was widely regarded as a repressive environment to practice political journalism. Reporters Without Borders ranked Egypt 143rd out of 175 countries in its annual report for 2009 ("Press Freedom Index 2009"). Comparatively, Egypt was a more dangerous place to be a journalist than Morocco, for instance, but much safer than Tunisia or Syria. However, the repression of high-profile journalists and activists does not tell us much about the actual discursive environment in which these actors are challenging state power. Rather, the way that Egyptian journalists moved seamlessly from personal blogs and media platforms to those of corporate-funded ventures, all the while effectively operating independently, suggested important and un-coopted digital spaces for the expression of political opinions.

The Rise of Multi-dimensional Media Systems

As of 2009, of 195 media systems in the world, 125 were either "not free" or "partially free." Despite the increasing attention paid to non-democratic media systems, particularly in the Middle East and Asia, scholars have yet to adequately and conceptually define such a system's basic parameters and characteristics. In democratic media systems, Becker has argued "it is the responsibility of a mass political media system to provide information to citizens to participate in processes of governance" (Becker 2004: 145). In such systems neither the state nor a small number of private market players should dominate the information marketplace, lest they limit the diversity of viewpoints and exclude voices from the public sphere. Scholars also note the importance of strong government institutions for the proper functioning of a democratic media system. As Waisbord argues, "the state remains a central institution for ensuring basic conditions for the functioning of the press" (2002: 106). In authoritarian media systems, then, the media exists primarily to advance the goals of the state and to serve the authoritarian regime's goals of stemming the flow of information and preventing ordinary citizens from having access to unfiltered information. For such regimes, "control of information is critical to maintaining power" (Price 2002: 17). Typologies of authoritarian media systems date to the 1950s and Seibert et al.'s famous (and problematic) framework of the four types of media systems: the *libertarian*, *authoritarian*, *social responsibility*, and *Soviet communist* models. Contemporary world politics have rendered this popular typology largely outdated, but no contemporary definitions of authoritarian media systems have yet reached scholarly consensus, particularly given the fragmentation of the media ecology since the adoption of digitally-mediated spaces.

Traditional media systems before the digital age were two-dimensional. One was the print media—largely corporate-controlled or state-controlled, heavily financed and steered by a relatively small elite of editors and writers. The other was radio and broadcast television, also quite amenable to state control. Thus, the height of the broadcast, mass-media era—the 1950s, to the 1970s—also represented the zenith of authoritarian control over media content. While challenges have been made to closed systems by enterprising pamphleteers or cassette-makers (Hirschkind 2006), the state could and did effectively control information. This is true for several reasons: the production of mass media during this period required heavy fixed investments—printing presses, offices, and large staffs of reporters and editors. This heavy cost of entry into the media environment led to media owners and authoritarian regimes quickly and successfully asserting their control in the period following the end of European colonialism.

Egypt was a relatively free-wheeling press environment during the Interwar period and after the Second World War, when the country was still ruled by an increasingly unaccountable monarchy. In 1952, the Free Officers revolution brought a military junta to power. While initially promising greater freedoms and democracy, the regime instead consolidated its control over all sectors of political, cultural and economic life. There is little evidence to suggest that international radio broadcasts seriously disrupted domestic politics during this period. Both radio and television continued to require enormous fixed costs to operation and because of those costs the state was able to control them (Rugh 2004: 181). The situation remained more or less unchanged for decades, with each segment of the broadcast system serving different but synchronized functions. As Castells argues:

> Until recently, and even nowadays to a large extent, the media constitute an articulated system, in which, usually, the print press produces original information, TV diffuses to a mass audience, and radio customizes the interaction. (Castells 2008)

This began to change, however, with the introduction of satellite broadcast television in the late 1980s and the 1990s. Satellite television ushered an era in which authoritarian media systems were subject to unwanted involvement by external media actors—in the Middle East by the widely-documented advent of the television station Al-Jazeera, which broadcasted frank reports and discussions of Arab political events directly into the homes of citizens across the region—citizens who normally did not have this kind of access to news and dissent about their own societies. The effects of that penetration have never quite been quantified, however, and are not without their critics. Kern and Hainmueller, for instance, argue that East Germans exposed to West German media before the fall of the Berlin Wall were more supportive of communism (Kern and Hainmueller 2009). In Egypt, the political environment was not quite as authoritarian as that in East Germany, but the state did try to prevent citizens from free access to information.

However, as the different dimensions of authoritarian mass media previously represented differences in degree, the introduction of the Internet represented a difference in kind: a fourth dimension to authoritarian media systems. In short, the Internet brought with it the age of media *multidimensionality*. The Internet has augmented the dimensionality of authoritarian media systems in several ways. First, it increases the reach of newspapers, and allows globally-produced newspaper information to penetrate state borders (Lynch 2006). It allows diasporas, exiles, and other members of the community to participate in politics in ways previously unimaginable (Brinkerhoff 2009). In the context of Burma, for instance, the Democratic Voice of Burma functioned "as an archive of public memory in a context where all political expression, including songs and popular political satire carry heavy penalties of imprisonment" (Pidduck 2012: 550). Digital media also allowed for access to the public sphere by political, religious, or ethnic minorities, who have otherwise been excluded from public deliberation (Faris 2010). Perhaps most importantly, it has wired citizens, even in authoritarian states, with the ability to form their own media outlet. Castells refers to this as a process and "rise of self-communication" (Castells 2008). Rather than serving as passive recipients of information in newspapers, or at best, as letter-writers or the lucky chosen few of the call-in satellite talk shows, the Internet allows citizens to co-produce and mediate information in direct and personal ways. While the state may still arrest individual writers or block web sites, the Internet and mobile technologies make it more difficult to shut down the *pathways of dissent.* For example, Mubarak's regime arrested bloggers and disrupted social media web site selectively, but there were always others writing and distributing information critical of the state and its affairs. Digital media tools, in the hands of ordinary citizens, made it possible for citizens to document and challenge abuses by the state by capturing images and videos of transgressions, and making them public information.

The Egyptian press environment prior to the uprising of January 2011 was much more open than one would gather from most media freedom rankings, particularly because they focus on outdated standards, and particularly because they neglect the important ways in which digital media have provided safe and self-powered alternatives. Both digital media and independent media outlets (which are quickly becoming interdependent and overlapping) have presented routine challenges to state power, and practitioners in both systems are subject to interference and harassment by state authorities. The Egyptian media system under Mubarak was thus a battleground where set-pieces about democracy, the proper reach of state authority, the scope of civil and political rights, and disagreements about foreign policy were performed much more rigorously than over-reading definitions of authoritarian media systems might suggest. To explore this important issue, it is important to consider a prototypical example of such professional yet independent media outlets present in contemporary Egyptian politics.

Al-Masry Al-Youm and the Challenge to Egyptian State Media Hegemony

Al-Masry Al-Youm emerged in 2004, after a loosening of press laws in Egypt that coincided with the Bush Administration's short-lived period of democratization in the Middle East. No coherent theoretical rationale has successfully explained why the Egyptian state at this particular juncture decided to open its press system to media outlets which almost immediately began to offer readers more critical evaluations of state policies than had traditionally state-run media. However, the events of 2003–6 do suggest strongly that authoritarian regimes react to pressure from their primary patrons, in this case the United States (Brownlee 2008). Unlike most newspapers in Egypt, which either are operated indirectly by the state, like the flagship state paper, *Al-Ahram*, or by the licensed political parties, *Al-Masry Al-Youm* offered a model which had not been seen in Egypt in decades—a privately-financed company staffed by journalists and editors who appeared to be independent from the state security apparatus. *Al-Masry Al-Youm* was followed in short order by the founding of the opposition weekly *Al-Dustur*, which was widely regarded as having an Islamist bent, and the daily newspaper *El-Badeel* in 2008, a left-leaning, secular outlet sympathetic to the burgeoning labor movement. Collectively these outlets comprised an entirely new sector in the Egyptian print environment—the independent press.

Collectively these papers were instrumental in breaking or giving in-depth coverage to countless stories that put the government in a bad light and which originated in the country's rich and vociferous blogosphere—from the torture scandal originally broken by the blogger Wael Abbas, to the sexual harassment of women in downtown Cairo, and more recently the killings of Baha'is in an Upper Egypt village, and the fatal police beating in June 2010 of Khaled Said (his murder would spark a Facebook movement that contributed heavily to the uprising). Journalists at these papers often worked hand-in-hand with bloggers—who were even more willing to cross the so-called red lines of Egyptian journalism (Faris 2010a). Some of these bloggers eventually came to work for *Al-Masry Al-Youm*, and some *Masry* journalists have their own blogs. *Al-Masry Al-Youm* was a pioneer in creating digital content in Egypt prior to the uprising—years before the events of January 2011, the paper had transformed itself into a hypermedia operation, complete with video journalists and an extensive online archive. This last point is crucial. Even if a reporter for a paper was arrested, his article was likely to be left online for anyone to see. The digital components of *Al-Masry Al-Youm* reinforce the idea that we cannot artificially separate digital media from traditional (broadcast) media.

One of the primary stories told to push the narrative of an Egyptian media environment descending into greater repression in the years 2007–10 was the arrest and imprisonment of *Al-Dustur* editor Ibrahim Eissa over reports of President Mubarak's death in the summer of 2007. Eissa's trial followed closely on the heels of the 2007 sentencing of four newspaper editors to prison for "defaming" President Mubarak and his son Gamal. Rumors of the President's ill health and possible demise swept through the Egyptian public sphere late July of 2007, facilitated by text-messaging and social media (Faris 2008). Press outlets—particularly those in the independent press—aggressively pushed this story line and openly inquired about the health of the president and his whereabouts. It certainly did not help matters that Muburak himself went into a kind of occultation for weeks and made no public appearances, leaving the stage open for various performances of concern, celebration, and speculation. The newspaper that ran with this story most aggressively was Al-Dustur, the independent paper that had recently transitioned from a weekly to a daily paper. Its editor, Ibrahim Eissa, wrote a widely-read daily column in which he skewered the hypocrisy, corruption, and ineffectiveness of the Egyptian state. His dispatches, no doubt irksome to those in power, were allowed to be printed with little interference until the emergence of panic concerning the health of President Mubarak. The state, claiming that rumors of the president's death negatively impacted the state's standing in international markets, arrested Eissa and charged him with spreading false rumors, one of the few press red lines to survive the opening of the press environment in 2004. The state blamed all sort of potentially interested parties for the rumors, including bête noirs Hamas and of course the Zionists (Lynch 2007). The crisis came to an end when Mubarak himself finally made a public appearance on August 30th, although there were some who questioned the legitimacy of the resulting video.

If the media situation in Egypt is in serious decline *systemically*, as Freedom House indicates, one would expect that decline to be borne out in available statistics. For instance, if newspapers were reporting on torture in 2008, and the situation has declined, one might expect there to be less reporting on torture in 2009. Or if journalists are getting in trouble for reporting rumors about President Mubarak's health in 2007, one might expect journalists to stop speculating about President Mubarak's health, for fear of their own safety and to ensure that they remain free to do their other work. Yet reporting on both torture and the health of President Mubarak continues to take place at significant rates in *Al-Masry Al-Youm* and in digital media. Bloggers continued to speculate about Mubarak's death, and *Al-Masry Al-Youm* continued investigating rumors of Mubarak's ill health. This is not to say that the legal environment for journalists was not also in decline, as Freedom House claims, but rather that both of these things can co-occur simultaneously.

We can also see this by comparing coverage of the 2007 Death Crisis reportage and the reports of the president's illness in July 2010. If there was, in fact, a chilling effect on journalists of the 2007 Eissa affair, we should be able to see it in the 2010 coverage. Yet Ibrahim Eissa himself—who spent time in prison precisely for reporting on Mubarak's health—devoted an entire column to addressing the question of Mubarak's health. Unlike reporting in the official press, which typically concludes with platitudes, like "He was full of energy. May God grant him good health," Eissa took the president head-on and suggested that he was too old to capably lead the country (Attalah 2010).

Journalists at *Al-Masry Al-Youm*, *Al-Dustur*, and *Al-Sharouq* covered the story as well. Mohamed Amin exclaimed in disgust, "There is no information!" and blamed the president and the secrecy surrounding his health for the persistence of rumors (2010). Columnist Osama Haykel claimed that "the intensity of the controversy is greater this time [than in 2007]" (Haykal 2010). Over the course of the crisis, *Al-Masry Al-Youm* ran dozens of stories and published videos—from news items to man-on-the-street interviews to op-eds—about the president's health. All of these items existed online even when Eissa was in prison and when journalists everywhere were probably fearful for their safety if they contributed to this debate. These hybrid print-digital artifacts were largely impervious to regime interference, since no one tried to take down the paper's web site, and if they had, there was an army of bloggers and digital activists waiting to excerpt, re-post or Tweet the content.

What this refusal to end speculation suggests is that the Egyptian media system itself was largely impervious to state repression of individual editors and journalists, and that digital activists and journalists were leading the charge in crossing red lines. The system is able to maintain a *contested multidimensionality*. Pathways of public dissent, even when interrupted by state repression, were quickly rerouted to other press outlets, or even to the same outlets where new editors and writers stepped into the line of fire and risked their own persecution for the cause of open dissent. Digital media enable this multi-dimensionality.

First it ensures that offending stories live on in Google caches, or more typically on the sites themselves, where they are rarely if ever removed by Egypt's comparative technically weak censorship strategy (in contrast to China's). The best Egyptian newspapers either have already transformed themselves into hypermedia entities—complete with blogs, videos, and interactive, participatory content, or exist only online to begin with. The Egyptian independent press, despite constraints, was one element of this multidimensionality. Bloggers continued to write about Mubarak's health, and about his possible death, including a well-trafficked Facebook page called "Mubarak is Dead." The digital media were a source of constant rumor-making, speculation and rumination about Mubarak's ill health and the future of Egypt after his death. And the willingness of digital activists and traditional reporters to cross red lines and to investigate state misbehavior reinforced one another in a mutually constitutive way that could be seen most clearly when bloggers, Facebook activists and independent journalists at *Al-Masry*

Al-Youm and elsewhere all seized on the story of Khaled Said's unjust death in the summer of 2010. The Facebook group *We Are All Khaled Said*, and general disgust with the practices of the Egyptian police, would be a major contributing factor in the uprisings (Snider and Faris 2011).

Egypt is a peculiar authoritarian environment in the way that it has incorporated the Internet. The regime made little effort to interfere with content on the Web directly, through keyword filtering or blocking. Other authoritarian regimes in the region have learned from the Egyptian regime's decision not to close down its media system. Bahrain, for instance, also witnessed an uprising in the winter of 2011. But with the help of Saudi and Emirati troops and a sophisticated digital filtering and surveillance system, the regime was able to maintain its grip on power (Mitchell 2012). Since 2011, that same regime has moved aggressively against all journalists. The country's 2002 Press Law imposed harsh restrictions on journalists who violate the country's red lines, and those measures have been even more punitively enforced since the Arab Spring began. Yet, despite ranking definitely as "Not Free," Freedom House notes, "the Bahraini media's coverage of news and politics is more critical and independent than reporting in most other Gulf countries" (2012). For example, the arrest of the owner of an online news organization called Rasad News in Bahrain, like many similar outfits in Egypt and Tunisia, is effectively a Twitter and Facebook based boutique media outlet. While the Bahraini regime did shut down the pages, Rasad News was operational again with a new Facebook page, and actively pursuing its critical work. Digital entrepreneurs and their partners in Bahrain's independent press seem willing to press on in spite of repression, and the costs for doing so are significantly alleviated with the mass diffusion of participatory social media platforms.

Standard indices of press freedom have failed to capture some of the dynamism and individual agency characterizing contemporary authoritarian media systems, like Egypt's. The recent history of the Egyptian media system indicates that digital technologies were crucial factors in creating a general climate of dissent and criticism that went beyond official regime determined red lines. Our understandings of authoritarian media systems have focused too heavily on state responses and policies, and not enough on the ability of individual journalists and activists to produce and share content with their fellow citizens. Enterprising journalists and digital activists have contributed to long-run changes in political systems, even while facing political repression. Future research must further investigate the content of authoritarian media systems more openly, and more closely consider the ways that individuals can now create, share, and act upon political information on social media platforms, as well as the ways those platforms may and may not effectively escape state control.

Chapter 8
Communicating Politics in Kuwait

Fahed Al-Sumait

Since the Arab uprisings that began in December 2010, scholars, pundits, and policymakers have given considerable attention to the role of digital media technologies in facilitating political change across the Middle East. However, prior to those momentous events such technologies where already altering the political landscape in several countries within the region. In this chapter, I describe one such country, Kuwait, and the ways in which oppositional political actors have been utilizing digital technologies in tandem with other localized venues for several years to circumvent mass media obstacles, interact with constituents, mobilize activism, and ultimately contest specific forms of power. I concentrate primarily on a time period preceding the Arab uprisings by drawing on insights from key political actors in Kuwait, where a constitutional monarchy has been incrementally ceding power to one of the oldest and most autonomous of Arab parliaments.[1] I focus on three groupings that represent significant political forces in both Kuwait and the region and whose discourses are increasingly influencing public sphere debates and, consequently, impacting political dynamics.

Analysis of the Arab Middle East tends to focus on political hotspots, leaving in-depth discussions of peaceful, indigenous political change—such as that found in Kuwait—largely absent from mainstream discourse. Yet, Kuwait is a particularly interesting case to examine with regard to the issues of political power and information infrastructure. This constitutional emirate—with a population of 2.6 million and about 10 percent of the world's oil reserves—has the region's longest existing democratically elected legislature and some of its highest levels of per-capita media usage (Al-Roomi 2007, Mellor 2005). It is often described among the most free of Arab states, with significant development toward political liberalization (Al-Roomi 2007, Brown 2009, Rizzo 2005, Salem 2008, Tetreault 2000). In 1938, Kuwait became the first Arab country to experiment with a formal consultative council called a *majlis* (Herb 1999), and in 1961, it established the

1 Most Arab countries have some form of parliamentary or congressional council, though their degree of legislative power or even formal consultative role is generally limited in comparison to Kuwait or to more advanced democracies. There is an Arab Inter-Parliamentary Union which was established in 1974 and on which 21 Arab countries plus Palestine have representatives. However, like the vast majority of its individual members, the union itself has limited powers or influence.

Gulf's first constitution. These efforts at political liberalization have been achieved with little violence or continuous external pressures to democratize.

Kuwait's media conditions are also indicative of a relatively robust information infrastructure for the Arab Middle East. The country is continually ranked among the most free of media environments in the region (Freedom House 2012, Reporters Without Borders 2010, 2011). Local newspapers and satellite stations are partisan and often driven more by political interests than economic concerns which, for example, helps explain why its per-capita distribution of local newspapers is nearly three times that of any other Arab country. Mobile phone penetration exceeds the population by a ratio of 3:2 and its percentage of Internet users is in the top third percent among all Arab nations (Central Intelligence Agency 2009, Internet World Stats 2011, Mellor 2005). With regards to social media, Kuwait's percentage of Facebook users is second among all Arab countries and, despite its small population, the country currently generates more tweets than any other (Arab or non-Arab) Middle Eastern nation, except Turkey (Mourtada and Salem 2012). In short, it stands out as a well saturated, vibrant and largely free media environment in a region known for persistent authoritarianism and media controls.

In addition to its distinctions, Kuwait's struggle with political liberalization reflects similar and important dimensions in nearby states: mixed Sunni and Shi'a Muslim populations; an economy reliant on natural resources; a hereditary monarchy; entrenched tribalism and other identity-based political groupings; and a rapidly changing media environment. Like the entire Middle East, information and communications technologies are rapidly diffusing. Widely available and affordable satellite television has already changed the nature of regional political and social debates (Eickelman and Anderson 2003, Lynch 2006, Seib 2007) and Internet expansion continues to open opportunities for social networking, political blogging, information access, and even political change (Bunt 2003, Hofheinz 2007, Howard 2011, Wheeler 2006). Such conditions are as important in Kuwait as they are in the broader region. In short, Kuwait represents a combination of both unique and shared elements with neighboring countries, making its analysis important in itself and simultaneously relevant to larger discussions about information infrastructure, political power and, ultimately, the process of political liberalization.

To demonstrate this, I describe the various communication channels, or means, by which three important identity groups within the country's opposition send and receive messages to and from the Kuwaiti public. My intent is to illustrate how information infrastructure and political power intersect within the country's broader communicative environment. In-depth examination of such an environment inevitably involves other important facets, such as political messaging and targeting strategies, public opinion and reception, factors of political economy, the social and cultural context, and so forth, which are not dealt with here. That is to say, focusing exclusively on the medium can only tell part of the contemporary political story about Kuwait or the region, though I argue it is an important part of a larger narrative concerning government opposition forces and the evolving nature of their political communication within the Middle East.

The findings presented here are based on in-depth interviews with 51 political actors over a 10-month period beginning in June 2010. I categorize the respondents according to three primary groupings: Islamists, liberals and female politicians.[2] In terms of their (former or current) positions, the interviewees represented numbers approximating 40 percent of Kuwait's legislature and half of the cabinet (of a unicameral 50-member legislative assembly and 16 ministers per cabinet), as well as civil society leaders, political activists, academics, journalists and the leaders of each major political "party." Thirty percent of the respondents were Shi'a, which is roughly representative of the national composition, and just over 40 percent were female, which is similar to their representation in the country's workforce. All were Kuwaiti citizens ranging in age from the late 20s to the 70s. What follows are their descriptions of the traditional and digital forms of communication they use to interact with citizens and promote their political agendas.

Traditional Communicative Means

I segment the following analysis according to two overarching communication mechanisms: *traditional* and *digital*. The traditional is comprised of conventional means found in most political environments—mass media, personal networking, lobbying, etc.—as well as time-tested provincial means unique to Kuwait and similar Gulf countries—duwaniyyas, religious gatherings, and social events. That is followed by a digital section that describes the growing use of new media technologies with an emphasis on generational and gender differences. As I will demonstrate, each of the groups examined has adapted the available communication means to their particular needs, with more marginal groups—such as youth and women—effectively supplementing traditional politicking with innovative workarounds, of which digital media technologies are playing an increasingly critical role.

2 I focus on these three categories of actors who are defined according to their *primary* self-expressed political identity. Islamists are an assorted force but unified in explicitly defining their political agendas through their Muslim identities. Self-described liberals, represent a long-standing force in Kuwaiti politics often characterized by their calls for secularism, formal political parties, and improved minority rights. Female politicians are included due to their rapidly growing, though still marginal, role in Arab politics. While significant contributors to public sphere debates, it should be noted that each group, like any conception of "a public," has porous boundaries and participants are not always exclusive to a single domain.

Conventional Media

Print and broadcast sources were the most commonly relied-upon forms of conventional media in Kuwait, though respondents described these as heavily partisan. Such partisanship can be an advantage for organizations that share political orientations with particular outlets, but since the largest partisan position is pro-government, opposition groups had more difficulties than advantages in this domain of the media environment. One analyst described it this way: "The number of newspapers is far greater than the capacity of Kuwait, but most of these newspapers are political. They are politically motivated … The thing is, if you want to see the media at large, most of the media, especially the TV [stations], are clients of the government. So there is a problem." A respondent from a liberal political organization elaborated on the condition: "Listen. Three-quarters of the newspapers in Kuwait are not government-controlled, but [are] government-friendly. And they block most of our work. And in this day and age, you cannot reach the public face-to-face only. You need the media to reach the people. And we have a problem with the media. They are not a free and open media." Such partisanship is an obstacle for all opposition groups in Kuwait, but since women's political organizations and female candidates held a wide variety of political orientations, they were not systematically deprived of media coverage based on ideological grounds to the degree claimed by many of the Islamists and liberals.

Beginning with Islamists, these groups had limited media outlets directly affiliated with their political views, so they often supplemented their direct media communications—such as press releases and public statements—with pseudo-events created to garner media attention. The nature of such gatherings vary in location, size, and even the titles associated with them—rallies, lectures, conferences, and so on—but they follow a common pattern of public assembly in which political figures give impassioned speeches and statements on amplified podiums about current issues directed at both the attendees and the media. The leader of a Shi'a group and seven-time Parliament Member (MP) discussed his organization's efforts to reach people through these events; both directly and via the associated media coverage. "We have to go down to the streets … If we have any problem or issue we can [reach] the streets by using the media and radio-stations and TV. We do this with [public] conferences every one or two weeks. We announce that 'these people will come and speak and if anyone has questions they can come and ask him'." In a sense, these gatherings functioned somewhat like continuous campaign speeches with multiple speakers. They also carried the opportunity for personal networking with attendees.

As an added benefit for holding these events, media regularly turned out to cover them as news stories, thus amplifying the group's messages. This interviewee continued: "We are using these [public lectures] very effectively with the TV stations, which are the private stations, and the newspapers. [The media] come each time … We want something that people not only hear, but see repeatedly, so the picture will remain in [their] head all the time." Other Islamist groups described a similar process. Here, a prominent member of a conservative Salafi Alliance explained the mass media's indifference toward his group's messages and how they use regular public lectures to get around these. "[Journalists] are saying, 'Okay, say what you want to say, but we will not take this [issue] as our matter, our problem' ... So we also hold [public] lectures ... This is how to reach [the people]. And the media, they show these [events]." In such a manner, the Islamists and others depended on journalists' systemic attraction to news events, even if reporters did not ascribe to the content of the communicated messages. The net effect is that some degree of coverage was afforded despite ideological obstacles in the press.

Liberals, too, employed such public presentations to reach people and the press, but since they are less cohesive as a formal group than many of the Islamists organizations, they were less consistent at drawing regular media attention. One long-time liberal explained how traditional oppositional groupings of liberals began the practice of public lectures decades ago, which others later adopted. "We were one of the first groups to start holding meetings outside of duwaniyyas[3] [during an unconstitutional parliamentary suspension in the 1980s], so the government cannot control it ... It developed and now everyone is using this [approach of public lectures]. Now they are more sophisticated. These days they use a lot of gadgets [like podiums, microphones, TV screens, and social media coverage]." He went on to explain how these were only part of a broader strategy liberals used to reach the public. "We also go through newspapers, especially the opposition newspapers [to reach the public] ... and then direct contact through duwaniyyas and civil society groups like the graduate society, trade unions, and so on." Civil society organizations were frequently described by all groups as key targets of political messages, but as noted here, they also served as a type of communication venue to supplement efforts through the news media and public lectures.

Provincial Forums

A second important group of traditional communicative mechanisms are commonplace in Kuwait. I characterize these as provincial to draw attention to their local origins. I am not, however, suggesting that these are somehow unsophisticated, as the colloquial use of the term sometimes denotes. In fact, the opposite is the case; these localized mechanisms of communication are highly sophisticated and personally tailored to great effect. Given their localized nature, provincial channels were employed regularly by males. However, women were at a distinct disadvantage here. To illustrate both the shared and unequal forms of provincial communicative means I first discuss the most common elements and

3 *Diwaniyyas* are mainly family-owned gathering places central to Kuwait's social and political atmosphere. They vary considerably in formality, function, and composition but are a regular part of social life for the majority of Kuwaiti men.

then demonstrate the unique obstacles faced by women, as well as some of the solutions they adopted to overcome these.

Both funerals and weddings double as opportunities for political networking and two-way communication. As in most Islamic societies, funerals and weddings are public events at which people offer condolences or congratulatory messages to entire families. In Kuwait, both events are regular social "obligations" for many Kuwaitis and especially the male gatherings are announced in the daily newspapers, publicized through text services, and spread by word-of-mouth. In the case of a death, relatives observe a three-day mourning period wherein they receive visitors for condolences. Even if one only knows an extended family member of the deceased, it still is considered appropriate to show respect by attending the ritual. These events are held in gender-segregated spaces that accommodate a large number of visitors, traditionally in a duwaniyya or other large hall. Upon arrival, guests shake the hands of the deceased's close family and offer their condolences before sitting with the other guests for an unspecified period of time. In a similar fashion, part of the traditional wedding ceremony is usually held in a hotel hall, outdoor tent, or other large space. Any male who knows either side of the family will often attend. Like the funerals, guests first shake the hands of the groom's close family members and then mingle with other guests, usually over a buffet dinner. As with the funerals, these events are a culturally specific opportunity for face-to-face interaction between the elected and electorate. Most notably, during the mingling periods politicians are frequently approached by other attendees to discuss issues of concern.

Since both events are part of social life in Kuwait, political actors utilize these opportunities to interact with the general public. One former minister, in his sixties, explained the frequency with which he attends such events, which was common for the average male of his generation and status. "I go to maybe 10 or 15 condolences a week and maybe two to three weddings." He then elaborated on the political capital to be gained. "MPs like to go to the weddings because they meet so many people. It is a free gathering with a free dinner. It is worth going to because [the MP] will get their photos taken with the groom's family and it might be in the newspaper the next day. And the family will keep the photo forever to remember that MP came to their wedding … With the condolences, [politicians] still go even if [they] are not close to the family. It shows a gentle psychological touch. It's good PR."

Beyond the publicity associated with these events, they are also opportunities for politicians to explain their initiatives. A Salafi MP stated: "Of course, we have to go to the condolences. We have to visit people, either in the hospitals or at the weddings. And this is one of the ways that we are contacting people … and also some of [the attendees], they come and ask questions, 'what is going on in the Parliament,' and I have to explain." A four-time independent MP described yet another benefit of these events. "Sometimes we get comments, very good comments, great comments—let me say—in the weddings. When we stop in any reception, some guys they give me their opinions. And also sometimes when I go to condolences they sit beside me and they say maybe two words, but these two words are very important for us … All these things I do normally [as social obligations], I also get [political] feedback." The combined benefits of good public relations, occasions to explain initiatives, and opportunities to collect valued feedback allowed these almost-obligatory social events to double as effective provincial communicative mechanisms.

Another localized means of communication are the *duwaniyyas* themselves. Every male with a political position interviewed for this research described these as a primary means for interacting with the public. These family-owned spaces function as sites for condolences and sometimes wedding receptions. They are used to socialize, organize, and campaign. They help people share, and expose one another to, competing political views, and they form the backbone of Kuwait's interpersonal communicative infrastructure among men (Al-Roomi 2007). In short, a great deal of social and political life in Kuwait occurs in and around the country's duwaniyyas. As one MP and former minister aptly summarized: "Duwaniyyas are our life." Another quote from a Salafi Islamists was characteristic of most people's descriptions. "I have my own duwaniyya every Saturday. So sometimes about 100 to 200 people come every week, they enter the duwaniyya to either say hello or they have some problems that they want me, of course, to help them with. Or sometimes I get new ideas [from attendees]. Of course, I also visit duwaniyyas almost every day." Thus, for male politicians these are among the most important venues in the country and cannot be overstated.

Women faced at least two distinct disadvantages by not regularly participating in duwaniyyas. They did not have the same opportunities to interact with large segments of the population as did their male counterparts, and women's issues were less likely to be discussed in these male-dominated spaces. Women did, however, have some exceptions and alternatives. Beginning with the exceptions, in the last elections female candidates increasingly campaigned in duwaniyyas to present their agendas and get feedback from male attendees. One of the female MPs, who wore a traditional hair covering (*hijab*), talked about her initial concerns in attending these forums. "Especially in the last elections [of 2009], more men's duwaniyyas were welcoming women with certain positions, mainly MPs. When I was running for election, I was very reluctant to enter men's duwaniyyas for the first time. I was really questioning myself. 'What should I wear? Should I dress the way I usually do or wear the Islamic *abaya*.'[4] I don't want to offend [the men]. I don't want to embarrass myself, so I was a bit reluctant. But now I enter the men's duwaniyyas the same way I am entering the women's duwaniyyas or the mixed duwaniyyas, and people are accepting me the way I am."

Another female MPs took a different track. "Even when I ran for the parliament, I decided not to go to the duwaniyyas. This was my decision. I even announced it

4 An *abaya* is a black body-covering worn by traditional Muslim women that goes over the clothing and symbolizes modesty. It does not cover the hair or face but it does cover everything from the shoulders down, including the arms.

[publicly]. I talked with my family and a number of people. Because of our family [honor], I decided not to go to duwaniyyas. But if I get a private invitation, I do go … but I did have different kinds of gatherings with women and men, [or just] women. Sometimes I had such gatherings in NGOs or in some public areas. So I meet people everywhere." This strategy had limitations in comparison to other candidates, but the fact she won a seat suggests that avoiding duwaniyyas was not a guarantee for failure. Her success might be due, in part, to the alternative communicative options women employed.

Indeed, women have some exclusive social forums that female candidates have used effectively as communicative means. A third female MP described these as a direct counter to the male duwaniyyas: "Way back to the first establishment of Kuwait, the duwaniyya was there, and at that time, definitely, the duwaniyya is okay for men. But women, they have their own gathering inside the houses at special hours of the day, usually in the early morning about this time, where they'll call it [midday tea] and again before sundown." The earlier female tea sessions were mainly the domain of older, non-working women, but the younger generations were more accessible at the evening tea sessions. A campaign manager for one of the successful female MPs explained how they used these along with existing female social networks to rally support for her candidate. "We had [our candidate] visit many duwaniyyas and spend time at our [campaign] headquarters, but we also had her meet with the older women at afternoon tea, because many women they have nothing [to do] in the day. So they go to [afternoon tea] and talk and spend time with friends … Some women also had the [religious gatherings] in their homes [to talk] about the *Quran* and the *hadith.* We had good success with these." In such a fashion, women candidates gained some advantages over their male counterparts. Whereas women could increasingly participate in male duwaniyyas, men did not have the option of visiting women's tea or religious sessions. This may not have been enough to counter the intrinsic disadvantages women faced with regard to the duwaniyyas, but it was an innovative attempt to work around the problem. However, an even more important communicative workaround employed by all the successful female candidates—as well as many of the men—was an increased reliance on digital media technologies, to which I now turn.

Digital Communicative Means

In 2006, a popular movement erupted which sought to change Kuwait's electoral districts from 25 to 5. The existing districts divided the polity in such a way that state-sponsored clientelism—the exchange of votes for money or favor—and the dominance of specific groups in key districts made it relatively easy to influence electoral results. A five-district division was seen as a path to fairer representation and less gerrymandering. What was especially noteworthy was that this change was driven by an independent youth movement and facilitated by digital media technologies. One of the young bloggers behind the movement illustrated the mobilizing capacity of these technologies with his telling of the events. “I’m a blogger to begin with. So it all started with the blogs and interactions that you have with your readers ... So when the issue [of redistricting] was discussed within parliament, naturally I picked up on it in my blog, and started writing and writing about it, and with that, creating levels of frustration among the readers ... So from that came the website *Kuwait5.org*.” Using his website and blog, this activist and his colleagues developed customizable content to maximize the effect of their political message. “We basically had easy steps on how you can get involved in the campaign. We had parliament members who we wanted to pressure ... and we had different options to contact them, email if they had an email, or fax, or SMS messages, or calling them. And you had the choice of what you wanted. And when you click on the option you wanted, you’d get a script that says exactly what you have to do.” Following their success in spreading the message of a need to redistrict, the online activists eventually began physically mobilizing people. “And it picked up really well ... and it was tremendous. Pressure was directed exactly where we wanted it, but then you reach a point that the people want more. So then we started with the rallies ... so with this, coupled with pressure from outside, we started driving people to the first rally. We managed to get 250 people, and from one rally to the other it kept building. We came up to 3,000 [demonstrators] at some point.” This so-called “orange revolution” has been noted for its innovative use of technology (Salem 2008, Tétreault 2006) and its success encouraged other Kuwaitis to take note of the power of online activism.

Cases like this demonstrate how digital media technologies are playing an increasingly political role in Kuwait. By digital media, I refer to the various forms through which digital information is transmitted using electronic technologies, such as the Internet, mobile communications equipment, and satellite television. Of particular interest here are media over which political actors exert a significant degree of control in the creation and distribution of messages. This includes Internet-enabled platforms like websites, blogs, emails, and social networking sites, as well as hand-held technologies such as cell phones. Digital technologies have had a variety of effects on the growth and forms of political activism around the world (Bennett 2007, Bennett 2008, Hick and McNutt 2002, Norris 2000) and are seen as central to the creation of a public sphere and the process of liberalization in Muslim countries (Eickelman and Anderson 2003, Howard 2011, Lynch 2003, Seib 2007). Both digital activism and liberalization are also evident in Kuwait, where political actors are progressively turning to new media to circumvent conventional media obstacles, target specific segments of the population, and contribute to a more robust public sphere. With regard to these digital media, two noteworthy patterns were evident among the groups interviewed. Islamists and liberals were divided in their utilization of these technologies, mainly along generational lines, while women, regardless of generation, embraced them with potent effect.

Generational Differences

Both Islamists groups and liberals were heavily split along generational lines in their descriptions about the effectiveness of digital media for communicating with the public. Older members were generally less apt to utilize these, even if they recognized their growing importance. An elder member of the Salafi Alliance and three-time MP declared: "Not yet, we're not so active [in the use of digital media]. We will be. Some of our young people used this in the last election to counteract the smear campaign [against us] that some people thought the government used. But this is something that I intend to make better use of next time [there is an election], to organize for it." Likewise, an elder figure in a Shi'a alliance acknowledged the importance of new media in general, but his group had yet to make a concerted effort to tap its potential. "Because of the technological revolution, the whole world is just like a small crystal ball. With the iPhone and Google you can get almost any information. Everything … We have a website [for our group], and there are some people who look at this, but this is not very advanced until now. It's not very effective." While such actors gave lip service to the importance of digital media, they were not priorities in their communication arsenal.

A long-time figure in the liberal movement and former five-time MP was in agreement with the older Islamists when asked about digital media. "It is there. It is being used now. But what role or how effective the influence is in political activities, though, is questionable. Their effects in promoting democracy or in political activities are limited because [the people who use these technologies] are dispersed. It's mostly individualistic and I don't see any coordinated efforts [by political groups] to use these yet." Even if this particular political figure did not see coordinated new media efforts, they did exist in Kuwait and around the region. In fact, despite older politicians' general lag in adopting these technologies, a growing number of Kuwaitis were turning them—especially the younger generations.

Not surprisingly, younger political actors were the most likely to talk about, and demonstrate, the political importance of digital media. The youngest Salafi member in Parliament responded this way when asked if he used new media: "Of course! We have our own divisions [of volunteers] in these areas, and for myself, I also have to follow up and to answer the questions which are raised by either the Facebook or the Twitter every day. And especially the emails. But for the Twitter and Facebook, because they don't wait, so I deal with them immediately. Of course the SMS is also very important." The leader of the liberal National Democratic Alliance, in his early 40s, confirmed the value of new media for his group. "We're trying to reach [the public] by the new trend, which is social networking, the Internet, by Facebook, Twitter, and blogs, and by face-to-face [interaction], and inviting people [to lectures through these means]. When we have an event here, we start using Twitter and Facebook and blogs and [text] messaging services to reach the people, as much as we can." He then discussed how these technologies sometimes generated interest even beyond the intent of his group. "I'll give you an example. We had an event here and we invited some of the MPs to talk [about a specific issue] but we didn't open it to the public. What we did, we sent messages to our members through our email system and SMS. And some people who got this message put it on Twitter and Facebook and stuff, retweeting it. Without even putting any certain advertisement about it, we had around 600 people here [for the lecture]." Both of these political actors, and others of their generation, worked directly to tap into the potential of new media. These technologies helped generate crucial feedback, community interactions, and general publicity. As the opening story to this section demonstrated, they also held great potential to mobilize people to action.

Twitter is a particularly interesting case of social media in Kuwait that serves as both an outgoing and incoming political communication tool. As noted, mobile phones outnumber people by a ratio of 3:2 and Kuwaitis, like people in other wealthy countries, are increasingly dependent on their phones for a variety of purposes. This makes Twitter an especially useful means of instant communication that some MPs have been quick to capitalize on. Indeed, as also mentioned, despite its small population, last year Kuwait was second only to Turkey when it comes to total volume of tweets by a Middle Eastern country (Internet World Stats 2011). One MP described how Twitter worked with surprising effect for some of her parliamentary colleagues. "I'll tell you an example of how powerful [Twitter] is. A few days ago [one group] proposed a grilling for the Prime Minister for not sending troops to Bahrain [in response to recent protests]. At night was when the press release came out … In the following few hours, at night, there was a huge wave against this [proposed grilling] on Twitter … immediately, the next day, they changed their tune because they saw that was going to hurt them. It started in Twitter … I mean, how would you monitor public opinion that quickly if it wasn't on Twitter?" Like many older sophisticates, the MPs she described were quickly realizing the benefits associated with new media, though some tentative users delegated their oversight to junior staffers. Even though some actors were still coming to terms with the power of new media, it was clear that female politicians of all ages had embraced these technologies with zeal.

Gender Differences

Female politicians relied heavily on digital media technologies to communicate their messages. Despite an almost 30-year gap between the oldest and youngest of Kuwait's female MPs, each successfully used new media technologies in their political campaigns and continued to do so once in office. Age, it seems, was less of a determining factor in their adoption of digital communications than with the men. All the females to serve in Kuwait's parliament had personal websites outlining their key messages, personal profiles, and showing reposted media coverage about them. The sites included feedback mechanisms, volunteer signups, and other interactive features. Each site also contained cross-media integration with Facebook accounts, YouTube videos, and email subscriptions. One of the female MPs responded this way when asked about new media. "Oh yeah, oh yeah, I have a website, you can see my long journey [leading to politics] and some of my speeches on YouTube, and my Twitter [account]. [These media helped me] to expand the number of people who see me and support me. From young people … to everyone who uses the Internet, which is most the people in Kuwait these days." She also described these platforms as mechanisms for getting around what she characterized as a biased media environment, though the oldest female MP had a slightly different view on the media scene. For her, new media were simply part of a robust and relatively free mediascape. "Yes. The new media is important. We use the media more and more now to express our ideas and our point of view, especially having more TV channels, private TV channels, the Internet. We feel more free to criticize the political practices, whether for our fellow MPs or to criticize the government's policies. So, having these open media channels, whether it's TV channels, or also newspapers, or new media, I think politics is getting more active in Kuwait and more reachable to the ordinary men and women." These women both saw digital media as useful tools for communicating their messages and reaching different segments of the population, even if they differed in the innovative credit they gave to new media technologies.

The campaign manager of a female MP explained their use of such technologies during the 2009 campaign. "So we had the website, we had YouTube, we had Facebook, we had Flickr, we had Twitter—although it had just started to pick up in Kuwait. We made really good use [of these media] and dedicated a lot of the campaign resources to new media and online ads." He then described the critical importance of these media for sending targeted messages. "And it wasn't just collecting members; we were actually utilizing [these technologies]: sending out messages, targeted messages … where we would ask people for a certain action and the response was amazing. We had email lists that we kept piling up throughout the campaign. Even with SMS—although SMS I wouldn't consider new media anymore—but the way we targeted people with it was new: geographically, demographically." The benefits of this strategy were apparent in his candidate's success, demonstrating that a host of new media technologies supplement and circumvent existing media channels. The general consistency with which all the female MPs used such media speaks to the power of digital technology to overcome some of the communicative obstacles faced by female politicians.

Conclusion

Like many parts of the world—and especially in the Middle East—political communication in Kuwait appears to be transitioning to a new era. This era is one in which the means of communication are continually evolving with some potent effects. I have focused the analysis primarily on means, since this is both the lynchpin of communicative strategies and an area where unique local adaptations are highly apparent. As well, communicative means provide insight into Kuwait's information infrastructure and the process of political debate in the country. The traditional mechanisms outlined in this chapter exemplified a robust set of historical pathways for reaching the public and remained the most important tools for communicating political intentions. Digital media increasingly augmented these channels and created new venues for reaching the electorate. Kuwait's political actors exhibited specific patterns as to who employed which media and to what effect. Ideology may have determined the levels of access these groups had to traditional means, but it explained little about political actors' motivations in using some communication channels over others. Islamists and liberals were mainly divided along generational lines and female politicians of varied ages ardently embraced them as part of a larger strategy for circumventing traditionally gender-biased communicative obstacles.

In terms of infrastructure, the relative openness of Kuwait's political and information environment allows significant space for groups to openly debate one another and contest specific forms of power with little fear of direct repression from the state. This is due, in part, to the fragmented nature of the opposition groups, which ensures that political battles are often between themselves and rarely pose a direct threat to the monarchy itself. As noted, the government also possesses distinct advantages over the traditional means of communication in comparison to the various political groups described here, and it has more resources at its disposal for employing digital means—this is in addition to its control over the larger media infrastructure through licensing and legal authority. So despite the innovate communication strategies of the political actors outlined in this chapter, there will always be an asymmetrical relationship between them and the state in terms of access, resources, and power. This is not to say such groups are powerless or their innovative forms of communication are irrelevant; in fact if one measures political success in terms of legislative victories and social mobilization, these groups have been very successful at times. However, in Kuwait, such victories represent only one realm where the state's authority is explicitly affected. Structurally speaking, the state's other modes of power—such as control over the economy, the police, military, and intelligence services, etc.—are not publicly contested. Put another way, the information infrastructure in Kuwait has done little to directly erode the state's "hard power" and it is not likely to do so in the foreseeable future.

Perhaps as important as infrastructure, then, is the geopolitical and historical context. The regional uprisings have illustrated the fragility of some Arab autocrats in the face of an angry and (at least temporarily) unified public. Each of the countries which underwent a recent political transition, or that is currently in a state of instability, has a unique set of conditions comprising its political and information environment. Furthermore, countries like Kuwait, have witnessed social mobilization and significant political debates both online and offline for several years now. In either case, information infrastructure is not a mono-causal variable capable of explaining authoritarian erosion any more than it can explain its persistence. However, when domestic political conditions, regional context, and information-communication technologies combine with human agency and a desire for change, then a potent recipe brews. This was obvious in the case of countries like Tunisia and Egypt where long-standing dictators where rapidly deposed, but has also been evident in countries like Kuwait where political change has been temperate in comparison. For example, when the Arab uprisings achieved a sufficiently high level of momentum and attracted the world's media attention, opposition MPs in Kuwait took their issues out of the parliament and on to the streets, organizing several street protests that eventually succeeded in the dismissal of Kuwait's Prime Minister. Kuwait's stateless citizens, called the Bidun, also capitalized on the moment to organize demonstrations and demand more political rights. In both cases, digital technologies played a critical role in terms of mobilizing protestors, declaring unified goals, documenting the protests and reactions to them, and then disseminating this information to the broader global community. As important as digital technologies were in each case, it was ultimately the regional context that made their actions successful.

Even when media-facilitated political change does happen on a significant scale, the Arab uprisings have demonstrated that such change is only one of the many steps necessary toward creating more accountable forms of governance and eroding authoritarianism. If and when such a difficult first step is accomplished, there are still no guarantees that the resulting direction will continue on a path toward democracy or even greater liberalization. In Kuwait, digital media are playing a critical role in the country's political debates, but for the foreseeable future it is still a supporting role alongside conventional and provincial forms of media. Despite the innovations of gendered and generational political actors, Kuwait, like much of the world, is still reliant on traditional mass media for reaching the broadest audiences and attempting to persuade political behavior. This is an especially point for the broader Arab Middle East where access to technology, literacy limits, economic disparities, ineffectual educational, political indoctrination, and a history of oppression are rampant. Therefore, media like TV continue to be paramount to regional politics. In assessing the political communication used by opposition groups within Kuwait, it can be concluded that the state's hard power is little eroded. Even with the introduction of new communication technologies being adapted to the local context, the likelihood that a more robust and free information infrastructure by itself will trigger further democratization is unlikely; a statement that I would argue is applicable well beyond the national and regional context described here. Such conditions can, however, open up new pathways that are necessary, if not sufficient, for political change. Based on countries like Kuwait, it can be surmised that communication technologies are not enough to guarantee political transformation in the region, but certainly political change in this part of the world will increasingly be reliant upon them.

Chapter 9

Social Media and Soft Political Change in Morocco

Mohammed Ibahrine

During the "third wave" of democratization around the world in 1990s, the Internet did not figure prominently. This has changed in the context of rapid digitalization since late 2010, especially in countries where authoritarian political structures and traditional cultural patterns still predominate. In the Arab region, social movements, dissidents and activists adopted social media, following the example of the revolutions in Iran (small media) and Eastern Europe (Samizdat) to trigger the long-awaited "fourth wave" of democratization. After his accession in 1999, Morocco's Mohammed VI initiated a "new concept of authority" that promised a free press, the respect of human rights and individual freedom. The post-Hassan II Morocco has been more democratic in form and substance. However, many authoritarian features have re-emerged as their cultural and institutional foundations turn out to be more resilient.

To understand contemporary Moroccan politics, analysts must focus on the effects of the emerging digital communication technologies. The thesis of this chapter is that digital media constitute a new site of power configuration in Morocco. The crucial moment of power construction is meanwhile decisively determined by the control of the pipelines of images and messages along with extensive formal and non-formal networks of distribution. Communication power, in the form of the ability to create and disseminate information, has been given to relatively powerless segments of society through the use of digital technologies (Castells 2009).

This chapter provides insight into Islamists' digital communication strategies by investigating the tactics of informing, interacting, mobilizing, recruiting and networking with their audiences, members and constituencies. By Islamists, I mean organizations that seek political power by using Islamic religious discourse and reference. The chapter also examines how and why Islamists have adopted these digital technologies to mediate, edit and frame their political discourses. In countries where the authoritarian grip over the channels of political communication is tight, Islamists have turned to digital platforms as an efficient tool for creating and distributing political messages to targeted audiences, especially to younger supporters, and for mobilizing followers and supporters for demonstrations. What is striking about Moroccan Islamists is that they are well integrated in the political field and system by publicly distancing themselves from political violence and by participating in the parliamentary elections since 1998. Secondly they were among the first Islamists in the Arab region to adopt and adapt their communication strategies to the digital environments.

The chapter also examines the recent use of social media and digital platforms by dissidents, activists and social groups other than the Islamist. These groups are getting their inspiration from Islamists application of digital platforms. While Islamists are creatively capitalizing on the decentralizing effects of the Internet for the quick dispersion of political information into all directions regardless of the authoritarian and highly hierarchical control of the information, the Moroccan regime was facing serious challenge to understand to how to control the explosion of the digital free flow of information and keep its tight grip, control and monopoly of the media landscape. The chapter concludes that the ascension of Moroccan Islamist power in 2012 gave credit to the information and communication technologies in eroding the origins of Moroccan authoritarianism.

Islamist Movements as "Resistance Identity" and "Project Identity" Movements

The concept of "identity of resistance" is particularly useful in providing a first framework for analysis of political collective action in the digital age and then in understanding the ongoing transformation in the networked public sphere and in the hierarchy of political power in Morocco. An appropriate starting point for interpreting the implications that the use of the Internet by Islamist movements have for politics in Morocco is Manuel Castells's suggestion that "the rise of the network society calls into question the process of construction of identity" (Castells 1997: 11). Castells himself applies this theoretical assumption on Islamist movements. He notes: "The search for meaning takes place then in the reconstruction of defensive identities around communal principles" (Castells 1997: 11). He goes on to point that: "In the network society, project identity, if it develops at all, grows from communal resistance." The Castellian argument is that cultural battles are the power battles of the information age. He identifies power as a "battle around cultural codes, symbols, which relate political and social actors, institutions and cultural movements, through religious leaders and symbols" (Castells 1998: 348). Castells argued that Islamists are engaged in a serious battle for the reconstruction of cultural identity. To win the hearts and minds of their target audiences, Islamists realized the strategic importance of digital and direct communication channels. Similarly, cultural forces armed with digital political communication strategies can produce, legitimate and implement political contents. Islamist movements in Morocco "seek the transformation of the overall social structure" (Castells 2004: 8).

The use and role of the Internet in recent Moroccan political transformation is to be understood in the context of the ongoing conflict between the Moroccan regime and social movements, especially Islamists. Before the arrival of the

Internet, Islamist movements in Morocco did not use digital platforms and social media but small media first to spread their messages to their target audiences through extensive informal networks in mosques and souks and secondly to overcome systematic censorship. The Iranian Revolution can be regarded as a role model with regard to the impact of small media on political change. With the publication of "Small Media Big Revolution" in 1994 by Sreberny-Mohammadi and Mohammadi, small media have become a serious agent for political revolution. By small media, I mean cassette tapes, photocopies, tape recorders, and telephone usage (Sreberny-Mohammadi and Mohammadi 1994). The distribution of audiocassettes with religious sermons of Ayatollah Khomeini in the late 1970s contributed to the fragmentation of political as well as the cultural authority of the Shah's regime. The Iranian Revolution of 1979 has illustrated the particular impact of audiotapes at spreading the messages of Ayatollah Khomeini and the importance played by small media in fostering political and religious discontent, thus triggering radical political change.

Eastern Europe is another region where small media in the form of *Samizdat* triggered great political and societal transformations the late 1990s. Samizdat, a Russian word, refers to privately and clandestinely printed and distributed in contrast to the state owned printing and distributing channels (Joo 2004: 572). Citizens of these countries were unable to publish because of the state rigid rules of control and censorship. By samizdatising, they typed their work and then passed the copies to other people in the samizdat network. A successful samizdat should have a powerful appeal to snowball through many regions, networks and audiences and spread the voices of freedom (Feldbrugge 1975: 5). While it originated in literary circles, samizdat was designed to convey a clear political message that defied the Stalinist *status quo* (Joo 2004: 572). Vladimir Bukovsky, a leading member of the Russian dissident movement of the late 1980s caught the essential kernel of the context and concept when he said: "I myself create it, edit it, censor it, publish it, distribute it, and … get imprisoned for it" (Bukovsky 2012). The inherent idea on which Samizdat relied is self-publishing. Passing along copies by hand depended on the intensive informal communication networks, which were of central significance for the functionality of this type of media activism. Dissidents and activists produced their documents and tracts and passed them from reader to reader to avoid the state tight censorship.

The French Political Islam expert, Gilles Kepel demonstrated the extent to which Islamist preachers, activists and groups exploit communication channels for their political goals and objectives. He showed the role of cassette recordings of the sheikh Abdal-Hamid Kishk's sermons in circulating Islam, thus creating a mass following for Islamist movements (Kepel 1984). The Egyptian and famously charismatic Sheikh Kishk popularized the teachings and tenets of Islam through his cassettes, which still echo in the population not only in Cairo's streets but also throughout the Arab and Islamic world. Islamists around the world realized the usefulness and effectiveness of cassettes as a political mass communication medium and started to follow suit. Moroccan Islamists operate with similar media strategies.

In Morocco, Islamist movements were also pioneers in the use of small media. Situated outside the strict regime's control, small media provided during the last third of the twentieth century, the much-needed means of political communication for political opponents, activists and preachers, who have been blocked off by rigid and restrictive media policies since the independence in 1956. Given the high rate of illiteracy, it were especially audiotapes, that easily reached the illiterate population and functioned as a resource of political, religious and cultural resistance. By dint of these alternative small media tools, Moroccan Islamist movements created for themselves a place in the "communication sphere" to influence the Moroccan public opinion in favor of Islamist perspectives. As stated above, since the late 1970s and early 1980s Islamist movements actively engaged in communicating with Moroccans to introduce their messages in to social and political circulation. Since they had been strictly barred from accessing the mainstream mass media, they resorted to small media, including books, private published magazines and audio and videotapes to disseminate their religious sermons and political information.

Digital Platforms and Islamization of Public Sphere

Over the last 50 years, Moroccan contemporary politics has been shaped by two conflicting ideologies, namely secularism and Islam The cultural and political fragmentation in Morocco accounts for the pressing need of an articulation of identity in terms of "identity of resistance." Islamist movements' undertakings with respect to identities involve antagonism. Their identity-building preserving antagonism aims at enhancing Islamic identity, which they perceive not just as different from that promulgated by the regime, but threatened by it. Social and economic as well as religious themes are the site of political antagonism. The Internet's arrival was heralded as an important force in the Moroccan political life. The potential power of the Internet did not go unnoticed by Islamist movements. Given the fact that Islamist movements in Morocco had no direct access to the public sphere by means of mass media, the importance of the Internet has grown rapidly. Armed with the belief in the strategic importance and high utility of the Internet, both actual and potential, Al-Adl Wal-Ihsan, the leading Islamist political organization in Morocco, set up a variety of websites beginning in the year 2000.

The Internet gained momentum for Islamist movements in Morocco on 28 January 2000, when Al-Adl Wal-Ihsan, launched a website to release a memorandum, a voluminous and a critical letter, entitled "To Whom It Concerns" translated in many European languages. After the regime banned the private newspapers, which published the full text of the memorandum, Al-Adl Wal-Ihsan went online and published the memorandum. It also launched other websites that contained a range of information concerning its religious writings, cultural activities and political discourses. According to Alexa.com, in 2012, Al-Adl Wal-

Ihsan website is ranked 236th in Morocco, making it the most browsed political website in Morocco (Ben Moussa 2011: 76).

Among the most important cases of political use of the Internet in Morocco was that of Nadia Yassine, the daughter of the leader of the most famous political opponent of the Moroccan regime. She launched a website in Arabic, English and French containing detailed information about her life, ideas, and activities (including audio clips of her public lectures—for example one given at the University of California at Berkeley). Al-Adala Wat-Tanmiya party also set up an array of websites with different objectives and target audiences: one website for the party, another for the election campaign, and also for the newspaper At-Tajdid, the central organ of the Party of Justice and Development (PJD).

The political, social and religious discourse reflected in dozens of Islamist movements' websites challenged traditional identifications of Moroccan identity. The process of identification took place when the websites exposed unjust situations and renew group commitments. In 2002, Islamists websites covered the second Aqsa Intifada in a way to incite organized collective political action by invoking an injustice frame that highlighted moral indignation and traces problems to specific actors. At the same time, Al-Adala Wat-Tanmiya and Al-Adl Wal-Ihsan have been proven able to transmit large amounts of political and religious content via their digital platforms. The volume and speed at which they transmitted political information about the election of 2002, the second Aqsa Intifada, and Al-Mudawana means that they have continually improved their strategies and tactics in informing, communicating and campaigning.

Political, social, religious and economic issues were deconstructed, reconstructed and discussed through the digital presence of Islamists (Ben Moussa 2011). The websites became new platforms where conflictual polarizations of the pre-existing identity are played out anew. Al-Adl Wal-Ihsan succeeded to integrate the websites with an overall communication plan (especially the use of email and email lists). The use of Internet added to the other forms of political communication. Since the Internet became popular, especially for young Moroccans to communicate, Islamists benefited greatly from this trend in matters of the political communication. On March 12, 2000, Islamists mobilized an estimated 500,000 participants to demonstrate and during the second Aqsa Intifada demonstration on April 7th, 2002, they mobilized about one million. On March 12, 2000 an estimated 40,000 supporters of the social reforms demonstrated in Rabat, the administration capital of Morocco. Islamist movements managed to mobilize 500,000 participants in Casablanca. This massive counter-demonstration by Islamist had put the regime and the then socialist-led government in a defensive position.

Many scholars argued that the new technologies of communication would allow religious and political identities to flourish (Eickelman and Anderson 1999). Eickelman and Anderson pointed out that "a proliferation of media and means of communication multiplied the possibilities for creating communities and networks among them, dissolving prior barriers of space and distance and opening new grounds for interaction and mutual recognition" (1999: 3). The potentialities of the political use of the Internet related not only to the number of people it could reach but to its impact on select and specific audiences.

In the case of Al-Adl Wal-Ihsan, the access to print media was at best extremely limited, censored, and controlled and at worst non-existent. In 1973 Yassine wrote an open letter Al-Islam Au At-Tufan: Risala Maftuha Ila Malik Al-Maghrib (Islam or the Deluge) and sent it to the king. Following the samizdat tactics, Yassine himself created it, edited it, censored it, published it, distributed it, and was imprisoned for it. Yassine's *nasiha* (morally religious advice) angered the king, who reacted by suppressing the text. It was widely known that to be in possession of the letter was punishable in Morocco so that the circulation of such material could be controlled. The regime successfully managed to stifle the circulation of the letter and thus minimized its effects on Moroccans. While the Nasiha originated in religious circles, Nasiha like the samizdat was designed to convey a clear political message that defied the authoritarianism of the Moroccan political regime.

In 2000, Yassine sent a new nasiha to the new king. The regime again quickly attempted to censor the circulation of this letter. Yassine published his memorandum in many independent newspapers, a new communication channel that have offered the Islamists a new chance to voice their concerns. Generally, Moroccan media have a negative orientation towards Islamist movements. The official media as well as the socialist and the liberal party press have never granted the Islamists a space to articulate their political and religious accounts. Further, they negatively portray the Islamists and present them pejoratively as "barbus" or "mouvance." The Internet leveled the field and offered the Islamists a direct channel to present their discourse directly to Moroccans without being reedited, misrepresented and gated. Islamists targeted specifically highly educated Moroccans such as students and professionals. This specific group of people was among the highest users of the Internet and is politically engaged in cyberspace. Digital platforms triggered a renaissance of the watchdog function and paved the way again for it to act as the fourth estate in controlling the misconduct of the political regime. Islamist movements in Morocco purposively spread unmediated literature for political purposes. One of the strengths of their websites had not been the content alone but the richness in terms of variations and organization of information. For Graham Meikle, the success of digital activists demands soft skills not in the state-of-the-art design or animation, but in information management and provision (Meikle 2002: 78). The provision of information is a crucial element of the development of activist politics. Islamist movements in virtual spaces had increasingly become more efficient in publishing and distributing religious and political information and discourse.

A public space is in the process of being formed around the intersection of political, social and religious issues. With these topics, Islamists aim at appealing primarily to middle-class professionals such as educators, engineers, doctors and administrators. These sets of issues attract youthful educated audiences and thus fit the information-seeking behavior of young Moroccans. Islamist movements framed their verbal and visual messages on the Internet to get and hold the attention of their target audiences and thus have a desired communication impact. Islamists' websites have been used successfully in promoting a coherent, collective assessment of what these events mean within the overall process of political change. A traditional concept of authority has come under attack, and has been shaken in many forms. Consequently, political power has become a contested domain, rather than an accepted reality. The growth of religiously based political identities is paralleled with a decrease of nationally based political identities. The internalization of these religious messages via new electronic media has increased the salience of Islamic and pan-Arab political identities at the expense of national identities (Nisbet and Myers 2010).

The Internet and digital platforms greatly contributed to the creation of an Islamized form of public space beyond the official broadcast media and mainstream print media. The dynamic shift of the content from offline to online has caused a change in the overall structure of Moroccan public sphere in favor of Islamic discourses. The changes in public sphere towards more opening and participation are contingent upon change in the communication strategies of Islamist movements. The increasingly assertive autonomy of Islamists by dint of the new digital media platforms brought into the open a new understanding of how these movements regularly circulated their religious tracts and material. One of the most significant consequences of the use of the Internet by Islamists has been the creation of mediated culturally and religiously based networks of identities and collective belonging.

The recent parliamentary elections of 2012 have led to the creation of the first ever elected Islamist-led government in modern Morocco's history. The PJD, a moderate Islamist party won 107 out of 395 seats in the parliament, 27.1 percent of the seats, a record victory for the PJD. This election was free and fair and the voter turnout was up from 37 percent in the last elections to 45 percent. The Justice and Development Party (PJD) led by Prime Minister Abdelilah Benkirane formed a coalition government with the Istiqlal Party (IP), National Popular Movement (MNP) and the Progress and Socialism Party (PPS). Many observers interpreted the win as a result of the Arab Spring's calls for political change, and the PJD's not yet tarnished reputation by the corruption scandals and political maladroitness so commonly associated with the other established parties.

Youth Engagement and Digital Activism

In Morocco, Internet access was initially limited to social, educated and urban elites, but since 2010, the Internet has become the communication platform preferred by Moroccan youth. Forums, blogs, wikis, and YouTube videos are in vogue. Young people started to generate their own media contents, practicing new kinds of journalism and becoming "citizen amateurish journalists." Blogs,

Forums, and social websites are contributing to the development of the media in Morocco; citizens increasingly use it as a samizdat-platform for their news and views. Also, dissidents and activists are capitalizing on these new digital media because they have learned from the Islamists' best practices in the application of digital communication strategies and tactics. They saw how creative, aggressive and effective Islamists used digital media over the last decade. Civil society groups and new social movements, including feminists are using social media to inform, mobilize, campaign, recruit, and build coalitions.

Considering that youth unemployment in Morocco has grown over the last few years, because of the exogenous and endogenous conditions, recent estimates suggest that 41 percent among Moroccans aged 15–24 are unemployed. In response to the protests of 2011, the new Constitution stated the creation of the Youth Council. The Ministry of Youth and Sports has been working in designing and developing proposals for an effective implementation of this council. The goal of this Youth Council is to engage young Moroccans in participating in the process of decision-making. The top issue on the agenda of the Youth Council is youth unemployment. The access to higher education has contributed to the emergence of better-educated youth who is more responsible and more active politically. With the help of mass media and social media, these young Moroccans started to organize themselves for collective civic and political action.

The recent use of social media by Moroccan activists and dissidents triggered a revival of the watchdog function of the media and paved the way for it to act as a *fourth estate* or even *fifth estate* (Dutton 2009) in monitoring political abuses by the regime. In summer 2008, an amateur cameraman filmed traffic police taking bribes from drivers. The so-called Targuist Sniper video was uploaded on the video-sharing website YouTube, where it was widely viewed. This led to a police investigation and the subsequent arrest of the police officers involved. This episode raised cyber-activism against routine corruption to a new level, setting an example that was followed in other cities. In the historical context of the Arab Revolutions, Morocco has been witnessing significant political transformations. Triggered and inspired by the uprisings in the two North African countries, Tunisia and Egypt, a protest movement known as the February 20 Movement held rallies and marches throughout the country during 2011 to demand democratic reforms, a parliamentary monarchy, social justice, the end of absolutism, and the abolition of corruption. The triggering demonstration occurred on February 20, 2011. The February 20 dissidents and activists adopted the Internet to organize and mobile protesters. According to Bashir Hazzam, a Moroccan blogger, blogging "enables people to publish their ideas easily, without control and for free."

The ideal type of a modern protester in Morocco is Mouad Belghouat, who is a rapper and hip-hop artist, anti-monarchist and key figure in the February 20 Movement. Belghouat is known as "Lhaqed" (The Spiteful) and he was famous for his parodies of royal speeches and the authorities. He also popularized the slogan: "Live Long the People." This slogan was set to compete with the national slogan, "Live Long the King." This is the first time in Moroccan contemporary political history that people shout, "Live Long the People." One of his titles modified the Moroccan motto in the end of the national anthem "Allah, Al Watan, the king" to "Allah, Al Watan, liberty." Belghouat was very active in the Moroccan blogosphere, using his YouTube channel to upload YouTube video-clips like the famous "Kilab Ed-Dowla" (Dogs of the State). Equally revolutionary are his popular songs, which deplore injustice and inequality. They harshly criticized the king and the ministers. Some big families that are related traditionally to the palace are also targets of his satirical parodies. In September 2011, he was arrested while distributing leaflets and protesting and sentenced to one year in prison. After public protests over his incarceration, his sentence was reduced to four months. Supporters accomplished this by creating a Facebook group with thousands of members who demanded the liberation of The Spiteful. They called for demonstrations and most protesters wore t-shirts that read "Free the Spiteful," and "We are all Spiteful." His arrest attracted national and international media coverage. The *New York Times* described the whole situation a "banal enough affair."

Dissidents and human rights activists doubted the genuineness of the charges advanced by the regime. In the same vein, yet more emotional, his mother voiced in a YouTube video her anger and ascribed his arrest to his political engagement and digital activism. In the context of the Arab Spring, the February 20 Movement accumulated strong formal and non-formal networks. During its consecutive demonstrations in the streets and squares throughout the country, the February 20 Movement had posters with slogans that targeted the rampant corruption in Moroccan public institutions, and particularly public broadcasting. Digital platforms offer an increasingly important addition, since every person can turn every digital device into a broadcasting or narrowcasting space. Moroccan social media users more and more carried out the role of grassroots reporter, fact-checker and critics of the traditional media coverage of events. Thus Internet users have grown from observers to commentators, and sometimes even shapers and producers of events.

During the recent Arab Spring protests, the Moroccan movement was fractious yet it made one great contribution to political reform in Morocco. The triggering demonstration occurred on February 20, 2011. A few weeks later, the monarch Mohamed VI responded by announcing and introducing constitutional reforms. In his "historic" speech of on March 9, 2011, the Monarch Mohammed VI demonstrated a political will to transform his monarchy from an "executive monarchy" to a constitutional monarchy. For the first time in Moroccan, a new constitution was drafted by Moroccans and was approved by a referendum by more than 95 percent of voters. In the context of the Arab Spring, which was characterized by hectic political instability, digital activism has gained momentum and shaped political outcomes. The demonstrations organized and coordinated by the February 20 Movement with the help of social media made the Moroccan regime respond to the events in a top-down approach. This time, the regime understood that the Internet is a powerful political communication medium that empowers civil society groups and thus undermines the entrenched authoritarianism of the Moroccan regime.

Regime Reaction to Digital Activism

Morocco has a long tradition of offline surveillance and suppression of political opponents. The regime has always attempted, with the help of several strategies, to re-center the distribution of information and narrow channels of the national information system. It did not, however, fully realize the power of an Internet-enabled civil society. As demonstrated in the case of *Al-Adl Wal-Ihsan*, the regime apparatus lacked imagination in how to respond to the new situation, where digital platforms were used *in lieu* of print media. While the regime took active and quick measures to sensor the print media, it remains passive and idle when it came to the publication of the same document on the Internet.

The regime passivity in matters of digital censorship continued, the Moroccan regime has not attempted to disconnect Internet choke points or mobile phone systems. Remarkably enough, the regime passivity went along with the issuing a few restrictive legal censorship mechanism such as the 2002 Press Code, the 2004 Audiovisual Communication Law, and the 2003 Anti-Terrorism Bill as a legal framework for regulating media contents and for news delivery on the Internet and mobile platforms. For instance, the Anti-Terrorism Bill addresses the legal liability for Internet content. The legal liability rests with the author, the site, and the Internet Service Provider (ISP). The three ISPs are Maroc Telecom, Medi Telecom, and Wana. Moroccan ISPs have the obligation (via the Anti-Terrorism Act) to screen and filter the contents on the Internet and must block infringing contents when aware of them. They bear joint liability with the Internet site that must also filter and screen contents posted on their sites. The site owners are also legally liable for Internet content. For example, if one user posts a comment on a newspaper site, and if the comment is deemed a threat to national security, both the author and the site are legally liable.

There are several explanations for the regime's reluctance when it comes to Internet censorship. One is that the Moroccan regime is, possibly, cognizant of the lasting economic consequences and losses that are closely intertwined with a temporarily shut down of telecommunications networks. The economic logic might be so powerful and pervasive as to make the regime enact to opt for interrupting the Internet. Another reason might be the underestimation of the political communication dimension of the Internet. The Moroccan regime failed to realize the interactive and networking potentials that the Internet offers to its users. The third explanation is that the regime did not perceive the Internet as a mass communication medium and wrongly thought that it was used exclusively by the Moroccan elites.

Digital censorship has gradually gained the regime's attention under the combined impact of the Arab revolutions and the growing mobilization of the

Moroccan civil society. Over the last two years, Internet censorship has become a more frequent practice and a more common feature. As Howard, Agarwal, and Hussain conclusively point out, the literature on digital censorship makes a distinction between four typically different political systems and regimes including democracies, emerging democracies, authoritarian regimes and fragile states (2011). Despite the globalization of digital censorship along the line with its rising rates in all four types, authoritarian regimes are more aggressive than other types of regimes (Howard, Agarwal, and Hussain 2011: 6). One can also observe that the less democratized the country, the greater the impact of digital censorship on civil society actors.

However, armed with digital devices, Moroccan Islamists are transforming the cultural foundations of politics and authority by contesting the hegemonic (and official) interpretations of religious discourses as well as the relation between the triad of religion, authority and politics. Changes in digital communication technologies have a significant influence in a number of political communication areas. The new era of digital political communication is marked by an increasing flow of political information, which has made political actors rethink their communication strategies and tactics to react to every issue in real time, to predict the direction, intensity, and form of that influence. The Internet has transformed the form and function of the political communication strategies of Islamists, by enabling them to deliver their political and religious message without being censored by the regime's administrative mechanisms. In the digital age, Islamists are using digital platforms to continue their management of information, communication, networking and relationship with their constituents. Islamists have managed to turn their emailing lists and online forums among other digital platforms into the most vibrant digital communities.

Since 1927, *Time Magazine* used to select the Man of the Year. This tradition has made its impact in 2006 and 2011 respectively. In 2006, *Time* selected as the Man of the Year "You" and in 2011, the "Protester." Both "You" and "Protester" reflected the zeitgeist of the time, because it shifted the focus from the powerful elite to virtually mobilized mobs and networked masses. The constitution of 2011 had created a democratic political system that will make Morocco different. When the King appointed the Islamist Ben Kirane as Prime Minster, he decidedly acted in the spirit of the new constitution and broke with the authoritarian tradition. He made it clear that Morocco's incremental change is uniquely exceptional in the Arab region. Abdelilah Benkirane regarded what happened in Morocco as a "peaceful revolution." Regional experts, like Kenneth Pollack, Director of the Saban Center for Middle East Policy, also referred to the recent changes in the Moroccan political field as a 'quiet revolution.' However, contrary to optimistic predictions, the "Arab Awakening" has turned into an "Islamic Awakening." The advance of the well-organized Islamists in electoral processes in Tunisia, Morocco and Egypt has marked a "religious turn" in politics—and in interesting ways, it is a digitally-enabled one.

Chapter 10
Leninist Lapdogs to Bothersome Bloggers in Vietnam

Catherine McKinley and Anya Schiffrin

This chapter investigates how a vibrant blogging community developed in Vietnam over the last decade, and explains who the bloggers are and what they write about. It also discusses why Vietnam now wishes to control the flow of information through the blogosphere, what information it wants to control, and how it tries to do so. Drawing on a close analysis of Vietnamese-language blogs as well as interviews, the chapter includes a number of case studies to illustrate the points it makes.

In Vietnam, as in many other closed societies, the Internet has brought about rapid transformation. Although the Vietnamese government has always been sensitive to public opinion, the Internet has forced it to become more immediately responsive to public sentiment and accountable in new ways. The rapid rise of new technology has showed the ruling Communist Party that it can no longer control how information is disseminated and even less how it is perceived publicly. This is a dramatic change for a system in which the media was tightly controlled and expected to follow the party line.

Since Vietnam began a period of economic reforms (known as "doi moi") in 1986, the ruling Communist Party has emphasized rapid economic growth. As part of the reform process that opened up Vietnam to the world economy, the government allowed private enterprise to grow, signed international trade agreements, opened a stock exchange, let some unprofitable state-owned enterprises fail and closed down or merged some of its unprofitable banks. The result was unprecedented GDP growth, which from 1992 to 2008 was generally between 8–10 percent a year, according to the World Bank. The rate of poverty fell to 14.5 percent of the population in 2008 from 58 percent of the population in 1993 while per capita income soared to $1,130 by the end of 2010 compared to below $100 in 1986. Not only was this growth essential for what was a poor country ravaged by decades of war, but delivering economic growth became the justification for the Party's existence (Elliot 2012, Thayer 2009). Vietnam's leadership aimed at forging a Singapore-type bargain in which increasing standards of living made up for the lack of free expression and human rights. The system worked relatively well: Vietnam kept growing, standards of living kept rising and while the government has been repeatedly criticized for human rights violations, the country was relatively stable and secure.

But a recent slowdown in economic growth, coupled with the development of an urban middle class that is willing to question its government's motives and actions, has begun to change all that. Growth in 2011 was 5.89 percent and in 2012 it is expected to fall to around or below 5 percent (although it may pick up again after that). In addition, high inflation, weakening exports, concerns over currency stability, and the exposure of massive debts at large state-owned companies that are damaging the nation's sovereign credibility are raising concerns that the government is mismanaging the economy and allowing corruption and nepotism to thrive while ordinary people struggle. The unspoken deal, firm for so long, is showing signs of strain and "the party probably recognizes that it is now more vulnerable than at any point in the last decade," according to the Associated Press.

It is within this context that the Internet is becoming an ever-more powerful tool used by many from small businesses to anti-government bloggers and social networkers. Bloggers weigh in on policy matters and criticize corruption, land seizures, and environmental problems. They force the government to respond to localized complaints while still focusing on overall economic growth, and the momentum generated by the Internet means the Party has to respond quickly, something it is not accustomed to doing. The amount of information and opinion available online is new to this closed and secretive society and problems can no longer be sealed off and dealt with quietly behind closed doors as in the past. Hanoi's leaders are between a rock and a hard place. They want to stifle online dissent and deal with controversy privately but they know they must support the growth of a communication tool so vital to the economy.

Historical Background

In order to understand what a shift this move to public discussion has been for the Party, it is helpful to look back at how information was managed before the Internet. As in many colonized countries, the media played an important role in the struggle for independence (Marr 1981) and newspapers were used both to provide information about the cause and to mobilize support for the anti-colonialist movement (Peycam 2012).

The Communist Party of Vietnam which came to power in the north of the country in 1954 and in the South in 1975 was influenced by the Leninist model of media control. Throughout the Vietnam War, the Party had a network of reporters and photographers who produced pictures and articles about the war for supporters overseas (Schiffrin 2002) and for domestic consumption. Once the Communist Party of Vietnam took control of the country it changed the structure of the media as well. There were no private media houses allowed and television, radio and newspapers were run by the government/Communist Party of Vietnam (Heng 1998). The Leninist approach was a top down approach in which party officials oversaw the coverage and made decisions as to what could be covered (Brooks 2000, McNair 1991). There were several enforcement mechanisms:

1) weekly news meetings in which news workers were told what they could cover; 2) sporadic releases of news by government agencies; and 3) the appointment of Party members to oversee the organs. All of these control mechanisms remain in place and continue to guide news coverage by the official media (Crispin 2012).

As well as national newspapers published by the Communist Party (*Nhan Dan*) and the military (*Quan Doi Nhan Dan*), different government agencies and party organizations had their own publications. The quality, professionalism, frequency of publication and circulation varied widely but included magazines and newspapers published by the Police Department, and then smaller agencies such as the customs office, the State Bank of Vietnam and so-called mass organizations such as youth organizations (which publish popular dailies like *Tuoi Tre* and *Thanh Nien*) Women's Union, Farmer's Union and Trade Unions (publisher of the daily *Lao Dong*). The publications were funded by direct government subsidies, subsidies provided by the management organizations and by mandatory subscriptions taken out by universities, state-owned enterprises and other government offices (Heng 1998). As in China, the Vietnamese government began scaling back financial support for media houses in the eighties and the media began publishing more sensationalistic and entertaining news in the hope of raising circulation (Heng 1998). The media also began to expose corruption (Heng 1998, Heng 2003). From the turn of the current century, when Vietnam gave the official nod to private enterprises, corporate advertising has also been allowed and has played an increasingly important role on the financing of newspapers as state subsidies fall. The Press Law of 1989 further opened up the media space. By the 1990s, Vietnamese readers could find women's magazines and home décor titles on newsstands in major cities. Thanks to widespread education, literacy rates are high in Vietnam with around 93 percent of the population classified as literate.

Their increasing financial independence from the state, coupled with the growth of a more demanding and complex urban readership, slowly both allowed and pushed some newspapers to break from the official mold and begin to cover stories that had not been provided by the official Vietnam News Agency and may not have received prior approval from censors, in particular stories about low-level official corruption.[1] As in many other countries where television and radio often remain tightly under state control because of the expensive cost of setting up parallel structures (Djankov 2003), radio and television never made this change. By the 2000s, the government responded to this change and began to officially endorse press coverage of corruption and other 'social evils' as part of an Anti-Corruption campaign. It named the media as an anti-corruption tool of the state and tried to guide coverage and be seen to be addressing corruption within its apparatus. It

1 Vietnam does not technically operate a system of pre-publication press censorship. However, the weekly meetings between government officials and editors in chief are a route through which instructions are shared regarding the types of stories that are deemed to be acceptable or unacceptable. Editors are expected to ensure that coverage remains within these bounds.

allowed foreign development partners to train local journalists in investigative reporting skills and slowly but surely gave news editors greater freedom to nudge against the glass ceiling that limits coverage of controversial issues, creating slow but constant pressure on censors (Mckinley 2008).

In 2008, this snail-pace reform of the media came to an abrupt end as a small number of papers began to point fingers at senior government officials, accusing them of corruption and nepotism and drawing the anger of powerful vested interests. Two journalists were arrested and one jailed on charges of 'abusing democratic freedoms' and 'propagating false information' following their reportage of a case known as the Project Management Unit 18 (PMU18). Myriad others were questioned by police, who demanded to know their sources and made it clear that the editorial freedoms enjoyed until then were no longer on offer. The crackdown in the wake of PMU 18 coverage clarified for journalists that their new freedoms had been at the discretion of the Communist Party and could be withdrawn at any time. A door had been opened, showing what might be possible and allowing reporting staff and news editors to experience a degree of "free press," and then closed again. At the time of writing, the post-PMU 18 media controls remain in place and many senior writers have either left the industry or complain that about the onerous restrictions. The brief opening had shown audiences that a new kind of news is possible, and piqued the interest of educated readers who questioned the news published by the Party organs. Journalists frustrated with the limits placed upon their professional activities responded to growing audience demand by moving online.

The Birth and Reach of the Blogosphere

Vietnam joined the Internet in 1997, at first allowing only state-owned businesses and government ministries to use it but in 1999 opening the web up to the public. In 2002, the government allowed the creation of up to 40 Internet Service Providers (ISPs), up from only four previously. The growing competition reduced prices and made the Internet more accessible with use of the Internet growing by 30 percent/year from 1997 to 2007, according to Thayer (Thayer 2007). Internet penetration by 2012 was estimated at around 34 percent of the population, according to figures by the Vietnam Internet Network Information Center.

Early converts used email and online chats to communicate with family and friends overseas because "the post was slow and the telephone was expensive," said a blogger in Ha Noi. Once online, people began to discover other online services, such as games, overseas news sites and blogs, but there was no Vietnamese-language blogging platform and those who wrote their own blogs were dispersed among different overseas platforms (Blogspot, Wordpress, etc.). In 2004 Yahoo! responded to demand for Vietnamese services by launching a Vietnamese-language version of its 360° blogging platform. The platform attracted millions of users and facilitated creating an online community not seen before in Vietnam.

Since then Vietnam's blogosphere has grown to a thriving online community of several million people, with most of the growth taking place in less than a decade. While the majority of bloggers confine themselves to discussion of non-controversial issues like friendship, fashion, gossip and shopping, a small but significant number blog about news and current affairs, often focusing particularly on issues like economic governance, policy, politics, and Sino-Vietnamese relations that the official media is unable to report effectively because of editorial controls imposed by the government.

The audience for these political blogs can be broken into four groups, the smallest of which is most directly influenced by what they read and the largest of which is usually only reached indirectly. The smallest group of readers is a relatively tight-knit "self-contained group" of fellow bloggers who regularly monitor each other's posts. Broadening the reach of blogs is a second group: the family and friends of each blogger who read both for the blogs' news value and to maintain ties of kinship and friendship. "My family, my friends, journalism students, people who see my by-line in the paper …," said one journalist blogger listing her main readers. This group probably contains several million, often influential, people who are "30–60 years old, educated, frustrated, and want to share ideas," added another.

They, in turn, forwards posts to a third group: their friends and contacts, who spread content more widely through a mostly urban and relatively young group of readers, particularly young professionals and urban students (some of whom may have returned from overseas study where they were exposed to other Vietnamese- and foreign-language blogs). These people will "jump in and out of favourite blogs … if there's something new they will share it immediately," said a retired journalist in Ha Noi. The forth audience group is mainly reached indirectly, as urban readers take home the information they have read and discuss it with family members who are unlikely to access blogs themselves. "Although I don't expect farmers and workers to read blogs because they don't know how to use (or have access to) computers, the population is very young and young people all over will begin to use the web. Then they'll start talking to their parents and grandparents," said one veteran blogger.

Because of their reach and because their authors tend to hail from the country's intellectual and sometimes political elite, the few hundred political blogs discussed here are believed to have a disproportionately powerful influence over public opinion, which in turn influences policy. Writers include professionals such as writers, lawyers, doctors, teachers, and academics. "I think they blog because they used to write, and there are no (longer) any official outlets for their writing," said a Vietnamese-American academic who follows the blogosphere inside Vietnam and maintains a popular blog himself. The largest sub group of professionals is thought to be journalists who "blog because they have access to news" they are no longer able to publish through the mainstream media, said a journalist in Ha Noi. They upload news stories from official sources, provide personal comments and/or content, or combine these activities.

The Official Response to Vietnam's Growing civic Voices

As editorial controls over the state-owned media have tightened, blogs have played an increasingly important role in uncovering and disseminating information about corruption and other controversial issues that has no other route into the public domain. This has earned some bloggers a wide readership and considerable public respect, but also official ire. A series of arrests and the growing harassment of bloggers is evidence that Ha Noi wants to wrest control over information flows back from the blogosphere and into state hands. In a sign of how the repression of the Internet has grown, Vietnam was included in "The 2012 list of the Enemies of the Internet" released by Reporters without Borders. Others include Burma, China, Cuba, Iran, North Korea, Saudi Arabia, Syria, Turkmenistan and Uzbekistan which "combine often drastic content filtering with access restrictions, tracking of cyber-dissidents and online propaganda" (Reporters without Borders 2012). Reporters without Borders also noted that after China, and Iran, Vietnam now has the third largest number of bloggers in jail. Vietnam has been influenced by China for decades and followed a number of its economic policies. Unsurprisingly, many believe China to be the role model followed by Vietnam's government as it tries to control the blogosphere.

It wasn't always this way. The government was initially slow to recognize the potential threat posed to information control by the unofficial online media, and for some years ignored it altogether. In an interview with a newspaper writer in the early 2000s, one senior official was confused when the writer asked him to comment on the impact of blogs on news flows: "He thought I meant 'block calendars,' he'd never heard of blogs," the writer said.[2] Later, as blogs became better known and more widely read, the government began to monitor those written by Vietnamese living overseas but targeting readers inside the country. Some of the more scholarly blogs that commented on public policy were viewed as a useful resource. They were read regularly by senior ministers and their advisors, who saw them as windows on public opinion and sources of academic and scientific information that could be used to inform the policy making process. There is "not enough evidence to judge" how many of Vietnam's leaders personally read blogs, said a blogger in Ha Noi, although he and other interviewees believe several key leaders either monitor or instruct their secretarial staff to monitor blogs they think may be opinion-forming and/or critical of the government: "They don't speak about it but they do read blogs. I have personally printed some out and given (copies) to them," said a newspaper executive in HCMC.

But several events in the mid 2000s soured this relationship. First, the rapid development of Yahoo!'s online community worried the government because it created a forum where people gathered without government approval or supervision. The creation of early news blogs made "bloggers realize they didn't

2 In Vietnamese, the word "blog" is pronounced the same as the word "block"—the name given to the kind of calendars that have a tear-off page for each new day.

have to own a newspaper to express their opinion," said one blogger. In 2006, blogger Ha Kin, who worked for the Ministry of Foreign Affairs, blogged about her experience organizing the Asia Pacific Economic Cooperation (APEC) forum held in Ha Noi. The blog was a personal view of an official event, and its publication demonstrated how information dissemination about such an event was no longer the exclusive domain of the official media. "She got up to 26,000 hits a day, as much as a popular article on VietnamNet," said a second Ha Noi blogger. In 2007 Co Gai Do Long blogged gossip about popular singer Phuong Thanh and was promptly sued for damage to Thanh's reputation. The mainstream media, which had until then avoided coverage of Thanh's personal life because of strict editorial controls on such tabloid writing, received readers' complaints that they were missing a story. Papers were forced to respond by picking up the story and covering the resulting lawsuit. This early demonstration of the blogosphere's influence on the mainstream media showed "people who hadn't blogged before the power of blogging … everyone wanted that notoriety," the blogger added.

After building a following interested reading about celebrities, some bloggers upped the ante, using their sites to organize public demonstrations. Anti-China protests in 2007 gained significant online coverage and organizational backing and became a rallying point for journalists who wished to support the demonstrators but were unable to do so via their state-owned news organizations: "Blogging became a political activity … In late 2007 the government realized that the blogging community could do something to threaten (it). There were many anti-government blogs and personal attacks on top leaders," one blogger recalled. These cases came shortly before the post-PMU18 crackdown on the mainstream media and increased the appeal of an alternative online outlet for mainstream media writers: "When journalists found they had an outlet to express their opinion without censorship they did it," said a journalist who maintains her own blog.

What happened next is unclear: some interviewees believe that the government began to more closely monitor and attempt to control the blogosphere at the urging of the Chinese authorities, which were keen to suppress support for and news of anti-China demonstrations. Others believe a senior Vietnamese official who had come under attack by bloggers persuaded the Ministry of Culture and Information to issue regulations to curb blogging. Whatever the details, "officials are now quite aware of blogs," which they increasingly view as unofficial news sites and wish to regulate like online newspapers, noted a blogger and journalist in Ha Noi.

A number of regulations to control blogs have been issued in recent years or are currently under discussion in draft form. In 2008, Decree 97 on the "Management and use of Internet Services and Electronic Information on the Internet" was published. It formalized management of the Internet under two ministries: the Ministry of Information and Communication and the Ministry of Public Security. Prior to this, the Ministry of Posts and Telecommunication had been responsible for technical management of the net, but there had been no comprehensive provision for the management of its content. In an early attempt to limit the publication of sensitive information online, Article 6 of the decree prohibits acts including the sharing of state secrets, opposing the state, and slandering or "hurting the prestige" of citizens (whether or not the information about that person or people is accurate). The decree also classifies Internet Service Providers as "Internet agents" and makes them responsible for monitoring content and user activity and reporting users in convention of Article 6. The decree clarifies that both the civil and penal codes might be used to punish infringement, making Internet use a potentially criminal act.

In 2010, a piece of lower-level legislation, Circular 14, was enacted to clarify some of the provisions of Decree 97. It stated that one of the "unlawful acts" for which Internet users might be punished was the "propagation of unlawful press." Websites and social networks were told to store information about those who used/read them and to make this information available to the authorities when requested. Foreign service providers such as Yahoo! and Facebook, and blog hosts such as BlogSpot and Multiply—all of which are commonly used in Vietnam—came under pressure to bring their servers onshore inside Vietnam. All refused.

The following year, in February 2011, Decree 02 collated a number of media management rules, including one that clearly delineated between the official press and the unofficial online media, giving a degree of protection to the former but making it clear that these legal protections did not apply to the latter. Since then, a growing number of bloggers and online critics of the government have been arrested, harassed and jailed, mostly on charges of Anti-State Propaganda, a vaguely worded criminal offense. In early 2012, a draft decree was published by the Ministry of Information and Communication for comment by other government offices that, at the time of writing, remains in draft form. If published it will force offshore service providers to bring servers onshore to be overseen by the government and will make the use of pseudonyms and anonymous writing illegal.

Much of this legislation is unenforceable: For example, Yahoo! and Facebook both refused to consider bringing servers used by Vietnamese clients onshore and the government lacks the human and technological resources to enforce demands for information from ISPs (which themselves often lack the technology to shore the information demanded). But journalists and bloggers say the aim is not current enforcement. Instead, the growing body of legislation is an arsenal the government plans to use over time to jail some dissenters and threaten others. The Criminal Code's all-inclusive 'anti-state propaganda' clause regularly comes under fire from international press freedom organizations and foreign governments that are lobbying Vietnam to improve its press freedom record. The new regulations provide legal tools with which critics of the government can be punished: "The regulations make it possible for them to harass people" in the hope that intimidation will slow the publication of critical information on the Internet, said one blogger.

To date there is little sign that these new laws are having the desired effect. In 2012 the increasingly vocal online community began to talk openly about corruption and nepotism within the prime minister's family, naming names and claiming to have access to high-level government information proving the prime minister's misdeeds. In response, in mid-September 2012 Prime Minister, Nguyen Tan Dung issued an order banning state employees from reading or forwarding blogs that it said contained "slanderous, fabricated, distorted, and untruthful information (designed) to paint a gloomy picture of the country's governing apparatus." The order named three blogs: Quan Lam Bao ("Officials doing journalism"), Dan Lam Bao ("Citizen Journalism"), and Bien Dong ("East Sea"—the Vietnamese name for the South China Sea, where disputes with China over ownership of the potentially oil-rich Spratley and Parcel islands are a highly controversial news topic in Vietnam).

The order told the Ministry of Information and Communication and the Ministry of Public Security to close the blogs, but an official in charge of media management within the public security ministry, who spoke on condition of anonymity, said his department lacks the technology to identify the compliers of these blogs, which are authored and edited anonymously. Immediately following the order's publication via Vietnam Television's main evening news program two of the blogs, Quan Lam Bao and Dan Lam Bao, posted notices on their sites saying they will continue to publish as usual: "Nobody can shut our mouth or stop our freedom of expression ... This is our mission, we will continue at any cost," Dan Lam Bao told the Associated Press. Indeed, far from slowing readership, the prime minister's order has piqued the publics' interest in these controversial blogs and their readership rose significantly the day after the order was published as curious members of the public and state officials logged on the see what stories they cover. Readership of Dan Lam Bao rose from 20,000 to 35,000 hits, according to statistics published by Google Analytics and quoted by Dan Lam Bao.

The Growing Influence of Online Media on Government and Governance

Today the Vietnamese blogosphere is firmly entrenched and performs multiple roles. The presence of the blogosphere is boosting government accountability, providing not just an outlet for unhappiness with the system but also a place where conflicts can be mediated. An example of how the blogosphere has affected government accountability can be seen in the very different ways a series of disputes over land and corruption have been made public in the past two decades: the Thai Binh protests of 1997, the Central Highlands protests of 2000, and the Ecoland Park protests of 2012. As is true of many developing countries, disputes over land are common especially as the government tries to transfer land that had been used by farmers over to big businesses and for real estate development. In Vietnam, land is also a sensitive issue. Until the French colonized Vietnam, land was publicly owned (Kerkvliet) and the equal distribution of land was a large part of the land reform that took place after the Vietnam Communist Party took power. The fights over land use in Vietnam today are fueled by anger over corruption but ultimately may make the government more accountable and even democratic (Wells-Dang).

Land in Vietnam is all owned by the state but as part of the 1986 Doi Moi reforms private land leases were introduced to encourage investment in agriculture and, later, private business. The granting of these leases has provided ample room for petty corruption as local authorities demand fees and favors in return for their allocation. Also, the prioritization of leases for ethnic Kinh majority families over ethnic minority groups has caused much public discontent in minority areas. The first agricultural land leases were issued in the late 1980s for 20 years and will soon expire. However, in some places local authorities, keen to transform farmlands into lucrative construction sites, are forcing farmers to give up their land early, and this has created a groundswell of public discontent around Vietnam.

The province of Thai Binh is in the Red River Delta and located some 80 kilometers southeast of Hanoi. In 1997, demonstrations broke out there as villagers protested fees levied on them by local officials and alleged corruption by these officials. The protests lasted for months and were discussed everywhere except the official media. Foreigners compared notes and rumors at diplomatic cocktail parties and the Vietnamese also talked about it a great deal. There is a Vietnamese expression along the lines of "the 10 cent cup of coffee goes around the world," that refers to how gossip was spread in the morning at the sidewalk coffee shops popular with urban Vietnamese. This was true in the case of the Thai Binh protests. The authorities had apparently sealed off the province and they imposed a complete news blackout on the events at Thai Binh. To this day it's not publicly known whether the police fired on the protestors or how many people were killed (Hayton 2010). But the fact that the protests had happened was confirmed to the outside world when in September 1997, the government admitted at a press briefing with foreign journalists that there had been some "incidents" in Thai Binh and that local officials had been disciplined (Schiffrin 1997). This was followed by a four-part series in the army's newspaper *Quan Doi Nhan Dan* suggesting that local officials had been levying fees for infrastructure construction and then pocketing some of the money, but with satellite television still banned and the Internet not yet connected, the State had a complete monopoly on the what news was reported inside Vietnam.

After the *Quan Doi Nhan Dan* article, newspapers announced that provincial governor and Central Committee member Vu Xuan Truong and 50 other officials were dismissed. Vietnamese media also ran articles about the great achievements of the province. The Grassroots Democracy Decree which was announced by the Party in 1997 was viewed as a response to the Thai Binh Protests (Hayton) and was meant to make local officials accountable.

Four years later in 2001, and again in 2004, more serious protests erupted: this time in the Central Highlands region, home to many of Vietnam's Hmong and other animist or Christian minority hill people who have traditionally offered little support to the Communist authorities and in some places were then still living a nomadic slash-and-burn life. As part of its economic transformation, Vietnam in the 1990s targeted coffee as a key export commodity and chose the central highlands region for its cultivation. To build and farm these new plantations, ethnic Kinh people were encouraged to move to the sparsely populated highlands region, and its population quadrupled from 1975 to the early 2000s (Human Rights Watch paper). The land they cleared for coffee was taken from minority people who, with no traditional concept of private land ownership, were forced onto marginal lands. Resources such as timber and grazing land were depleted, and the "net effect of these interlocking processes (was) a gradual dispossession and displacement of indigenous highlanders" (Salemink 2008). In response, Hmong church and other community leaders organized ongoing mass protests outside local government offices. The involvement of church leaders heightened tensions, as the Hmong community does not accept Vietnam's official form of Christianity, which incorporates loyalty to the Communist Party, but practices its own version of the faith. In 2001, and again three years later, the authorities responded with force, bringing in the military to suppress the protests and forcing hundreds of protest leaders and participants to flee over the border to Cambodia. Many were caught, returned, and jailed.

Through the period, the state media portrayed the protesters as enemies of the state supported by Anti-Communist lobby groups overseas, ungrateful of the benefits state policy had bought to their undeveloped region. The foreign press and diplomatic corps was barred from entering the region, although news agencies nonetheless covered the news in a limited manor. Inside Vietnam, a small number of urban Internet users were beginning to access these reports. Although the government blocked access to major foreign news sites, overseas Vietnamese communities bypassed this rudimentary firewall by emailing stories to relatively inside the country who then forwarded them to others. The State's grip on information flows was weakening.

A third major land dispute demonstrates how far the online media has come in forcing transparency upon the State. In April 2012, 3,000 police and private security guards were bought in to clear around 1,000 farmers from their land in Van Giang (Hung Yen province) ahead of the planned development of a luxury Ecopark housing development in which many high-ranking officials are believed to have invested. The 500-hectare project required the removal of thousands of farmers from their land. Media coverage of the land clearance operation was banned well before the event took place. But then a blogger, Nguyen Xuan Dien, "blogged about it live when the police came," according to a fellow blogger. Dien was later taken into custody and questioned by police, but the story had been broken. Although an embargo on official news about the park remained in place and was strictly enforced, the next day news organizations—pushed to cover the issue by readers who had learned of it online—began to write editorials relating to land tenure and government corruption in land management. Blogs now offer their readers access to news that mainstream news groups cannot. Indeed, they have become so institutionalized that they are now known as the "left lane" of information flows. While official news flows along the "right lane" (the correct driving lane in Vietnam), bloggers fill the left lane. "Readers access both, and when there's not much on the right lane they will go to the left," according to one journalist who also blogs. The forced release of information about the Ecopark case, as well as coverage earlier in the year of the unfair eviction of a tenant farmer near Hai Phong who protected his land using a homemade shotgun, have created such a public outcry that the government has promised to put reform of the land law on the legislative agenda.

This is not the first time bloggers have forced policymakers to act. In 2007 the prime minister approved a Bauxite mining project in the Central Highlands, granting most of the work to a Chinese contractor. Opponents believed that the project was environmentally unsound and, because much of the work would be done by Chinese laborers and profits repatriated to China, economically of little value to Vietnam. In early 2009, war Veteran General Vo Nguyen Giap wrote an open letter to the prime minster requesting additional impact studies and his letter was circulated online. Academics joined him, launching a blog, www.bauxitevietnam.info, to lobby for change. The state responded by blocking the site, which moved to another server, playing cat and mouse with the authorities until the lobbying momentum the blog had created eventually forced Hanoi to act. In April 2009/10 the Politburo agreed to review the project, which was sent back to the National Assembly (parliament) where normally passive members took the opportunity not only to re-evaluate the mine but also to openly question the prime minister's decision to split the $1.1-billion project into smaller parcels, which had allowed his office to bypass the legal requirement that projects worth more than $1 billion be scrutinized by parliamentarians before being approved. The Bauxite site showed that blogs "can have significant influence, especially when policy is being made. (National Assembly) delegates used to monitor the mass media to gauge public opinion, but they no longer trust it. Now they monitor blogs," said a well-known blogger.

It also exposed high-level intra-party discussions, forcing a degree of transparency not often seen in Vietnam. When a group of retired war veterans wrote to the Politburo demanding that officials tainted by the bauxite case be reprimanded or removed, their letter was circulated through the blogosphere. Senior Politburo officials responded by telling the veterans to air their concerns in private, and rumors circulated that Politburo member Trung Tan San had visited one retired general and a tense conversation had ensued. The general responded to these rumors by posting a note on the bauxite blog explaining that the conversation had in fact been cordial. Interviewees said that by doing so he dispelled rumors (and thus pacified the Politburo) while also keeping the discussion in the public domain. The extremely partisan nature of some more recent blogs, such as Quan Lam Bao and Dan Lam Bao, reveal the previously hidden disputes between high-level officials. The fact that the blogs currently under attack all oppose the prime minister suggests that the controversy is not coverage of politics, but coverage of personalities within the political structure. Blog Beo, a highly political blog written openly by the editor-in-chief of a large newspaper in Ho Chi Minh City, supports the prime minister and his policies and was not targeted under the recent administrative order.

Conclusion

By censuring some blogs and not others the government is performing a balancing act—allowing some freedom but trying to maintain limits on what is said. However, the anger and mistrust that is giving rise to the social tension being played out in the blogosphere is not going to go away. As Vietnam continues to develop economically there will likely be more inequality and more corruption, more land grabs and more damage to the environment. The perception that access to resources is a rigged game will continue to grow and anger over these issues is fodder for the blogosphere in Vietnam just as it is in many other countries. Given that Internet use is growing, the Communist Party of Vietnam will likely continue doing what it's been doing: allowing the Internet to thrive but cracking down on dissent when it perceives a threat.

However, the benefits of the blogosphere are greater than the risks. By holding the government to account and providing a space where people can air their grievances it may turn out that the Internet will help the Party more than it harms it. The CPV knows it needs it must address corruption and knows the media to help it fight against corruption (Cain 2012, McKinley 2008) but continues to try to control the way that "help" is given. An October 2012 politburo meeting, that before it met had been rumored to be preparing to oust Prime Minister Dung because of his alleged mismanagement of the economy, instead issued a public apology admitting its failure to contain corruption. President Nguyen Phu Trong ended the meeting by saying: "The politburo have seriously self-criticized and honestly apologize to the Central Committee for the shortcomings in party building, cases of moral decay among party members and cadres" (BBC, October 16, 2012). He said Vietnam's top decision-making body had decided not to "discipline one member." This unwillingness to upset the apple cart, even when the apples are believed by a growing number of people to be rotten, indicates Hanoi's overwhelming desire to ensure stability. But in order to do so, it must walk a fine line between controlling information flows and suppressing bad news, and allowing enough news to reach Vietnamese citizens to assure them that their government is really addressing the ever-growing problem of graft.

Chapter 11
Dynamics of Innovation and the Balance of Power in Russia

Gregory Asmolov

In recent years information technologies have played a variety of different roles in social and political movements. Information and communication technologies (ICTs) suggest new ways of manifesting both symbolic power, for example new ways of framing and agenda setting, and material power, for example new opportunities for simplifying the organization of collective action. Manuel Castells explores the role of ICTs in power relationships through the notion of mass self-communication. According to Castells (2007), mass self-communication is a "building of autonomous communication networks to challenge the power of the globalized media industry and of government and business controlled media" and, more generally, "the capacity by social actors to challenge and eventually change the power relations institutionalized in society" (2007: 248).

This chapter analyzes the Russian protests of 2011–2012 as a case study for examining the role of ICTs in the relationship between authoritarian power and citizens. From the mass self-communication perspective, the protests suggest another case study of the role of ICTs in the emergence of political counter-power. In this case, the question that should be asked is to what extent the application of a particular technology was able to challenge the balance of power. I also argue that an analysis of the role of ICTs role in political and social mobilizations should also focus on the process of emergence of new tools, rather than on analyzing functions of particular applications and platforms. Examining the dynamics of the process can help to understand the role of ICTs in a particular sociopolitical environment and to respond to the question of whether ICTs erode or strengthen authoritarian power. The process under investigation is political innovation, in other words the capacity of participants in a political conflict to create new tools that seek to challenge or protect the balance of power. Addressing the dynamics of political innovation requires us to address the following questions: To what extent are oppressed groups able to adapt to new political challenges and introduce new tools, doctrines and forms of organization? To what extent is a government able to introduce or respond to innovation? What is the nature of the dynamic in a balance of power, and do ICT innovations favor one side or eventually preserve the status quo? Does innovation suggest a temporary advantage for a particular side or does it lead to permanent changes in the balance of power?

There are a several reasons why Russia, and in particular the Russian electoral cycle of 2011—2012, provides a good case study for the analysis of the political innovation process. First, Russia provides a fruitful environment for innovation due to the relatively high penetration of the Internet and the degree of ICT literacy, especially in the big cities which are considered to be where the politically active middle class lives. Second, historically, since the end of the 1990s, the Internet has had a consistently significant political role in Russia. While the traditional media, and in particular television, are controlled by government, the Internet remains a relatively free space. Unlike the traditional media, the Russian online space has tended to have a more oppositional agenda and to suggest a contestatory framing of political events (Etling et al. 2010). In addition, Russian Internet users have already had experience of using online tools for the facilitation of collective actions to address social issues (Machleder and Asmolov 2011). Third, the period between the two rounds of voting in December 2011 and March 2012 constitutes a timeframe with a high concentration of political challenges and this served to accelerate the innovation process.

A Framework for the Analysis of Political Innovation

The role of innovation in the balance of power between the sides in a conflict is analyzed in the field of security studies, and particularly in terms of the Revolution in Military Affairs (RMA) concept. One of the questions for RMA concerns when a particular technology is able to empower one side in such a way that this substantively erodes the power of the other side. RMA refers to the "major change in the nature of warfare brought about by the innovative application of new technologies which, combined with dramatic changes in military doctrine and operational and organizational concepts, fundamentally alters the character and conduct of military operations" (Marshall cited in McKitrick et al. 1995). Similarly, the analysis of the dynamics of political innovation seeks to understand the extent to which ICTs can change the nature of political conflict and lead to substantial change in a balance of power between state and protesters. In the case of political conflict, the role of innovation is significant only if it is supported by changes in the organizational and doctrinal dimensions. For instance new tools can lead to new forms of protest. The framework for the analysis of the dynamics of political innovation suggests three layers:

a) The Structure of Political Challenges

The political environment is shaped by the structure and diversity of political challenges. Innovation is triggered, inspired and driven by these challenges. Therefore understanding the functions and dynamics of political ICT innovations requires an analysis of the structure of the political challenges. If the challenges are not considered sufficiently significant, this may mean there is a lack of incentive for innovation. In a situation of crisis and political instability, the challenges tend to become more significant. Innovation by the opposition side creates political challenges for the authorities, which may also respond with innovation.

b) The Structure of Innovation Opportunities

While innovation is led by the nature of the challenges, there are factors that may lead to opportunities being taken or cause them to be missed. Social movement literature introduces a variety of definitions of political opportunity structures. For instance, according to Garret, opportunity structures are "attributes of a social system that facilitate or constrain movement activity" (Garret 2006). In order to understand the role of ICT, we need to examine what capacity exists for using technology to address political challenges, in other words the innovation opportunity structure. That requires mapping the factors that allow or restrict innovation.

The innovation opportunity structure is associated with two factors. The first is whether the particular political challenge can be addressed through ICT-based tools. The second is whether the oppressed group has the technical capacity to develop such tools. This can include the capacity of programmers and activists to collaborate, the degree of information literacy and tech-savviness among political protesters, the level of Internet penetration, the degree of Internet freedom, the local legislation, and so on. We must also differentiate between two types of innovation. The first type is the development of original solutions by local programmers and activists. The second is the adaptation of existing solutions, including platforms, political strategies or tactics, from other countries. The latter requires the existence of "bridge persons" who are able to take experience from one political environment and apply it to another context (Zurckerman 2008).

c) The Role of the Balance of Power between Protesters and Authorities

An innovation process is a chain that starts with a challenge to one side in a conflict that provides new opportunities for the application of ICT and in turn creates a challenge for the other side. The degree of challenge to both sides depends on the extent to which a particular innovation changes the existing balance of power and thus the status quo. Innovation contributes to this dynamics, but also emerges as a part of the dynamics, while any response by the authoritarian power (whether it uses technological innovation or traditional forms of power) to innovation leads to the creation of a new political challenge that can be addressed by a new innovation. Consequently, innovation is a mutually reinforcing process, where both sides may use various applications or tools to increase their own power or decrease the empowerment of the other side. Therefore, in order to follow the dynamics of innovation we need to address the interrelation between innovative solutions deployed by power and counter-power. In what follows, I present four case studies exhibiting innovation practices and technologies related to expanding the abilities for *election monitoring, the organization and mobilization street protests, the consequent coverage and protests and opposition activities*, and finally, their impact on the *political solidarity and legitimacy of protest leaders and organizers*.

Election Monitoring

Election monitoring is a common political challenge in political systems with a low degree of transparency and a high probability of voting falsifications. Monitoring seeks not only to reduce the scale of fraud, but also to question the legitimacy of elections by exposing the scale of falsifications. In recent years the use of crowdsourcing platforms for election monitoring has become common. The Ushahidi crowdsourcing platform has been used in many election campaigns, from Kyrgyzstan to Egypt (Meier 2011a). The Russian case presents the role of innovation in the emergence of multidimensional monitoring systems with a variety of ICT-based tools and platforms.

The crowdsourcing platform Map of Violations (kartanarusheniy.ru) was launched by the election monitoring NGO *Golos*. This was a website developed from scratch to address the specific needs of Russian election monitoring. Its structure included a number of special features such as expert evaluation, the rating of popular violations and the incorporation of crowdsourcing content with traditional media content. Strong collaboration with an online liberal media outlet, *Gazeta.ru*, helped to engage more people in monitoring, as well as to incorporate the results of crowdsourcing into the media agenda. *Karta Narusheniy* was able to collect thousands of messages during each election cycle. Russian citizens also actively used social networks, Twitter and blogs to share first-hand information, documents, photos and video of violations. Citizen-based reporting and user-generated content surprise no one these days. Of greater interest are the scale, immediacy and value of the reporting. The outcome of monitoring depends on the relationship between the scale of falsifications and the capacity of citizens to cover these falsifications.

The crowd of Russian networked citizens was also able to collect, post, and share a critical mass of reports concerning falsifications including documents and video reports. For instance, a YouTube playlist posted after the elections included the 60 most viewed videos of documented violations. The capacity of the Russian networked crowd relied on well-developed Internet infrastructure that allowed users to share information online almost in real time, and on the structure of the Russian Internet space, where interconnectedness between various platforms led to the rapid proliferation of information. The significant public exposure to the scale of fraud in the parliamentary elections visibly resulted in an accelerated process of innovation in the three-month period leading up to the presidential elections. A variety of new tools for election monitoring were introduced, addressing a diversity of monitoring-related challenges:

a) New Methods for the Collection of Violation Reports

The NGO *Golos* developed a service (sms.golos.org) which allowed the collection of reports from observers in real time through text messages. A group of activists developed, a special election monitoring application for smartphones. The application Webnablyudatel (webnabludatel.org) classified all violations and made it possible to instantly share video, photos and reports of these. Later, a Tweet Observer platform was introduced in order to create better opportunities for Twitter users to report violations.[1]

b) Data Mining and Verification of Monitoring Results

A platform, *Svodny Protocol* (svodnyprotokol.ru), was created for the collection and analysis of election observers' reports and protocols. This system presents the idea of "bounded crowdsourcing," where information was collected from a limited number of contributors who have special access to the event of interest and whose identities have been verified.

c) Mobilization of Observers

A number of platforms were created to enable any individual to become an observer. One such platform, aimed at simplifying the procedure for becoming an observer, was rosvybory.org. A similar function was offered by the Citizen-observer project (nabludatel.org). In St Petersburg, a website, Saint Petersburg Observers (spbelect.org), was launched by a group of local activists.

d) Coordination of Monitoring

Russian developers introduced *Grakon* (grakon.org), a special social networking platform for election monitoring. The purpose of this platform was to make election monitoring and coordination between various groups of observers as simple as possible.

Analysis: Election-monitoring and Balance of Power

A number of actions were undertaken to reduce the impact of the Map of Violations (*Karta Narusheniy*) and other monitoring efforts. One of the authorities' strategies was to put pressure on the media. Gazeta.ru was forced to revoke its endorsement of *Karta Narusheniy*. Additionally, the authorities embarked on a court case against the platform, accusing it of distributing false information. Pro-Kremlin activists contributed false reports to the platform in order to demonstrate that it

1 The platform was used at regional elections in October 2012.

was not credible. A video distributed on YouTube showed how this was done and described the dots on the *Karta Narusheniy* map as a "disease on the map of Russia" (Meier 2011b). Additionally, on election day unprecedented distributed denial-of-service attack (DDoS) attacks blocked the crowdsourcing platform, as well a number of Russian online liberal media outlets.[2] Anton Nossik, a well-known Russian Internet expert, compared this attack with the long-time Soviet attempts to block reception of foreign radio broadcasts.

As a response to the DDoS attacks, online media began using Facebook, Twitter and other media that were not affected by the attacks for the proliferation of content related to the elections (Sidorenko 2011). *Karta Narusheniy* also used Google Documents to continue collecting information. The emergency migration to alternative platforms demonstrated that the opposition and the liberal media were able to adapt to the attacks and create new patterns of information distribution.

Following the parliamentary elections, the state's response strategy changed from one of legal prosecution and DDoS attacks to a more innovative track. Following an order from Putin, a special online system for election monitoring, webvybory2012.ru, was developed. This allowed people to follow the majority of Russian polling stations (about 95,000) online on the day of the presidential election. Every polling station was equipped with two cameras, one focused on the ballot box and the other giving a general view of the polling station. Once the voting was over, one of the cameras broadcast the counting of votes. The cost of this project was at least 13 billion rubles (around US$500 million).

Opposition activists argued that the most common election violations could not be monitored by webcams. Nonetheless, the cameras did allow numerous violations to be spotted. However, this did not finally lead to reconsideration of any election results. In this case the innovation served not to increase the transparency and accountability of the voting process, but primarily to create a widespread semblance of transparency and accountability. It is also important to note the enormous gap between the costs of the citizen-based crowdsourcing election monitoring systems and the system introduced by the authorities. The opposition also tried to use innovation to overcome the limitations of the new state system. Webvybory2012 did not allow any recording mode or function which would permit complaints about violations; however a few special applications were developed by protesters in order to increase the efficiency of the state surveillance. Additionally, relying on the state system, the Video Observer platform (http://videonabludatel.org/) allowed tasks to be distributed among a network of online observers.

Innovation in the election-monitoring field challenged the balance of power between state and citizens. Michel Foucault used Jeremy Bentham's concept of the Panopticon as a model for the total surveillance by a state of its citizens. Some experts argue that ICTs and the Internet contribute to a state's capacity to monitor

2 These attacks cannot conclusively be attributed directly to Russian authorities, but there is evidence indicating that Pro-Kremlin groups were involved in conducting them.

its citizens. As we can see from the Russian case, however, in a context where every citizen is potentially a networked broadcasting sensor the situation can also be the opposite, with an increasing number of citizens monitoring the state. Information technologies have empowered the other side of the Panopticon by creating self-organizing surveillance networks focused on the observation of the authorities (Asmolov 2011). The introduction of the Russian surveillance system, Webvybory2012, which is in fact the largest Panopticon in human history, can be viewed as the state's attempt to use innovation to restore the balance of power within the Panopticon structure through engagement of people's gaze within a state-backed network of sensors.

Innovation did not lead to a reconsideration of the voting results. However, ICTs enabled a questioning of the legitimacy of the elections and triggered political protests. Innovation in the field of election monitoring led to the emergence of new political opportunities and challenges that were in turn addressed by sets of innovations in other fields. The further case studies address the other elements in the innovation chain.

Mobilization and Organization of Protests

One of the common challenges for the organization of protests is mobilizing citizens. Following the parliamentary elections, Russian political activists used a range of existing online platforms, including Facebook, Twitter, Vkontakte, LiveJournal and others, to mobilize participation in protest rallies. One of the most successful Facebook event pages was created by a journalist, Ilya Klishin, for a protest at Sakharov Square in Moscow on December 24, 2011. More than 54,000 people joined the event page. The actual number of participants in the rally was somewhere between 29,000 (according to official police data) and 120,000 (according to organizers' data).

The use of traditional online mobilization tools, however, was not felt by Russian opposition activists to be sufficient. "The space of Facebook and Twitter became too narrow for us," says Klishin (in personal). He started a practice of creating dedicated websites for specific protest events by launching the dec24.ru website, providing up-to-date information and links to mobilization groups on different platforms, for a rally to take place on December 24, 2011. The need to expand the range of mobilization tools was also related to the structure of the political challenges faced. Organizers of protests faced pressure, including questioning, prosecution and arrest, from the Russian security services. Additionally, the authorities required legal approval for the organization of protest events. Both challenges demanded new forms of protest and new strategies for their organization—below are four such categories of new organizational forms.

a) Car protests

On a few occasions, social networks and blogs were used to organize simultaneous flash mob protests in few cities, during which people with white ribbons symbolizing the protest on their cars gathered at a specific time and location. Some of these protests attracted more than 1,000 cars. Pro-Kremlin movements later adopted the same form of protest.

b) Single Protest

According to Russian law, a protest by one person does not require special permission. An example of how this can be exploited through amplification by ICTs was provided by Olesya Shmagun, who made a poster that read "Putin, go out and take part in public debates!" and stood with this by the entrance to Vladimir Putin's office. She was questioned by the government security service, but was not detained. Later, she published the story of her protest, together with photos, on her LiveJournal blog. Just a few dozen people were able to see Shmagun's protest in the offline world, but the blog post drew attention and was shared by many blogs and media outlets.

c) Large-scale Decentralized Mobilization

In February 2012, the opposition initiated the Big White Circle action (Khoklova 2012a). The idea behind this was to cover the circular road around Moscow's center (known as the Garden Ring) with a chain of protesters. Unlike the previously mentioned protests, this did not receive a permit from the authorities. Additionally, it was a particular challenge to cover the entire Ring of about 15 kilometers. A special online tool, the Feb26.ru website, was developed to organize this protest. This allowed people to check in at locations of their choice on the map of the Garden Ring, and showed which locations were already occupied. Unlike other protests, the Big White Circle had no organization committee or individual leader. The role of leader was played by a website. Seven-thousand-eight-hundred-and-forty-three people registered for the action and the online circle showed a relatively equal distribution of check-ins. While this would not have been enough to cover the whole circle, the actual number of participants was more than 20,000.

The action had two layers: it included people standing in the road and hundreds of cars with symbols of the protest driving around sounding their horns. The police distributed their forces around the circle, but no action was taken against the protesters. The nature of protest required the mobilization of a large number of policemen dispersed over a wide territory; therefore, it was difficult to concentrate police forces in one place. This case demonstrates how ICTs enable new forms of protest which have no clear leader, are decentralized, can bypass some legal restrictions and create new challenges for the authorities. The ideas of the protest, as well as its leadership functions, are embedded within the online platform.

d) Migration of Occupy Protesters

Following the Russian presidential elections, protesters tried to create Occupy camps. This was an adaptation of the protest tactics used in the US and other countries. The police attempted to close the camps and arrest the activists. As a response, activists started to use Twitter and social networks to coordinate the migration of camps from one location to another. The migration was so fast and well-coordinated that police were not able to respond fast enough and follow protesters. At some point the security forces became exhausted and a camp, #OccupyAbay, succeeded in surviving in one location for a few days.

Analysis: Mobilization and Balance of Power

In order to understand the role of ICTs in a power relationship, it is crucial to examine the capacity of both sides to apply innovation to its mobilization tactics, as well to restrict counter-mobilization. One the one hand, the authorities tried to limit the opposition mobilization through a number of methods, including prosecution, intimidation, arrests, as well as DDoS attacks on the platforms used for mobilization. Later, new legislation was introduced that significantly restricted the freedom to hold demonstrations. On the other hand, the challenge for the authorities was to mobilize supporters of the Kremlin in order to show that the protesters were a minority. They used a different type of online tool to mobilize people. A website, massovki.ru, that was usually used to engage paid participants for different types of public crowd event, such as the filming of a movie crowd scene, was used for the mobilization of pro-government rally participants. However, the mobilization of pro-government crowds mostly relied on offline strategies using so-called "administrative resources," where various organizations including large factories and universities are required to send a particular number of people to a political event. For instance, this type of mobilization was used for a large pro-Putin rally at the Luzhniki Stadium on February 23, 2012 (Asmolov 2012).

The opposition response to this was on two levels. On the one hand, they continued to introduce new forms of protest, exploring the limits imposed by the authorities. For instance, in May 2012 a group of famous writers organized the *Kontrolnaya progulka* (Control walk) when thousands of people were just walking on the streets of Moscow following the writers. At another level, the activists used ICTs to question the credibility of pro-government protests. Bloggers sneaked into pro-government events and interviewed people who had been forced or paid to participate.

The Russian case represents a struggle between bottom-up strategies of mobilization by an opposition relying primarily on innovation, including technological tools and new ways of organizing protests, and top-down mobilization by a government using primarily traditional strategies, while at the same time trying to limit the innovative potential of the opposition. In some cases, as at the pro-Putin rally in Luzhniki, the top-down vertical mobilization used by the authorities was able to mobilize more people than the bottom-up mechanisms. However, what we can see is that different strategies for mobilization create very different kinds of crowd, and the difference in nature of the two kinds of crowd may be more important than the number of people.

Coverage of Protests and Opposition Activities

One of the challenges faced by opposition activists in an information environment with a high degree of state control over the traditional media is the coverage of protests. Obviously, user-generated content was widely used. However, innovation led to the emergence of new practices with greater capacity to influence framing and agenda-setting. The mobile-based, real-time broadcasting platforms ustream.com and bambuser.com were used to provide live coverage of the protests against the result of elections from the heart of the crowd. Some of the streams had an audience of more than 40,000 people at one time. A Russian blogger with the nickname *Vova-Moskva* became a "livestreamer" and provided real-time footage of protests, including clashes between the protesters and the police. At one of the protests he broadcast his own arrest. He also used crowdfunding to support his work. A member of the *Duma*, Ilya Ponomarev, broadcast live from the police station in Novosibirsk where he was detained for "illegal distribution" of his newspaper.

During the protests people detained in police cars used their mobile phones to broadcast live and to send photos. The detained participants of the rallies also actively used Twitter to update of their arrests, as well as to share information about the location of the police car taking them to the station. At the peak of the arrests, Twitter feeds were full of dozens of reports from those detained. The live broadcasting and tweeting of arrests increased transparency around the police actions. When an individual broadcast news that he had been detained, a group of his friends followed him to the police station and demanded his release. A group of volunteer lawyers was also following the information. A website, ovdinfo.org, aggregated information from different sources about arrests. When the number of arrests increased after the inauguration of President Putin, a political activist, Maxim Katz, created a center for the coordination of assistance to those detained, which sent lawyers as soon as information about arrests was received. The use of ICTs made it easier to hold the police accountable for their actions.

An additional challenge for the protest coverage was that of the representation of numbers of participants. The statistics on participation were highly contested, with the authorities always giving low numbers and the organizers arguing that the number of participants was very high. A programmer, Anatoliy Katz, created the White Counter, an application that was used to count protesters. The counter was based on an analysis of the large number of images taken every second. It was used first time on June 12, 2012 demonstration. While police sources claimed that 18,000 people participated in the protests, according to the counter it was 54,000.

While participants in the opposition rallies produced a lot of online content in real time, almost no user-generated content came from pro-government demonstrations. The traditional, state-controlled media covered pro-government rallies extensively, while limiting the coverage of protests and framing opposition rallies as marginal activities. The dominant presence of oppositional content online is challenged by a number of tactics that can be attributed to pro-government interests. One of the tactics used was "hashtag spamming," where pro-Kremlin activists used oppositional hashtags to distribute pro-government information or spam. The distribution of paid content in support of the authorities or against the opposition was also a popular method in the blogosphere. Additionally, armies of bots were leaving pro-government comments on various liberal websites and blogs.

DDoS, hashtag spamming and "bot renting" could not be directly attributed to the Kremlin. However, the tactics of pro-government activists and their links to the Kremlin were exposed when a group of hackers claiming to be a part of the international Anonymous network published email exchanges between a number of pro-Kremlin activists and members of the presidential administration. The contents of these individuals' mailboxes were published on a special website, slivmail.com. In this case hacking was also a part of the dynamics of innovation, aiming to decrease the credibility of pro-government activities online. This method was inspired by Wikileaks and can be viewed as an adaptation of international experience to the Russian political context.

Political Solidarity and Legitimacy of Protest Leaders

The activities of pro-government networks also included using technology to delegitimize the leaders of the opposition. For instance, the mailbox of a blogger and opposition leader, Alexey Navalny, was hacked several times. The content of email exchanges were used to argue that Navalny was getting paid for serving various "enemies of Russia." Navalny's Twitter account was also hacked and hackers started writing offensive messages purporting to come from him. However, the major legitimacy challenge faced by opposition leaders was not from the government, but from within the opposition. In the Russian political environment, many citizens have lost trust not only in government, but also in opposition politicians. The opposition forces are very diverse and divided. They include nationalists and liberals, social-democrats, anarchists, environmentalists and many more.

One of the most challenging issues for this type of opposition is coordinating activities between different factions and groups, as well as making decisions about the form and content of protests. To increase the transparency and legitimacy of decision-making around protests, the key discussions concerning the organization of protests were live-streamed on a new online channel, Networked Public TV (rusotv.org). Another tool that helped to increase trust and transparency in the organization of protests was the use of online voting to select rally speakers. However, despite claims that the nature of Internet protest is leaderless, the question of how to establish a legitimate group of leaders became increasingly relevant once the time of big protests passed and the struggle entered a routine phase. A few months after Putin's inauguration, activists decided to conduct online elections and create a "Coordination Board of the Opposition." A special concept, procedure and dedicated platform (www.cvk2012.org) were developed under the direction of an opposition politician from Yekaterinburg, Leonid Volkov.

Volkov developed a complex and sophisticated system that addressed a variety of challenges, including the verification of voters, for ensuring that every Russian citizen who participated in the process voted only once. A variety of existing online platforms were used, as well as those developed especially for voting. In addition to online voting, a network of offline polling stations was created all over the country. The Russian online liberal TV channel, *Dozhd*, provided space for debates between candidates. The system faced a number of challenges, including DDoS attacks on election weekend and efforts to compromise the system through massive participation by members of a Russian financial pyramid, MMM. Eventually 170,012 people registered on the system, 97,727 verified their identities and 81,801 voted. A board of 45 activists was selected. Once the opposition had failed to achieve an annulment of the official voting results, it had decided to create its own alternative voting system. While the outcome of the voting is still unclear, these elections were the most innovative and large-scale online political experiment to date initiated by the Russian opposition.

Conclusion

The outcome of the Russian protests demonstrates that ICTs alone cannot erode authoritarian power. The elected parliament and elected president remained in place. No political reform has begun. On the contrary, some new anti-liberal laws have been passed. However, this study also suggests that any evaluation of the role of ICTs that is dependent on a specific political outcome is misguided. The definition of success of political protests depends on expectations, which can vary greatly, as well as on dozens of political and socioeconomic factors existing in a particular political context. Moreover, any "cause and effect" evaluation focuses on short-term outcomes and ignores the possibility of long-term influence.

What is important for evaluating the role of ICTs is the extent to which society is able to address challenges and a consideration of state-citizen dynamics as a whole. This study suggests that in order to understand the role of ICTs in a power relationship between authorities and opposition we need to focus not on the outcome of particular ICT applications, but on the extent to which each side is able to use ICT-based innovation to address new political challenges, and the degree to which this is capable of disrupting the status quo. This process is conceptualized as the dynamics of political innovation.

Concerning the extent to which the oppressed are able to adapt quickly to new political challenges and introduce new tools, doctrines and form of organizations, we can note the diversity of ICT-based innovations introduced by the Russian opposition in response to political challenges. This has included not only new tools and applications, but also new forms of protest and new organizational strategies. In some cases, like those of the Occupy migration tactics or the Wikileaks-type activities, this was an adaptation of Western strategies. In other cases, like that of the feb26.ru website, it was a novel innovation that addressed particular Russian challenges and relied on local features of the protests.

In addition to opposition actors, the government also introduced some innovative responses. However, the characteristics of these innovations were very different. First, in most cases it was a response to innovation by the opposition. It focused primarily not on empowering the authorities, but on neutralizing the increasing power of the opposition. Second, some of these innovations were based on illegal methods and, while they served the interests of authority, could not be directly attributed to state institutions. Third, in comparison to the innovations of the opposition, some of the tools proposed by the authorities were disproportionately expensive. Fourth, unlike the cases of innovation by the opposition, the technological innovations introduced by the authorities did not lead to any real change in the state's own modus operandi. The organizational and doctrinal aspects remained unchanged.

Lastly, regarding shifts in the balance of power, we can observe that the way opposition activists used ICTs was in fact able to change the balance of power in many fields, including election monitoring, the mobilization of protests, and agenda setting. On the other hand, the innovations created by the opposition cannot be considered as effectively disruptive. It has not led to a primordial advantage for the opposition or to a strategic shift in the balance of power. Eventually, the state was able to the restore the status quo that had been challenged by the innovations of the opposition. However, in most cases the state action to restore that balance relied not on innovation, but primarily on traditional doctrinal and organizational strategies including the use of administrative resources for top-down mobilization, on new forms of regulation based on new legislation, and on the mobilization of traditional forms of power like the police to prosecute political activists and restrict demonstrations. The role of innovation in the state's restoration of the status quo was in most cases minor. While the state was able to restore the balance of power, its capacity to respond to opposition challenges with innovations of its own was more than limited.

With the opposition demonstrating a considerable capacity to address political challenges through innovation, including diverse solutions which can be implemented in a short time, the state may face a situation where addressing innovation without innovation of its own will require more and more radical forms of traditional power. However, offline administrative resources and other traditional power resources may become exhausted and more radical and repressive actions may be required. Eventually, this will contribute to destabilization and lead to the creation of new and significant political challenges, which will be addressed by a new wave of innovation. This may lead to a further proliferation of protests and to increasing opposition empowerment.

Consequently, an analysis of the dynamics of innovation in the case of the Russian elections may suggest that in the long term ICTs can contribute to the erosion of authoritarian power and the strengthening of opposition activism. At the same time, the significance of innovation and the realization of its potential depend on the structure of the challenges that arise and on a variety of socioeconomic and political factors. A few months after the 2012 presidential elections, floods in southern Russia caused the death of more than 170 people. While the response of the authorities was heavily criticized as insufficient (Lipman 2012), the Russian people were able to use the Internet and to create a variety of tools that helped to provide a self-organized emergency response (Khokhlova 2012b). The major role of volunteers in emergency relief was another example of a shift in the balance of power in a field traditionally dominated by state actors.

Any crisis situation can create new challenges and can trigger a shift in the balance of power. As a consequence, a crisis provides opportunities for ICT-based innovation and can be a driving force for development of the role of ICTs in social and political systems. Viewing crises as a fruitful time for ICT innovation suggests that the development of the sociopolitical role of ICTs is cyclical in nature, developing from one crisis to the next. This suggests that focusing on the analysis of the process may give more answers than focusing on particular situational functions. When a society develops the capacity to address challenges through innovation, this could lead in the long term to significant political transformations.

Chapter 12
Anonymous vs. Authoritarianism

Jessica L. Beyer

In June 2009, as the Iranian state cracked down on the election demonstrators, users around the world navigating to the popular file-sharing site The Pirate Bay discovered that its normal pirate ship logo was green and labeled "The Persian Bay." The new green pirate ship had a banner across it that said, "Click here to help Iran." The link led to a forum focused on supporting the Iranian protesters on a website hosted by a subset of Anonymous, Why We Protest. In the aftermath of the 2009 Iranian elections, widely believed to be rigged in favor of the Iranian regime, Iranian citizens began protesting the presidential election outcome. People outside Iran watched horrified as Iranian protesters were beaten, shot, firehosed, and violently taken into detention by the Basij (McDowall 2009), a plain clothed paramilitary organization (Anderson 2009). Many of these Iranian protesters were using the Internet to help coordinate their protests and spread information. Social networking sites, such as Twitter, became central to coordination efforts as protesters used such sites to organize flash mobs and spread information. Twitter became important enough that in June 2009, the US government asked that the site delay its regularly scheduled maintenance to stay online so Iranians could continue to use it, a request that Twitter honored (Grossman 2009). Scholars have also argued that while Twitter and the Internet did not cause anything to happen in Iran in 2009 it certainly facilitated protest (Howard 2010).

The Iran-focused section of the Why We Protest Anonymous site has remained online since 2009. On the website Anonymous users continue to offer how-to guides outlining ways for people to remain anonymous online. The site also provides instructions for citizens and activists outside Iran who want to create proxies for in-country Iranian protesters. Among the resources the site offers are practical protest advice, such as how to make do-it-yourself gas masks. The site also includes a place where protestors can upload videos and pictures so the media can access the material, hosts discussion areas where protestors can plan protests and promote the democratization cause, posts links to other places trying to help the Iranian protesters, and provides a forum to help protestors and others track missing people. While the decision to become involved in helping the Iranian protesters was debated, ultimately, the Why We Protest Anonymous participants decided that their primary motivation was supporting freedom of information. The Why We Protest Anonymous group is only one of the many Anonymous activist groups and other online actors working to support the Iranian protesters. Support for the Iranian protesters marked the beginning of Anonymous groups mobilizing on behalf of democratization efforts in general in the Middle East and North Africa, as well as in other parts of the world. Anonymous has since supported democratization movements in the "Arab Spring" countries, using names such as "Operation Syria," "Operation Egypt," "Operation Bahrain," and "Operation Algeria."

Undoubtedly, there are limitations to the effects that any online group can have in authoritarian contexts. However, because authoritarian governments attempt to project the image of an omnipotent state (Wedeen 1999, Yurchak 2005) the actions of Anonymous groups and other hacktivists pose a challenge to this image and serve to highlight the limitations of state power. Although the power of hacktivist groups such as Anonymous is limited to the online world, hacktivists facilitate protest, communicate international solidarity with beleaguered dissidents, educate novices to the potential of digital media, and erode the perception of power that authoritarian states have worked hard to create. Thus, groups such as Anonymous are important new actors in the sphere of political protest because they loosen the stranglehold that most authoritarian governments maintain on the media and other information sources.

The Origins of Anonymous

The birthplace of Anonymous is the image board system 4chan.org. 4chan.org's board design allows users to post without user name or other personal identifiers, an attribute that most of the other board systems that the 4chan community has spread to share. Thus, the "author" of nearly all posts on 4chan.org and other related online spaces is "Anonymous"—which is the origin of the name "Anonymous."

Before 2008 Anonymous' action was generally focused on a nihilistically-defined pursuit of entertainment for entertainment's sake (lulz) with the extreme anonymity of the community a double edged sword—fostering highly intelligent creativity at the same time as creating an environment testing boundaries of offensive and shocking speech and imagery (Bernstein et al. 2011, Beyer 2011, Knuttila 2012, Phillips 2012). Some Anonymous actions have had normatively good results, but tend to be framed as produced for the "lulz," or potential entertainment value. However, in 2008, Anonymous activities shifted to mobilize explicitly for political causes. Anonymous groups' first campaign was against the Church of Scientology, and most scholars and journalists define this as a major turning point for Anonymous (Beyer 2011, Coleman 2011, Norton 2012a, Olson 2012). Anonymous began its action against the Church of Scientology using the same tactics it had used in actions framed as "lulzy" prior to becoming an explicitly political force. In particular, it used Distributed Denial of Service (DDoS) attacks, hacking Scientology computers, ordering large numbers of pizzas to Church of Scientology centers, and faxing reams of black paper to Church offices, among other tactics.

However, Anonymous members also began protesting offline outside Church of Scientology offices across the world in highly organized and coordinated protests that obeyed local laws, contained a cohesive message, used the iconic Guy Fawkes mask popularized by the film *V for Vendetta*, and set forth an agenda framed in explicitly political terms. Of the many striking attributes of the Scientology protests, the most observable was the shift in using normative language to frame the protests, rather than speaking of the protests as the pursuit of entertainment for entertainment's sake. This does not mean that the idea of entertainment was annexed, rather, that for the first time, there were equally strong voices arguing for Anonymous to exercise its power to help citizens.

The Church of Scientology protests gave Anonymous a taste of its potential and after 2008 Anonymous began engaging in other political action. As part of the move into more explicitly political activities, the Anonymous community also splintered into three loose affiliation groups (Beyer forthcoming, 2011). The first to emerge argued Anonymous should refrain from using illegal tactics, such as DDoS attacks, and focus on using only legal means to achieve its ends. This group is represented on the Why We Protest website mentioned previously. Second, a large subsection of the Anonymous community rejected the idea that Anonymous should be involved with anything political and argued that Anonymous should only engage in collective action for the sake of entertainment. The third group argued that Anonymous should be engaged in political protest but that it had to stay true to its roots and continue to use online tactics such as DDoS attacks. This third group is the part of Anonymous that most frequently finds its way into the press and it is this group that is usually responsible for high profile Anonymous "hacktivist" actions. This part of Anonymous has continued to grow in numbers over time, but it also continues to defy quantitative measurement or definition.

The name Anonymous is now given to participants in any number of online communities as well as anyone who participates in a collective activity that is defined as an Anonymous action (Beyer forthcoming, Coleman 2011, Norton 2012, Phillips 2012). To further complicate the organizational definition of Anonymous, their media materials often communicate that Anonymous is not an individual or a group, but rather an idea whose "time has come." Some have asked whether anyone who expresses support for, agrees with, or identifies herself with Anonymous or its actions should be counted as one of Anonymous (Coleman 2012, AnonNews.org). As the illustrations suggests, Anonymous does not have a formal membership, or a leadership structure with clearly identifiable hierarchy, as well as no defined single agenda. Anonymous actors contain programmers, experts, IRC server hosts, press release writers, among other who engage in purposeful action. When Anonymous mobilizes, it is because someone has suggested a target and enough members have decided that the proposed action is important (and, often, entertaining). If the proposal fails to gather enough support, then nothing happens. Norton (2012b) framed Anonymous action in the following way:

> Anonymous is a classic 'do-ocracy,' to use a phrase that's popular in the open source movement. As the term implies, that means rule by sheer doing: Individuals propose actions, others join in (or not), and then the Anonymous flag is flown over the result. There's no one to grant permission, no promise of praise or credit, so every action must be its own reward. Anonymous action is facilitated by an array of online tools such as Internet Relay Chat (IRC), posting boards, Twitter, wikis, blogs, websites, and other software.

For any given Anonymous action there are likely Anonymous members who do not agree with that action, and there are high levels of disagreement within the community about partisan politics. For example, during the 2011 protests in Wisconsin against the Governor's efforts to remove public employee collective bargaining rights, some Anonymous members proposed that Anonymous mobilize on behalf of the protesters. In response to the suggestion, other members argued about whether Anonymous should involve itself in partisan politics when there was no way that all Anonymous members could agree on a political platform. In contrast, Anonymous members do tend to share a belief in freedom of information (Beyer forthcoming) and a belief in civil liberties in general. This shared belief is one of the reasons Anonymous has repeatedly challenged authoritarian governments all over the world, including working to support protesters across the Middle East and North Africa during the Arab Spring.

Anonymous and the Arab Spring

Anonymous actions in Iran, Syria, Tunisia, Egypt, and Bahrain offer an example of how a transnational network of Internet-based activists do challenge state power. Anonymous not only provides new conduits for information transfer in situations where states have attempted to completely close society off from the outside world, but it challenges the image of an omnipotent state.

Syria serves as an entry example of the challenge Anonymous poses to authoritarian regimes. In Syria, Hafiz al-Assad's state committed considerable resources to build a cult of Assad—a cult in which Assad knew "all things about all issues" (Wedeen 1999: 1). Following Hafiz al-Assad's death, Bashar al-Assad's government has continued to project the image of an all-powerful and unchallengeable state, responding to the increase in criticism of the regime that followed the so-called "Damascus Spring" with a severe crackdown on critics and others whom the regime perceived to be a threat (England 2008). As the Syrian government has waged war against its unarmed population and Syria has descended into civil war, Assad's government has continued to shape discourse around the violence. Externally, he has hired public relations firms to help shape his image (Carter and Chozick 2012). Internally, he has claimed that reporting on Syria is false, and has accused the United States of fostering the conflict (Baetz 2012) and claimed that the civil war is being perpetuated by terrorists (MacFarquhar 2012).

Tied to these efforts to shape discourses about and inside Syria has been an ongoing effort to surveil and curtail the political uses of information technology. Reporters without Borders (2012) reports that Syria has become one of the most dangerous places on the planet for journalists. The restrictions on information transfer have become so tight that activists must use Lebanese and Turkish proxy networks to upload information, moving close to borders to access international Internet cables. Much of the sensitive political information leaves the country using "sneaker networks" of people smuggling USB drives from person to person until contents can be safely uploaded online (Ulbricht 2012). Information and images are then shared with major news sources, such as the *New York Times*, as well as organizing online archives of the information for global distribution (Goodman 2012). In Syria, Internet cafés have been the site of state surveillance as owners have been compelled to log comments people posted online since 2007 (Steavenson 2012). Overall, the media environment in Syria is highly restricted and dangerous for anyone attempting to use any technology to show the world what is happening inside the country.

The Syrian government is also supported in its efforts to create a monopoly on information by a range of actors, including the Syrian Electronic Army (SEA). The SEA is a group of pro-government hackers that has been active online using many of the same tactics that Anonymous members use, including DDoS attacks as well as hacking websites and replacing the content (Fisher and Keller 2011). SEA also engages in "protests" on the Facebook pages of groups that it views as anti-Syrian. In two well publicized instances, the SEA hacked a Reuters-affiliated Twitter account (Fox 2012) and Al Jazeera's website in response to their reporting on the Syrian conflict. The SEA has targeted Anonymous websites, and Anonymous has also attacked the SEA website in response (Pavel 2012). Despite SEA's public statements that it is not affiliated with the Syrian government, in June 2011 Assad referred to the group in a speech saying, "There is the electronic army, which has been a real army in virtual reality" (Fisher and Keller 2011).

In response to the Syrian government and the SEA, Anonymous and other transnational Internet-based activists have actively challenged the state's attempt to maintain control over information. On June 3, 2011, the Syrian government "turned off" the Internet in Syria in response to the unrest in the country (Reporters without Borders 2012). Following this major initiative, the only Internet connections remaining were those used by the Syrian government. In response, Anonymous pledged to engage in attacks on Syrian government sites, in particular, Syrian embassy sites, announcing (AnonOpsSyria 2011):

> This is a message from Anonymous. It has come to our attention that the tyrant and human rights abuser Bashar Assad the so called president or dictator of Syria has shut down the internet within Syria, thus further isolating and terrorizing the freedom loving people of Syria who have already suffered so much from this evil regime. So today we will begin a program of removing from the internet the web sites of the Syrian Embassies abroad.

In the following weeks, Anonymous also engaged in other attacks on the Syrian government's online infrastructure, including the Ministry of Defense where Anonymous posted, among other things, one of the iconic Anonymous "logos," photographs of tortured protestors and the following message in English and Arabic (syrianona 2011):

> To the Syrian people: The world stands with you against the brutal regime of Bashar Al-Assad. Know that time and history are on your side—tyrants use violence because they have nothing else, and the more violent they are, the more fragile they become. We salute your determination to be non-violent in the face of the regime's brutality, and admire your willingness to pursue justice, not mere revenge. All tyrants will fall, and thanks to your bravery Bashar Al-Assad is next.
>
> To the Syrian military: You are responsible for protecting the Syrian people, and anyone who orders you to kill women, children, and the elderly deserves to be tried for treason. No outside enemy could do as much damage to Syria as Bashar Al-Assad has done. Defend your country—rise up against the regime!

Following this foray, in September 2011, Anonymous again hacked multiple Syrian government websites, this time including official "city" websites, replacing content with links to guides on how to remain anonymous online; information about the city, such as the number of people killed by the government in the city; and videos about government action against protestors (Pavel 2011). In early 2012, Anonymous, in collaboration with LulzSec and the Peoples Liberation Front, hacked into a mail server used by the Syrian Ministry of Presidential Affairs and released hundreds of emails. The initial email release in February 2012 was considered embarrassing to the regime and included emails discussing strategies to manipulate US public opinion, emails showing Assad had received advice from Iran, and texts revealing Assad was using a third party address to buy music on iTunes in spite of sanctions (Booth, Mahmood and Hardy 2012). In July 2012, WikiLeaks stated that it was working with news agencies[1] to release another block of Anonymous-obtained Syrian files—more than two million email messages (WikiLeaks 2012). Initial analysis of these email messages revealed that Western firms provided communications equipment to the Syrian regime (Satter 2012).

Other Internet-based activist groups are also working on behalf of the Syrian people. For example, Telecomix, a collective of hackers similar to Anonymous operating in Europe, revealed that the Syrian regime was using a BlueCoat (a US software company), for censorship and surveillance of the Internet (KheOps 2011)—something the US State Department has since investigated (Horowitz 2012). In mid-August 2011, Telecomix hacked the Syrian Internet. Users logging

---

1 The news sources include *Al-Akhbar*, *Al-Masry Al-Youm*, *L'espresso*, *Norddeutscher Rundfunk*, *OWNI*, and *Público*.

in and attempting to visit websites such as Google, instead, saw a page that stated, "This is a deliberate, temporary Internet breakdown. Please read carefully and spread the following message … Your Internet activity is monitored" (Greenberg 2011). The page then directed users to a new page that included information about strategies and tools to remain anonymous online (Greenberg 2011). It also offered advice, technical information, and strategy via IRC channels to interested activists around the world. Telecomix has engaged in types of activism similar to those Anonymous members use, although it began as an explicitly political project and does not affiliate itself with Anonymous (Greenberg 2011, Orange 2012).

Anonymous participants' action on behalf of Syrian protesters was just one of many organized Anonymous projects on behalf of citizens in authoritarian states. For example, Anonymous has also taken action against the Tunisian government. In a press release uploaded on January 5, 2011 and viewed over 43,000 times as of August 30, 2012, Anonymous announced (Anonymousworldwar3 2011a):

> To the Tunisian government: Attacks on the freedom of speech and information of your citizens will not be tolerated. Any organization involved in censorship will be targeted. Attacks will not cease until the Tunisian government hears the claim of freedom from its own people. It is in the hands of the Tunisian government to bring this to a resolution.

In response to the Tunisian state's attempts to stop protests and restrict the movement of information in Tunisia, Anonymous attacked Tunisian government websites using DDoS attacks and hacking, as well as helped to give people in Tunisia a conduit to move information out of country (Norton 2012a, Ryan 2011). As Anonymous attacked government websites, it replaced the pages with the Pirate Bay pirate ship image (a reference to Operation Payback, the umbrella campaign under which Operation Tunisia fell) and a message from Anonymous that stated (Derrick 2011):

> Anonymous has heard the cry for freedom from the Tunisian people. Anonymous is willing to help the Tunisian people in this fight against oppression. This is a warning to the Tunisian Government: violation of the freedom of speech and information of its citizens will not be tolerated. Cyber Attacks will persist until the Tunisian Government respects all Tunisian citizens' right to Free Speech and Information and ceases the censoring of the internet.

Anonymous also distributed tools to help Tunisian activists distribute information privately after discovering that the Tunisian government was harvesting usernames and passwords from online forums being used to coordinate protest (Ragan 2011). Anonymous released what an Anonymous member described to *Wired*'s Quinn Norton as a "care package" (Norton 2012a). This included a browser add-on allowing Tunisians to access Google's Blogger, Facebook, Gmail, Yahoo, and Twitter safely (Ragan 2011). It also included a technical manuals, like *How to Bypass Internet Censorship*, providing instructions for how to build homemade gas masks, information about how to use anonymizer tools like Tor, lists of links to proxies, and more (Ragan 2011).

Along with other hacktivist groups such as Telecomix, Anonymous was also active in supporting protesters in Egypt, using similar tactics field-tested in Tunisia (Wagenseil 2011). In line with standard Anonymous action, it began its work in Egypt with a press release, viewed by over 90,000 people as of August 30, 2012. The press release (mmxanonymous 2011) stated that Anonymous would be acting on behalf of the Egyptian people and continued with coordinated action on behalf of the Egyptian people similar to that in Tunisia (Somaiya 2011). Anonymous has also engaged in action in other Arab Spring countries, such as a smaller mobilization against the Algerian regime (Cushing 2011, Anonymousworldwar3 2011b), and is currently engaged in ongoing efforts to support protesters in Bahrain's violent crackdown. As part of this effort, Anonymous members have used DDoS attacks on government sites, brought down Bahrain's Formula One website, and engaged in other action to support Bahraini protestors (Mezzofiore 2012).

Despite Anonymous' successful innovations in supporting citizens in repressive political environments, there are limits to its political impacts. In the past, some—including Anonymous participants—have facetiously called Anonymous the "final boss of the Internet" (e.g. JC 2008). It is true that Anonymous exercises a certain level of cultural influence and power online. However, in its support of protesters in authoritarian contexts, Anonymous is limited by the very instrument that grants it power, as the Egyptian government illuminated in June 2011 when it "turned off" the Internet (Vanhemert 2011). Then, it is the citizens on the ground who were agents of change—and, as the history of revolution show, the Internet is not a monocausal condition for political change, but rather a mix of conditions. Anonymous members are aware of their limits to bring about political change, and many press releases state explicitly that they stand behind those who are the 'real' change agents. In a press release during Operation Tunisia, Anonymous members stated: "Anonymous has heard the claim for freedom of the Tunisian people. Anonymous is willing to help the Tunisian people in this fight against oppression."

Although there are limitations to the change that groups such as Anonymous can bring about in authoritarian regimes, overall, the net effect of information technology in this area is one of a challenge to state authority. As stated previously, authoritarian states combine their on-the-ground policies with a projected image of themselves as all-powerful, all-knowing, and impossible to challenge (Wedeen 1999, Yurchak 2005). However, every time Anonymous facilitated the movement of information from within an authoritarian state and into the hands of the global media, it publicly challenged the state's monopoly on the political narrative. Even more, when Anonymous members successfully took down government websites, and defaced official government websites with anti-government content, these acts highlighted the new limits of state power today.

As Anonymous continues to pose a challenge to state authority, it is also a growing movement that can and will adapt to learned lessons and new challenges.

Anonymous provides a conduit for individuals everywhere who want to work to support democratization efforts and activists. For transnational Internet-based activist groups, such as Anonymous, information technology has allowed for the curation of a world-wide "audience" to become directly involved in challenging restrictive regimes' information management practices. Anonymous' actions provide an opportunity structure that channels and empowers individuals who want to be directly involved in helping protestors in countries with repressive governments. Thus, as the Anonymous network or groups with similar aims continue to grow, the influence of transnational Internet-based activists poses a new set of actors and activities that erode the power of recalcitrant rulers.

It is also important to note that although this chapter focuses on the actions Anonymous has taken against authoritarian governments, Anonymous regularly uses the same tactics and rhetoric against democratic governments. For example, at 8am eastern Australian time on February 10, 2010, several Australian government sites crashed due to a DDoS attack, followed by a "storm" of pornography-related emails, faxes, and prank cell phone calls to government officials. The pornography was specifically chosen to match content that would be banned under a proposed Australian government Internet filtering plan. At the peak of the attack, the Parliament site received 7.5 million hits per second, rather than the normal hundreds per second. Observers estimated that about 1,000 people around the world participated in the attacks, which were carefully coordinated to occur at the same time to stress the operational limits of the system, even though the attackers were located globally in different time zones (AFP 2010). The attackers also sent emails to media outlining the reasons for the attacks on the government (Cheng 2010). One such statement noted the campaign would last "as long as the individuals that make up Anonymous decide that action needs to be taken to protect the freedom of the internet" (AFP 2010). This action was one of many that targeted the Australian government over the government's efforts to filter the Internet. The action against the Australian government was similar in tactics to the Anonymous action against the US government and major corporations on behalf of WikiLeaks in late 2011. The Australian government has responded by arresting Australian participants. Participants in other countries were not arrested, as they were living outside the jurisdiction of the Australian state. The examples of Anonymous members' actions against democratic regimes are as numerous as examples where these activists worked to challenge authoritarian power. Thus, it is important to recognize that Anonymous and other transnational Internet-based networks are using information technology to challenge and undermine the power of authoritarian states; but they are also using the same strategies, tools, and people to challenge any state, in the name of Internet freedom.

Bibliography

Abdulla, R.A. 2007. *The Internet in the Arab World: Egypt and Beyond.* New York: Peter Lang.

Abrougui, A. 2011a. "The Internet Is Freedom": Index speaks to Tunisian Internet Agency chief. *Index on Censorship* [Online]. Available at: http://uncut.indexoncensorship.org/2012/02/tunisia-internet-moez-chakchouk/ [accessed 10 August 2012].

Abrougui, A. 2011b. Tunisia: Internet Censorship Makes a Comeback. *Global Voices Online* [Online]. Available at: http://globalvoicesonline.org/2011/05/17/tunisia-internet-censorship-makes-a-comeback/ [accessed 20 August 2012].

Aday, S., Farrell, H., Freelon, D., et al. 2012. *Blogs and Bullets II: New Media and Conflict After the Arab Spring.* United States Institute of Peace.

Adelkhah, N. 2010. Iran integrates the concept of the "soft war" into its strategic planning. *Terrorism Monitor* 8(23). Available at: http://www.jamestown.org/programs/gta/single/?tx_ttnews%5Btt_news%5D=36482&cHash=a7a18f117e [accessed 15 August 2012].

Akhavan, N. 2014. Social Media and the Islamic Republic, in Farris, D. and Rahimi, B. (eds) *Social Media and Iran.* New York: State University of New York Press.

Al Arabiya. 2011. Lawyers call on the Tunisian Internet Agency to ban pornographic websites. *Al Arabiya* [Online]. Available at: http://www.alarabiya.net/articles/2012/01/22/189868.html [accessed 20 August 2012].

al-Aamri, K. 2012. Iranian government imposes new restrictions on media. *Al Monitor.*

Al-Roomi, S. 2007. Women, blogs, and political power in Kuwait, in Seib, P.M. (ed.) *New Media and the New Middle East.* New York: Palgrave Macmillan.

al-Saqaf, W. 2012. Circumventing Censorship in the Arab World, in *Liberation Technology*, edited by L. Diamond and M.F. Plattner. Baltimore: Johns Hopkins University Press, 124–138.

Al-Yahyawi, Y. 2012. Facebook and the Arab Uprisings. *Al-Jazeera*, July 27 [Arabic].

Almadhoun, S. 2012. Access to Information in the Middle East and North Africa Region: An overview of recent developments in Jordan, Lebanon, Morocco and Tunisia. World Bank [Online]. Available at: http://wbi.worldbank.org/wbi/Data/wbi/wbicms/files/drupal-acquia/wbi/Almadhoun-ATI_in_MNA_Region_ENGLISH.pdf [accessed August 2012].

Amamou, S. 2010. Mass Gmail Phishing in Tunisia. *Global Voices Advocacy* [Online]. Available at: http://advocacy.globalvoicesonline.org/2010/07/05/mass-gmail-phishing-in-tunisia/ [accessed 20 August 2012].

Amin, M. 2010. Talk … About the President's Health! *Al-Masry Al-Youm*, July 15. Available at: http://www.almasryalyoum.com/opinion/كلام-فى-صحة-الرئيس [accessed 14 August 2010].

Amnesty International. 2010. *Iran: Journalists Under Siege* [Online: Amnesty International].

Anderson, C. 2011. The hidden Internet of Iran: Private address allocations on a national network, *Cornell University Library*. Available at: http://arxiv.org/abs/1209.6398.

Anderson, J.L. 2009. Jon Lee Anderson: Understanding the Basij. *The New Yorker*. June 19. Available at: http://www.newyorker.com/online/blogs/newsdesk/2009/06/jon-lee-anderson-understanding-the-basij.html [accessed 25 August 2012].

Anderson, L. 2011. Demystifying the Arab Spring. *Foreign Affairs* 90(3), 2–7.

AnonOpsSyria. 2011. Operation Syria. *YouTube.com*, June 10. Available at: http://youtu.be/qiFGN2NlFGU [accessed 30 August 2012].

Anonymousworldwar3. 2011a. ANONYMOUS—OPERATION TUNISIA—A Press Release. *YouTube.com*, January 5. Available at: http://youtu.be/BFLaBRk9wY0 [accessed 30 August 2012].

Anonymousworldwar3. 2011b. ANONYMOUS—OPERATION ALGERIA—A Press Release. *YouTube.com*, January 21. Available at: http://youtu.be/5cgNoe-lOSY [accessed 30 August 2012].

Ansari, A. 2010. *Crisis of Authority: Iran's 2009 Presidential Election*. The Royal Institute of International Affairs.

Argüero, M.R. 2010. Acceso a Internet es un derecho fundamental. *La Nación/El país*, September 7 [Online]. Available at: www.nacion.com/2010-09-08/ElPais/NotasSecundarias/ElPais2514038.aspx [accessed August 2012].

Article 19. 2012. *Islamic Republic of Iran: Computer Crimes Law*. Available at: http://www.article19.org/resources.php/resource/2921/en/islamic-republic-of-iran:-computer-crimes-law [accessed 28 August 2013].

ASC. 1994. Internet in Tunisia. *University of Pennsylvania African Studies Center: Electronic Mail & Networks with Africa* [Online]. Available at: http://www.africa.upenn.edu/E_Mail/int_tun.html [accessed 8 August 2012].

Asmolov, G. 2011. Russia: Elections and the "other side of the Panopticon." *Global Voice Online* [Online]. Available at: http://globalvoicesonline.org/2011/12/07/russia-election-and-the-other-side-of-panopticon/ [accessed 9 September 2012].

Asmolov, G. 2012. The balance of crowds: Top-down and bottom-up mobilization strategies in the Russian election campaign. *POLIS blog* [Online]. Available at: http://blogs.lse.ac.uk/polis/2012/03/03/the-balance-of-crowds-top-down-and-bottom-up-mobilization-strategies-in-russian-election-campaign-guest-blog/ [accessed 9 September 2012].

ATI. 1998. Nos Services. *Agence Tunisienne d'Internet* [Online]. Available at: http://web.archive.org/web/19990117020555; http://www.ati.tn/service2.htm [accessed 8 August 2012 via Internet Archive Wayback Machine].

ATPDC. 2005. Freedom of expression in mourning. *Association Tunisienne pour la Promotion et la Défense du Cyberespace* [Online]. Available at: http://tounis.blogspot.com/2005/10/freedom-of-expression-in-mourning-la_03.html [accessed 20 August 2012].

Attalah, L. 2010. Thursday's Papers: The Health of the President and the Deeds of the Citizens. *Al-Masry Al-Youm*, July 22. Available at: http://www.almasryalyoum.com/en/news/thursdays-papers-health-president-and-deeds-citizens [accessed 14 August 2010].

Baetz, J. 2012. Syria Crisis: Assad Accuses U.S. of Fueling Opposition Uprising. *Associated Press*, July 8. Available at: http://www.huffingtonpost.com/2012/07/08/syria-crisis-assad-us-fueling-opposition_n_1657174.html [accessed 25 August 2012].

BBC. 2010. Egyptian Policemen Charged over Khaled Said Death, July 1. Available at: http://www.bbc.co.uk/news/10476720.

BBC. 2011. Egypt protests: Army rules out the use of force, January 31. Available at: http://www.bbc.co.uk/news/world-middle-east-12330169.

BBC. 2012. Vietnam PM Spared Action as Communist Party Meeting Ends. Available at: http://www.bbc.co.uk/news/world-asia-19957834 [accessed 18 October 2012].

BBC News Middle East. 2011. Profile: Egypt's Wael Ghonim, February 8. Available at: http://www.bbc.co.uk/news/world-middle-east-12400529 [accessed 1 September 2012].

BBC Persian. 2010. Explanation to Parliament about IRGC's Purchase of TCI Shares.

Becker, J. Lessons from Russia: A Neo-Authoritarian Media System. *European Journal of Communication* 19(2), 139–163.

Bellin, E. 2005. Coercive Institutions and Coercive Leaders, in *Authoritarianism in the Middle East: Regimes and Resistance*, edited by M. Posusney and M.P. Angrist. Boulder, CO: Lynne Rienner, 21–41.

Ben Moussa, M. 2011. The Use of the Internet by Islamic Social Movements in Collective Action: The Case of Justice and Charity. *Westminster Papers in Communication and Culture* 8(2), 63–92.

Bennett, L. 2007. Communicating global activism: Strengths and vulnerabilities of networked politics, in Negrine, R.M. and Stanyer, J. (eds) *The Political Communication Reader.* London/New York: Routledge.

Bennett, L. 2008. Engineering Consent: The Persistence of a Problematic Communication Regime, in Nardulli, P.F. (ed.) *Domestic Perspectives on Contemporary Democracy.* Urbana: University of Illinois Press.

Bernstein, M.S., Monroy-Hernández, A., Harry, D., et al. 2011. 4chan and /b/: An Analysis of Anonymity and Ephemerality in a Large Online Community. *Association for the Advancement of Artificial Intelligence.*

Beyer, J.L. 2011. *Youth and the Generation of Political Consciousness Online* (Doctoral Dissertation).

Beyer, JL. forthcoming. The Emergence of a Freedom of Information Movement: Anonymous, WikiLeaks, the Pirate Party, and Iceland. *Journal of Computer-Mediated Communication.*

Beygijanian, N. and Richardson, J.V. 2008. E-government in the Islamic Republic of Iran: Reaching out to the world? *IFLA Journal* 34(20), 20–33.

Bimber, B. 2001. *Information and American Democracy: Technology in the Evolution Political Power*. Cambridge: Cambridge University Press.

Bimber, B., Flanagin, A. and Stohl, C. 2012. *Collective Action in Organizations*. New York: Cambridge University Press.

Bimber, B., Flanagin, A.J. and Stohl, C. 2005. Reconceptualizing Collective Action in the Contemporary Media Environment. *Communication Theory* 15(2005), 365–388.

Booth, R. and Mahmood, M. 2012. How the Assad emails came to life. *The Guardian*, March 14. Available at: http://www.guardian.co.uk/world/2012/mar/14/how-assad-emails-came-light [accessed 15 October 2012].

Booth, R., Mahmood, M. and Harding, L. 2012. Exclusive: Secret Assad emails lift lid on life of leader's inner circle. *The Guardian*, March 14. Available at: http://www.guardian.co.uk/world/2012/mar/14/assad-emails-lift-lid-inner-circle [accessed 15 October 2012].

Bormann, N., Vogt, M. and Cederman, L. 2012. The Arab Spring and the Forgotten Demos. Working Paper No. 52. Switzerland: National Centre of Competence in Research (NCCR) Challenges to Democracy in the 21st Century.

Bounenni, B. 2011. The limits of silencing Tunisia. *Foreign Policy* [Online]. Available at: http://mideast.foreignpolicy.com/posts/2011/01/12/the_limits_of_silencing_tunisia [accessed 27 August 2012].

Boyle, J. 2002. Fencing off Ideas: Enclosure and the disappearance of the public domain. *Daedalus* 131(2), 13–25.

Boyle, J. 2003. The Second Enclosure Movement and the Construction of the Public Domain. *Law and Contemporary Problems* 66(33).

Brinkerhoff, J. 2009. *Digital Diasporas: Identity and Transnational Engagement*. Cambridge, UK: Cambridge University Press.

Bröning, M. 2011. The Sturdy House that Assad Built. *Foreign Policy*, March 7.

Bronner, E. and Slackman, M. 2011. Saudi Troops Enter Bahrain to Help Put Down Unrest. *New York Times*, March 14, p. 1.

Brooks, J. 2000. *Soviet Public Culture from Revolution to Cold War.* Princeton: Princeton University Press.

Brown, N. 2009. Moving out of Kuwait's political impasse. *Carnegie Endowment for International Peace* [Online]. Available at: http://www.carnegieendowment.org/publications/index.cfm?fa=view&id=23320 [accessed 12 March 2011].

Brownlee, J. 2007. *Authoritarianism in an Age of Democratization*. New York, NY: Cambridge University Press.

Bukovsky, V. 1999. Bukovsky Archives [Online]. Available at: http://www.bukovsky-archives.net/ [accessed 11 October 2012].

Bunt, G.R. 2003. *Islam in the Digital Age: E-Jihad, Online Fatwas and Cyber Islamic Environments.* London/Sterling, VA: Pluto Press.

Burks, R.V. 1961. *The Dynamics of Communism in Eastern Europe.* Princeton, NJ: Princeton University Press.

Byrne, D. 2007. Public Discourse, Community Concerns, and Civic Engagement: Exploring Black Social Networking Traditions on BlackPlanet.com. *Journal of Computer-Mediated Communication* 13(1), 319–340.

Caine, G. 2012. *Beyond the Fourth Estate: Marketization, Decentralization and the Press as the Party's Informal Police Force*. London: Unpublished MA thesis, School of Oriental and African Studies, University of London.

Campagna, J. 2008. Tunisia report: The smiling oppressor. *Committee to Protect Journalists* [Online]. Available at: http://cpj.org/reports/2008/09/tunisia-oppression.php [accessed 28 August 2013].

Carter, B. and Chozick, A. 2012. Syria's Assads Turned to West for Glossy P.R. *New York Times*, June 10. Available at: http://www.nytimes.com/2012/06/11/world/middleeast/syrian-conflict-cracks-carefully-polished-image-of-assad.html [accessed 25 August 2012].

Castells, M. 1997. *The Power of Identity: Economy, Society and Culture*. Oxford: Basil Blackwell.

Castells, M. 1998. *End of Millennium: Economy, Society and Culture*. Oxford: Basil Blackwell.

Castells, M. 2007. Communication, power and counter-power in the network society. *International Journal of Communication* 1, 238–266.

Castells, M. 2009. *Communication Power*. Oxford: Oxford University Press.

Central Intelligence Agency. 2009. *The World Factbook-Kuwait* [Online]. Available at: http://www.cia.gov/library/publications/the-world-factbook/geos/ku.html [accessed 17 March 2009].

Chatfield, A., Akbari, R., Mirzayi, N. and Scholl, H. 2012. *Interactive Effects of Networked Publics and Social Media on Transforming the Public Sphere: A Survey of Iran's Leaderless "Social Media Revolution"*. Paper to the 45th Hawaii International Conference on System Sciences, January 2012.

Cheng, J. 2010. Anonymous targets Australian government over porn filters. *Ars Technica*, February 10. Available at: http://arstechnica.com/tech-policy/2010/02/anonymous-targets-australian-government-over-porn-filters/ [accessed 28 August 2012].

Coleman, G. 2011. Anonymous: From the Lulz to Collective Action. *The New Everyday*, April 6. Available at: http://mediacommons.futureofthebook.org/tne/pieces/anonymous-lulz-collective-action [accessed 15 September 2012].

Coleman, G. 2012. Our Weirdness is Free, The Logic of Anonymous—online army, agent of chaos, and seeker of justice. *Triple Canopy*, January. Available at: http://canopycanopycanopy.com/15/our_weirdness_is_free [accessed 15 September 2012].

Committee for the Protection of Journalists. 2011. Bahraini Blogger Dies in Custody; Journalists under Attack, April 12. Available at: http://cpj.org/2011/04/bahraini-blogger-dies-in-custody-journalists-under.php.

Corm, G. 2012. The socio-economic factors behind the Arab revolutions. *Contemporary Arab Affairs* 5(3), 355–371.

CPJ. 2009. Naziha Réjiba, Tunisia, Kalima. *CPJ International Press Freedom Awards 2009* [Online]. Available at: http://cpj.org/awards/2009/naziha-rejiba-editor-kalima.php [accessed 27 August 2012].

CPJ. 2009. *Ten Worst Countries To Be a Blogger* [Online]. Available at: https://www.cpj.org/reports/2009/04/10-worst-countries-to-be-a-blogger.php [accessed 8 August 2012].

Crispin, S. 2012. *Vietnam's Press Freedom Shrinks Despite Open Economy.* New York: Committee to Protect Journalists. Available at: http://cpj.org/reports/2012/09/vietnams-press-freedom-shrinks-despite-open-economy.php [accessed 6 October 2012].

Curtis, R. 1996. National Institutes Concentrate on Developing Computer Geniuses. *Washington Report on Middle East Affairs* [Online]. Available at: http://www.wrmea.com/component/content/article/174–1996-november-december/2347-national-institutes-concentrate-on-developing-computer-geniuses-.html [accessed 8 August 2012].

Cushing, T. 2011. International Lulz: Anonymous Aids Rebellions in Tunisia, Algeria, and Libya. *Tech Dirt*, May 27. Available at: http://www.techdirt.com/articles/20110520/15384614363/international-lulz-anonymous-aids-rebellions-tunisia-algeria-libya.shtml [accessed 25 August 2012].

CWS. 2012. Tunisiana's Ken Campbell talks about his company's strategy ahead of his participation to North Africa Com. *Com World Series* [Online]. Available at: http://comworldseries.blogspot.nl/2012/03/tunisianas-ken-campbell-talks-about-his.html [accessed 27 August 2012].

Dabashi, H. 2010. *Iran, the Green Movement and the USA: The Fox and the Paradox*. London/New York: Zed Books.

Dayem, M.A. 2010. In Egypt, a Deplorable Press Freedom Climate. CPJ Blog, May 3. Available at: http://cpj.org/blog/2010/05/in-egypt-a-deplorable-press-freedom-climate.php [accessed 15 June 2012].

De Kloet, J. 2002. Digitisation and its Asian discontents: The Internet, politics and hacking in China and Indonesia. *First Monday* 7(9) (September 2).

Deibert, R. and Rohozinskii, R. 2010. Liberation vs. control: The future of cyberspace. *Journal of Democracy* [Online] 21(4), 43–57. Available at: http://muse.jhu.edu/journals/jod/summary/v021/21.4.deibert.html [accessed 27 August 2012].

Deibert, R., Palfrey, J., Rohozinskii, F. and Zittrain, J. (eds) 2010. *Access Controlled: The Shaping of Power, Rights, and Rule in Cyberspace.* Cambridge, MA/London: MIT Press.

Deibert, R.J. 2009. The geopolitics of internet control, in Chadwick, A. and Howard, P.N. (eds) *Routledge Handbook of Internet Politics*. New York: Routledge, 323–336.

Deibert, R.J., Palfrey, J.G., Rohozinskii, R., et al. 2010. *Access Controlled: The Shaping of Power, Rights, and Rule in Cyberspace*. 1st edn. Cambridge, MA: MIT Press.

Derrick, L. 2011. Anonymous Shuts Down Tunisia Government Websites after Violence and Web Censorship. *Huffington Post*, January 4. Available at: http://www.huffingtonpost.com/lisa-derrick/anonymous-shuts-down-tuni_b_804342.html [accessed 30 August 2012].

Desmukh, F. 2012. The Internet in Bahrain: Breaking the Monopoly of Information. *Foreign Policy*, September 20. Available at: http://mideast.foreignpolicy.com/posts/2010/09/21/bahrain_government_vs_the_internet.

Diamond, L. 1994. Rethinking Civil Society: I. Toward Democratic Consolidation. *Journal of Democracy* 5(3), 4–17.

Djankov, S., McLiesh, C., Nenova, T. and Shleifer, A. 2003. Who Owns The Media?, *Journal of Law and Economics* 46(2), 341–382. Available at: http://www.nber.org/papers/w8288 [accessed 11 October 2012].

Dutton, W. 2009. The Fifth State Emerging through the Network of Networks. *Prometheus* 27(1), 1–15.

Dutton, W., Dopatka, A., Hills, M., et al. 2011. *Freedom of Connection Freedom of Expression*. Paris: UNESCO Publishing.

Dutton, W.H., Dopatka, A., Hills, M., et al. 2010. *Freedom of Connection—Freedom of Expression: The Changing Legal Regulatory Ecology Shaping the Internet* [Online: Social Science Research Network]. Available at: https://papers.ssrn.com/sol3/papers.cfm?abstract_id=1654464 [accessed 28 August 2012].

Earl, J. and Kimport, K. 2011. *Digitally Enabled Social Change: Activism in the Internet Age*. Cambridge, MA: MIT Press.

Ehsani, K. 1999. Municipal Matters: The Urbanization of Consciousness and Political Change. *MERIP* 212, 22–27.

Ehsani, K. 2009. The urban provincial periphery in Iran: Revolution and war in Ramhormoz, in *Contemporary Iran: Economy, Society, Politics*, edited by Ali Gheissari. Oxford/New York: Oxford University Press, 38–76.

Eickelman, D. and Anderson, J. 1999. *New Media in the Muslim World: The Emerging Public Sphere*. Indianapolis: Indiana University Press.

Eickelman, D.F. and Anderson, J.W. 2003. *New Media in the Muslim World: The Emerging Public Sphere*. Bloomington: Indiana University Press.

El Gazzar, S. 2011. Government Restores Internet Service After a Weeklong Shutdown. *The Wall Street Journal*, February 2. Available at: http://online.wsj.com/article/SB10001424052748703960804576119690514692446.html.

Elkin, M. 2011. Exclusive: Tunisia Internet Chief Gives Inside Look at Cyber Uprising. *Wired* [Online]. Available at: http://www.wired.com/dangerroom

/2011/01/as-egypt-tightens-its-internet-grip-tunisia-seeks-to-open-up/ [accessed 20 August 2012].

Elliott, D.W.P. 2012. *Changing Worlds: Vietnam's Transition from Cold War to Globalization*. Oxford: Oxford University Press, 289.

Enayat, M., Smith, B. and Wojcieszk, M. 2012. How Iranians reach for news and information. The Iran Media Program's 2011–2012 report on media consumption, Center for Global Communication Studies, *Annenberg School for Communication.*

England, A. 2008. "Damascus Spring" Fades from Memory. *Financial Times*, September 13. Available at: http://www.ft.com/cms/s/0/2f085060-810d-11dd-82dd-000077b07658.html [accessed 25 August 2012].

Etling, B., et al. 2010. *Public Discourse in the Russian Blogosphere: Mapping RuNet Politics and Mobilization* [Online]. Available at: http://cyber.law.harvard.edu/publications/2010/Public_Discourse_Russian_Blogosphere [accessed 9 September 2012].

Farhi, F. 2010. Electoral miscalculations in Iran. *Woodrow Wilson International Center—Middle East Program Occasional Paper Series*, Spring, 14–17.

Faris, D. 2008. The President is Dead! Long Live the President! The Web, the Cell Phone and the Mubarak Death Crisis of 2007. *Technology and Politics Review* 1 (March 2008), 51–60.

Faris, D. 2010. (Amplified) Voices for the Voiceless. *Arab Media & Society*, Summer 2010.

Faris, D. 2012. *Dissent and Revolution in a Digital Age: Social Media, Blogging and Activism in Egypt*. London: I.B. Tauris and Co.

Farivar, C. 2012. *The Internet of Elsewhere: The Emergent Effects of a Wired World.* New Brunswick, New Jersey/London: Rutgers University Press.

Feldbrugge, F. 1975. *Samizdat and Political Dissent in the Soviet Union.* Sijthoff: Leiden.

Finkle, J. and Bartz, D. 2009. Twitter hacked, attacker claims Iran link. *Reuters* [Online]. Available at: http://www.reuters.com/article/2009/12/18/us-twitter-idUSTRE5BH2A620091218 [accessed 21 August 2012].

Fisher, M. and Keller, J. 2011. Syria's Digital Counter-Revolutionaries. *The Atlantic*, August 31. Available at: http://www.theatlantic.com/international/archive/2011/08/syrias-digital-counter-revolutionaries/244382/ [accessed 15 October 2012].

Fisk, R. 2011. What now for Egypt? *The Independent*, February 11. Available at: http://www.independent.co.uk/voices/commentators/fisk/robert-fisk-as-mubarak-clings-on-what-now-for-egypt-2211287.html.

Foreign Policy. 2007. Caught in the Net: Tunisia's First Lady. *Foreign Policy Magazine* [Online]. Available at: http://www.foreignpolicy.com/articles/2007/12/13/caught_in_the_net_tunisias_first_lady [accessed 20 August 2012].

Fox, Z. 2012. Reuters' Twitter Hacked by Pro-Assad Activists. Mashable.com, August 6. Available at: http://mashable.com/2012/08/06/reuters-hacked/ [accessed 15 October 2012].

Freedom House. 2009. Methodology, in *Freedom of the Press*. Available at: http://www.freedomhouse.org/template.cfm?page=350&ana_page=359&year=2009 [accessed 27 August 2012].

Freedom House. 2011. *Freedom on the Net 2011: Tunisia*. Available at: http://www.freedomhouse.org/sites/default/files/inline_images/Tunisia_FOTN2011.pdf [accessed 27 August 2012].

Freedom House. 2011a. *Iran: Freedom on the Net 2011*. Available at: http://www.freedomhouse.org/sites/default/files/inline_images/Iran_FOTN2011.pdf [accessed 23 August 2012].

Freedom House. 2011b. *Tunisia: Freedom on the Net 2011*. Available at: http://www.freedomhouse.org/report/freedom-net/2011/tunisia [accessed 28 August 2013].

Freedom House. 2012. *Freedom of the Press Scores and Status, 1980–2012*. Available at: http://www.freedomhouse.org/report-types/freedom-press/.

Freedom House. 2012. *Tunisia: Freedom of the Press 2012*. Available at: http://www.freedomhouse.org/report/freedom-press/2012/tunisia [accessed 23 August 2012].

Galloway, A.R. 2004. *Protocol: How Control Exists After Decentralization*. Cambridge, MA: MIT Press.

Garrett, R. 2006. Protest in an Information Society: A Review of Literature on Social Movements and the New ICTs. *Information, Communication & Society* 9(2) (April), 202–224.

Gause III, G. 2011. Why Middle East Studies Missed the Arab Spring. *Foreign Affairs* 90(4), 81–90.

Gharbia, S. 2008. Silencing online speech in Tunisia. *Global Voices Advocacy* [Online]. Available at: http://advocacy.globalvoicesonline.org/2008/08/20/silencing-online-speech-in-tunisia/ [accessed 20 August 2012].

Gharbia, S. 2010. Tunisia: Flickr, Video-sharing Websites, Blog Aggregators and Critical Blogs are Not Welcome. *Global Voices Advocacy* [Online]. Available at: http://advocacy.globalvoicesonline.org/2010/04/28/tunisia-flickr-video-sharing-websites-blogs-aggregators-and-critial-blogs-are-not-welcome/ [accessed 20 August 2012].

Gharbia, S. 2010b. Anti-censorship movement in Tunisia: Creativity, courage, and hope! [Online]. Available at: http://ifikra.wordpress.com/2010/05/28/anti-censorship-movement-in-tunisia-creativity-courage-and-hope/ [accessed 20 August 2012].

Gheytanchi, E. 2010. Symbols, signs, and slogans of the demonstrations in Iran, in *Media, Power, and Politics in the Digital Age: The 2009 Presidential Election Uprising in Iran*, edited by Yahya, R. and Yahya, K. Lanham: Rowman & Littlefield, 251–264.

Gheytanchi, E. and Rahimi, B. 2008. Iran's Reformists and Activists: Internet Exploiters. *Middle East Policy* 15(1), 46–59.

Goodman, D.J. (ed.) 2012. Watching Syria's War. *New York Times*. Available at: http://projects.nytimes.com/watching-syrias-war [accessed 25 August 2012].

Gordon, N. 2008. *Israel's Occupation*. Berkeley: University of California Press.

Greenberg, A. 2011. Meet Telecomix, The Hackers Bent on Exposing Those Who Censor and Surveil the Internet. *Forbes*, December 26. Available at: http://www.forbes.com/sites/andygreenberg/2011/12/26/meet-telecomix-the-hackers-bent-on-exposing-those-who-censor-and-surveil-the-internet/ [accessed 25 August 2012].

Grossman, L. 2009. Iran Protests: Twitter, the Medium of the Movement. *Time Magazine*, June 17. Available at: http://www.time.com/time/world/article/0,8599,1905125,00.html [accessed 25 August 2012].

Hanafi, S. 2009. Spacio-cide: Colonial politics, invisibility and rezoning in Palestinian Territory. *Contemporary Arab Affairs* 2(1), 106–121.

Hanlon, Q. 2012. Security Sector Reform in Tunisia a Year after the Jasmine Revolution. United States Institute of Peace: Special Report 304, March 2012.

Hayton, B. 2010. *Vietnam: Rising Dragon*. New Haven: Yale University Press, 42–43.

He, B. 2006. Western theories of deliberative democracy and the Chinese practice of complex deliberative governance, in *The Search for Deliberation Democracy in China*, edited by in E. Leib and B. He. New York: Palgrave Macmillan, 133–148.

Heng, R. 1998. *Media in Vietnam and the Structure of its Management in Mass Media in Vietnam*, edited by Marr, D. Canberra: Department of Political and Social Change, Research School of Pacific and Asian Studies, The Australian National University.

Heng, R. 2003. Vietnam, Status of Media, in *Encyclopedia of International Communications*. Elsevier Science (USA), 561–571.

Herb, M. 1999. *All in the Family: Absolutism, Revolution, and Democracy in the Middle Eastern Monarchies*. Albany: State University of New York Press.

Hick, S. and McNutt, J.G. 2002. *Advocacy, Activism, and the Internet: Community Organization and Social Policy*. Chicago: Lyceum Books.

Hirschkind, C. 2006. *The Ethical Soundscape: Cassette Sermons and Islamic Counterpublics*. New York: Columbia University Press.

Hofheinz, A. 2007. Arab Internet use: Popular trends and public impact, in Sakr, N. (ed.) *Arab Media and Political Renewal: Community, Legitimacy and Public life*. London/New York: I.B. Tauris.

Horowitz, S. 2012. Syria using American software to censor Internet, experts say. *The Washington Post*, October 22. Available at: http://www.washingtonpost.com/world/national-security/syria-using-american-software-to-censor-internet-experts-say/2011/10/22/gIQA5mPr7L_story.html [accessed 25 August 2012].

Howard, P.N. 2002. Network Ethnography and the Hypermedia Organization: New Media, New Organizations, New Methods. *New Media & Society* 4(4), 550–574.

Howard, P.N. 2010. *The Digital Origins of Dictatorship and Democracy: Information Technology and Political Islam*. Oxford/New York: Oxford University Press.

Howard, P.N. and Hussain, M.M. 2012. Digital Media and the Arab Spring. *Journal of Democracy* 22(3), 35–48.

Howard, P. and Hussain, M. 2012. Egypt and Tunisia: The role of digital media, in *Liberation Technology*, edited by L. Diamond and M.F. Plattner. Baltimore: Johns Hopkins University Press, 110–123.

Howard, P.N. and Hussain, M.M. 2013. *Democracy's Fourth Wave? Digital Media and The Arab Spring.* Oxford; New York: Oxford University Press.

Howard, P., Agarwal, S. and Hussain, M. 2011. The Dictators' Digital Dilemma: When Do States Disconnect Their Digital Networks? *Issues in Technology Innovation* No. 13, October.

Howard, P.N., Duffy, A., Freelon, D., et al. 2012. Opening Closed Regimes: What was the role of social media during the Arab spring? *Project on Information Technology and Political Islam* [Online]. Available at: http://www.scribd.com/doc/66443833/Opening-Closed-Regimes-What-Was-the-Role-of-Social-Media-During-the-Arab-Spring [accessed 21 August 2012].

Huang, C. 2011. Facebook and Twitter key to Arab Spring uprisings: Report. *The Nation*, June 6. Available at: http://www.thenational.ae/news/uae-news/facebook-and-twitter-key-to-arab-spring-uprisings-report.

Human Rights Watch. 2012. Bahrain: Revoke Order Dissolving Rights Group's Board, September 9. Available at: http://www.hrw.org/news/2010/09/09/bahrain-revoke-order-dissolving-rights-groups-board.

Human Rights Watch. 2012. Egypt Country Report 2012. Available at: http://www.hrw.org/world-report-2012/world-report-2012-egypt.

Huntington, S. 1991. *The Third Wave: Democratization in the Late Twentieth Century*. Norman: University of Oklahoma Press.

Huntington, S. 1993. The Clash of Civilizations? *Foreign Affairs* 72(3) (Summer), 22–49.

Internet World Stats. 2011. *Internet usage statistics* [Online]. Miniwatts Marketing Group. Available at: http://www.internetworldstats.com/stats5.htm#me.

ITU. 2012. Data Explorer: ICT Data and Statistics. *International Telecommunications Union* [Online]. Available at: http://www.itu.int/ITU-D/ict/statistics/explorer/index.html [accessed 27 August 2012].

Jacobs, F. and Parag, K. 2012. The New World. *New York Times*, September 22. Available at: http://www.nytimes.com/interactive/2012/09/23/opinion/sunday/the-new-world.html?ref=opinion.

JC. 2008. Anonymous: Final boss of the Internet? *Romhack.net*, October 8. Available at: http://www.romhack.net/index.php?post/2008/10/03/Anonymous%3A-final-boss-of-the-Internet [accessed 25 August 2012].

Jelassi, T. 2010. ICT in Tunisia: A strategic lever for building a knowledge-based economy, in *Global Information Technology Report 2009–2010*, edited by S. Dutta and I. Mia [Online: World Economic Forum], 153–164. Available at: http://www.itu.int/wsis/implementation/2010/forum/geneva/docs/publications/GITR%202009-2010_Full_Report_final.pdf [accessed 4 August 2012].

Joo, H.-M. 2004. Voices of Freedom: Samizdat. *Europe-Asia Studies* 56(4) (2004), 575.

Joyce, M.C. 2011. Book Review: Digitally Enabled Social Change: Activism in the Internet Age, *Meta-Activism*, October 3. Available at: http://www.meta-activism.org/2011/10/book-review-digitally-enabled-social-change-activism-in-the-internet-age/.

Kamoun, F., et al. 2010. Tunisia ICT Sector Performance Review 2009/2010: *Towards Evidence-based ICT Policy and Regulation.* Vol. 2, Policy Paper 12. *ResearchICTAfrica.net* [Online]. Available at: http://www.researchictafrica.net/publications/Policy_Paper_Series_Towards_Evidence-based_ICT_Policy_and_Regulation_-_Volume_2/Vol.%202%20Paper%2012%20-%20Tunisia%20ICT%20Sector%20Performance%20Review%202010.pdf [accessed 27 August 2012].

Kampfner, J. 2012. The fight for control of the internet has become critical. *The Guardian*, July 22 [Online]. Available at: http://www.guardian.co.uk/profile/johnkampfner [accessed August 2012].

Kaplan, A. and Haenlein, M. 2010. Users of the World, Unite! The Challenges and Opportunities of Social Media. *Business Horizons* 53(1), 59–61.

Karlekar, K.D. and Cook, S.G. 2009. *Access and Control: A Growing Diversity of Threats to Internet Freedom* [Online]. Available at: http://old.freedomhouse.org/uploads/specialreports/NetFreedom2009/FOTN%20Overview%20Essay.pdf [accessed 23 August 2012].

Karpf, D. 2012. *The MoveOn Effect: The Unexpected Transformation of American Political Advocacy.* New York: Oxford University Press.

Katz, S. 2002. *The Hunt for the Engineer: The Inside Story of How Israel's Counterterrorist Forces Tracked and Killed the Hamas Master Bomber.* Pompano Beach, FL: The Lion Press.

Kavanaugh, A. 1998. *The Social Control of Technology in North Africa: Information in the Global Economy.* Westport, CT: Greenwood Publishing Group.

Kepel, G. 1984. *Légitimation et délégitimation de l'autoritarisme dans le Moyen-Orient contemporain.* Grenoble.

Kerkvliet, B. 1995. Village-State Relations in Vietnam: The effect of everyday politics on decollectivization. *Journal of Asian Studies* 54(2), 396–418.

Kern, H.L. and Hainmueller, J. 2009. Opium For the Masses: How Foreign Media Can Stabilize Authoritarian Regimes. *Political Analysis* 17(4), 377–399.

Khalidi, R. and Samour, S. 2011. Neoliberalism as Liberation: The Statehood Program and the Remaking of the Palestinian National Movement. *Journal of Palestine Studies* 40(2), 6–25.

Khamis, S. and Vaugh, K. 2011. Cyberactivism in the Egyptian Revolution: How Civic Engagement and Citizen Journalism Tilted the Balance. *Arab Media and Society* Issue 14 (Summer 2011).

KheOps. 2011. BlueCoat's Presence in Syria Finally Uncovered. *Reflects.info*, October 29. Available at: http://reflets.info/bluecoats-presence-in-syria-finally-uncovered/http://reflets.info/bluecoats-presence-in-syria-finally-uncovered/.

Khokhlova, V. 2012a. Russia: The "Big White Circle" protest in Moscow. *Global Voices Online* [Online]. Available at: http://globalvoicesonline.org/2012/02/27/russia-the-big-white-circle-protest-in-moscow/ [accessed 9 September 2012].

Khokhlova, V. 2012b. Russia: Netizens respond online and offline to devastating Krymsk floods. *Global Voices Online* [Online]. Available at: http://globalvoicesonline.org/2012/07/09/russia-netizens-trying-to-explain-the-devastating-flooding-in-krymsk-helping-the-victims/ [accessed 9 September 2012].

Khosravi, S. 2008. *Young and Defiant in Tehran*. Philadelphia, PA: University of Pennsylvania Press.

Khun, T. 1962. *The Structure of Scientific Revolutions*. Chicago: Chicago University Press.

Kirkpatrick, D.D. 2011. Chief of Tunisian Army Pledges His Support for "the Revolution." *New York Times*, January 24. Available at: http://www.nytimes.com/2011/01/25/world/africa/25tunis.html.

Knuttila, L. 2011. User Unknown: 4chan, anonymity, and contingency. *First Monday* 16(10). Available at: http://firstmonday.org/htbin/cgiwrap/bin/ojs/index.php/fm/article/view/3665/3055.

Lev-On, A. and Hardin, R. 2008. Internet-Based Collaborations and Their Political Significance. *Journal of Information Technology and Politics* 4(2), 5–27.

Li, D. 2006. The Gaza Strip as Laboratory: Notes in the Wake of Disengagement. *Journal of Palestine Studies* 35(2), 38–55.

Lipman, M. 2012. Floods and suspicion in Russia. *The New Yorker* [Online]. Available at: http://www.newyorker.com/online/blogs/newsdesk/2012/07/floods-and-suspicion-in-russia.html [accessed 9 September 2012].

Lipset, S. 1959. Some Social Requisites of Democracy: Economic Development and Political Legitimacy. *The American Political Science Review* 53(1), 69–105.

Luciani, G. 2009. Oil and Political Economy in the International Relations of the Middle East, in *International Relations of the Middle East*, 2nd edn, edited by L. Fawcett. Oxford: Oxford University Press, 79–184.

Lunat, Z. 2009. The Palestinian Hidden Transcript: Domination, Resistance and the Role of ICTs in Achieving Freedoms. *The Electronic Journal on Information Systems in Developing Countries* 37(1), 1–22.

Lupia, A. and Sin, G. 2003. Which Public Goods are Endangered?: How Evolving Communication Technologies Affect the Logic of Collective Action. *Public Choice* 117, 315–331.

Lynch, M. 2003. Beyond the Arab street: Iraq and the Arab public sphere. *Politics & Society* 31.

Lynch, M. 2006. *Voices of the New Arab Public: Iraq, Al-Jazeera, and Middle East Politics Today*. New York: Columbia University Press.

Lynch, M. 2007. Rumors of Mubarak's Death. *Abu Aardvark*, September 2. Available at: http://abuaardvark.typepad.com/abuaardvark/2007/09/rumors-of-mubar.html.

MacFarquhar, N. 2012. Assad Condemns Houla Massacre, Blaming Terrorists. *New York Times*, June 3. Available at: http://www.nytimes.com/2012/06/04/world/middleeast/assad-condemns-houla-massacre-blaming-outside-terrorists.html [accessed 28 August 2012].

Machleder, J. and Asmolov, G. 2011. Social change and the Russian network society, redefining development priorities in new information environments. *Internews Network* [Online]. Available at: http://www.internews.org/research-publications/social-change-and-russian-network-society [accessed 9 September 2012].

Mackinnon, R. 2012. *Consent of the Networked: The Worldwide Struggle for Internet Freedom*. New York: Basic Books.

Maher, K. 2011. What's Happening in Tunisia? *NDItech: DemocracyWorks* [Online]. Available at: http://www.demworks.org/blog/2011/01/whats-happening-tunisia [accessed 27 August 2012].

Market Access Database. 2002. Tunisia Telecoms Market Access Study. Trade, European Commission. Available at: http://madb.europa.eu/madb_barriers/viewDoc.htm?type=study&filename=29.doc [accessed 27 August 2012].

Marmura, S. 2008. A net advantage? The internet, grassroots activism and American Middle-Eastern policy. *New Media & Society* 10(2) (April), 247–271.

Marr, D.G. 1981. *Vietnamese Tradition on Trial, 1920–1945*. Berkeley and Los Angeles: University of California Press.

Marshall, M. and Jaggers, K. 2010. *Polity IV: Political Regime Characteristics and Transitions, 1800–2009*. College Park, MD: Center for International Development and Conflict Management.

Mashal, M. 2011. Pakistani troops aid Bahrain's crackdown. *Al Jazeera*, July 30. Available at: http://www.aljazeera.com/indepth/features/2011/07/2011725145048574888.html.

McCarthy, J.D. and Zald, M.N. 1973. The Trend of Social Movements in America: Professionalization and Resource Mobilization. Social Organization, Center for Research on—Working Paper Series, no. 164.

McCarthy, J.D. and Zald, M.N. 2001. The Enduring Vitality of the Resource Mobilization Theory of Social Movements, in Turner, J.H. (ed.) *Handbook of Sociological Theory*. New York: Kluwer Academic/Plenuim Publishers, 533–565.

McDowall, A. 2009. Iran's Basij force: The shock troops terrorizing protesters. *The Telegraph*, June 21. Available at: http://www.telegraph.co.uk/news/worldnews/middleeast/iran/5588291/Irans-Basij-force-the-shock-troops-terrorising-protesters.html [accessed 25 August 2012].

McKinley, C. 2008. Can a State-owned Media Effectively Monitor Corruption? A Study of Vietnam's Printed Press. *Asian Journal of Public Affairs* 2(1).

McKitrick, J., et al. 1995. The revolution in military affairs, in *Battlefield of the Future: 21st Century Warfare Issues*, edited by B. Schneider and L.E. Grinter. Maxwell Air Force Base, Ala: Air University Press. Available at: http://www.

airpower.maxwell.af.mil/airchronicles/battle/chp3.html [accessed 9 September 2012].

McLaughlin, W. 2003. The use of the Internet for political action by non-state dissident actors in the Middle East (computer file). *First Monday (Online)* 8(11) (November), 1.

McNair, B. 1991. *Glasnost, Perestroika and the Soviet Media.* London: Routledge.

Meier P. 2011a. *Do "Liberation Technologies" Change the Balance of Power between Repressive States and Civil Society?* Fletcher School, Tufts University.

Meier, P. 2011b. *Crowdsourcing vs. Putin: "Mapping Dots is a Disease on the Map of Russia"* [Online]. Available at: http://irevolution.net/2011/12/04/crowdsourcing-vs-putin/ [accessed 9 September 2012].

Meier, P. 2012. The Role of Ushahidi as a Liberation Technology in Egypt and Beyond, in *Liberation Technology: Social Media and the Struggle for Democracy*, L. Diamond and M. Plattner (eds). Baltimore: Johns Hopkins University Press.

Mellor, N. 2005. *The making of Arab news,* Lanham, MD, Rowman & Littlefield Publishers.

Messieh, N. 2011. Tunisian government got discounts on surveillance software in exchange for bug-tracking. *The Next Web* [Online]. Available at: http://thenextweb.com/me/2011/10/04/tunisian-government-got-discounts-on-surveillance-software-in-exchange-for-bug-tracking/ [accessed 20 August 2012].

Meyer, D.S. 2004. Protest and Political Opportunities. *Annual Review of Sociology*, August (30), 125–145.

Mezzofiore, G. 2012. Bahrain Formula 1: Anonymous Attacks Official F1 Website. *International Business Times*, April 20. Available at: http://www.ibtimes.co.uk/articles/331151/20120420/opbahrain-anonymous-official-formula-1-websites-protest.htm [accessed 25 August 2012].

Mitchell, M. 2012. The Aborted Revolution. *Harvard International Review*, Spring, 32–36.

mmxanonymous. 2011. OPERATION EGYPT—ANONYMOUS PRESS RELEASE 26/01/2011. YouTube.com, January 26. Available at: http://youtu.be/yOLc3B2V4AM [accessed 30 August 2012].

Mohammadifar, M.R. 1992. Computers in Persia: Electronic data-processing equipment, in Persia. *Encyclopaedia Iranica.* Available at: http://www.iranicaonline.org/articles/computers-in-persia [accessed 14 August 2012].

Moqaddem, A. and Naja, F. 2011. Anti-cybercrime police established in all provinces. *Weblog News* [Online]. Available at: http://weblognews.ir/1390/01/ngo/13985/ [accessed 27 August 2012].

Morozov, E. 2011. Net.Effect: Tunisia, social media and the politics of attention. *Foreign Policy* [Online]. Available at: http://neteffect.foreignpolicy.com/posts/2011/01/14/tunisia_social_media_and_the_politics_of_attention [accessed 27 August 2012].

Morozov, E. 2011. *The Net Delusion: How Not to Liberate the World.* London: Allen Lane.

Mourtada, R. and Salem, F. 2012. *Arab Social Media Report* [Online]. Dubai School of Government. Available at: http://tips.fohmics.com/asmr2011/Twitter/LineChart.aspx?&PriMenuID=18&CatID=25&mnu=Cat.

Mourtada, R. and Salem, F. 2012. *Arab Social Media Report* [Online]. Dubai School of Government. Available at: http://tips.fohmics.com/asmr2011/Twitter/LineChart.aspx?&PriMenuID=18&CatID=25&mnu=Cat.

Nisbet, E. and Myers, T. 2010. Challenging the State: Transnational TV and Political Identity in the Middle East. *Political Communication* 27, 347–366.

Norris, P. 2000. *A Virtuous Circle: Political Communications in Postindustrial Societies.* Cambridge, UK/New York, NY: Cambridge University Press.

Norton, Q. 2012a. 2011: The Year Anonymous Took on Cops, Dictators, and Existential Dread. *Wired Magazine*, January 11. Available at: http://www.wired.com/threatlevel/2012/01/anonymous-dicators-existential-dread/ [accessed 15 September 2012].

Norton, Q. 2012b. How Anonymous Picks Targets, Launched Attacks, and Takes Powerful Organizations Down. *Wired Magazine*, July 3. Available at: http://www.wired.com/threatlevel/2012/07/ff_anonymous/all/ [accessed 15 September 2012].

Nouri, K. 2010. Tehran's unplugged internet plan. *Payvand Iran News* [Online]. Available at: http://www.payvand.com/news/10/oct/1189.html [accessed 27 August 2010].

NSRC. 1995. Connectivity Providers Database: Tunisia. Tunisia Networking Update. Available at: http://nsrc.org/db/lookup/report.php?id=890202326514:497426987&fromISO=TN [accessed 27 August 2012].

O'Brien, D. 2011. Tunisia invades, censors Facebook, other accounts. *Committee to Protect Journalists* [Online]. Available at: https://cpj.org/internet/2011/01/tunisia-invades-censors-facebook-other-accounts.php [accessed 20 August 2012].

Olson, M. 1971. *The Logic of Collective Action: Public Goods and the Theory of Groups.* Cambridge, MA: Harvard University Press.

Olson, P. 2012. *We Are Anonymous: Inside the Hacker World of LulzSec, Anonymous, and the Global Cyber Insurgency.* New York: Little, Brown, and Company.

ONI. 2005. *Internet Filtering in Tunisia in 2005: A Country Study* [Online: OpenNet Initiative]. Available at: http://opennet.net/studies/tunisia [accessed 20 August 2012].

ONI. 2007. *Internet Filtering in Tunisia in 2006–2007* [Online: OpenNet Initiative]. Available at: http://opennet.net/studies/tunisia2007 [accessed 23 August 2012].

ONI. 2009. *Internet Filtering in Bahrain* [Online: OpenNet Initiative]. Available at: http://opennet.net/sites/opennet.net/files/ONI_Bahrain_2009.pdf.

ONI. 2009. *Iran* [Online: OpenNet Initiative]. Available at: http://opennet.net/research/profiles/iran [accessed 23 August 2012].

ONI. 2009. *Tunisia* [Online: OpenNet Initiative]. Available at: http://opennet.net/research/profiles/tunisia [accessed 23 August 2012].

ONI. 2011. *West Censoring East: The Use of Western Technologies by Middle East Censors 2010–2011* [Online: OpenNet Initiative]. Available at: http://opennet.net/sites/opennet.net/files/ONI_WestCensoringEast.pdf [accessed 20 August 2012].

Orange, R. 2012. Battle of the hacktivists: Anonymous vs. Telecomix. *Global Post*, June 1. Available at: http://www.globalpost.com/dispatch/news/business/technology/120531/anonymous-telecomix-hackers-arab-spring [accessed 30 August 2012].

Oslo 2, Annex III, Article 36, *Israeli-Palestinian Interim Agreement on the West Bank and the Gaza Strip*, 28 September 1995.

Pars Times. *Press Law* [Online]. Available at: http://www.parstimes.com/law/press_law.html [accessed 21 August 2012].

Paust, J. 2012. International Law, Dignity, Democracy, and the Arab Spring. *Cornell International Law Journal* 46, 1–38.

Pavel, T. 2012. Assad vs. Anonymous. *The Guardian* via *Maariv*, July 23. Available at: http://www.guardian.co.uk/media-network-partner-zone-publici/assad-anonymous-syria-war [accessed 15 October 2012].

Payvand. 2012. Iran cyber army hacks former president's websites. *Payvand* [Online]. Available at: http://www.payvand.com/news/12/feb/1282.html [accessed 27 August 2012].

Perry, E.J. 2007. Studying Chinese Politics: Farwell to Revolution? *The China Journal* 57, 1–22.

Peterson, S. 2010. *Let the Swords Encircle Me: Iran—a Journey Behind the Headlines*. New York: Simon & Schuster.

Peycam, P. 2012 *The Birth of Vietnamese Political Journalism: Saigon (1916–1930)*. New York: Columbia University Press.

Phillips, W. 2012. The House That Fox Built: Anonymous, Spectacle, and Cycles of Amplification. *Television & New Media*. Published online before print, August 30. Available at: http://tvn.sagepub.com/content/early/2012/08/27/1527476412452799.abstract.

Pidduck, J. 2012. Exile media, global news flows and democratization: The role of Democratic Voice of Burma in Burma's 2010 Elections. *Media, Culture and Society* 34(5), 537–553.

Posusney, M. and Angrist, M. 2005. *Authoritarianism in the Middle East: Regimes and Resistance*. Boulder, CO: Lynn Rienner.

Press Freedom Index. 2009. Reporters sans Frontiers. Available at: http://en.rsf.org/press-freedom-index-2009,1001.html [accessed 29 August 2012].

Press TV. 2012. Leader decrees establishment of Supreme Council of Cyberspace. *Press TV* [Online]. Available at: http://www.presstv.ir/detail/230425.html [accessed 24 August 2012].

Price, M. 2002. *Media and Sovereignty: The Global Information Revolution and Its Challenge to State Power.* Cambridge, MA: MIT Press, 2002.

Price, M. 2012. Iran and the Soft War, International Journal of Communication 6, Feature 2397–2415. Available here: http://ijoc.org/ojs/index.php/ijoc/article/viewDownloadInterstitial/1654/79 [accessed 5 June 2013].

Prusher, I. 1996. Palestinians Sprint to Break Israeli Grips on Phone Lines. *The Christian Science Monitor*, 10 August.

Ragan, S. 2011. Anonymous offers support to Tunisian protestors. *The Tech Herald* [Online]. Available at: http://www.thetechherald.com/articles/Anonymous-offers-support-to-Tunisian-protestors-(Update-2)/12403/ [accessed 20 August 2012].

Ragan, S. 2011. Tunisian government harvesting usernames and passwords. *The Tech Herald* [Online]. Available at: http://www.thetechherald.com/articles/Tunisian-government-harvesting-usernames-and-passwords/12429/ [accessed 27 August 2012].

Ragan. 2011. *How to Bypass Internet Censorship* [Online]. Available at: http://www.howtobypassinternetcensorship.org/ [accessed 30 August 2012].

Rahimi, B. 2003. Cyberdissent: The internet in revolutionary Iran. *Middle East Review of International Affairs* [Online] 7(3), 1–12. Available at: http://meria.idc.ac.il/journal/2003/issue3/jv7n3a7.html [accessed 9 August 2012].

Rahimi, B. 2008. The Politics of the Internet in Iran, in *Media, Culture and Society in Iran: Living with Globalization and the Islamic State*, edited by M. Semati. London/New York: Routledge, 37–56.

Rahimi, B. 2011. The agnostic social media: Cyberspace in the formation of dissent and consolidation of state power in postelection Iran. *The Communication Review* [Online], 14(3), 158–178. Available at: http://www.tandfonline.com/doi/full/10.1080/10714421.2011.597240#tabModule) [accessed 27 August 2012].

Rahimi, B. 2011a. The Agonistic Social Media: Cyberspace in the Formation of Dissent and Consolidation of State Power in Post-election Iran. *The Communication Review*, 14, 158–178.

Rahimi, B. 2011b. Facebook Iran: The carnivalesque politics of online social networking. *Sociologica* 3.

Rahimi, B. 2012. Iran's Declining Influence in Iraq. *The Washington Quarterly*, Winter.

Rao, M. 2001. E-Dinars, E-Tijara: Tunisia Embarks on Ambitious Internet Plan. *eOTI* [Online]. Available at: http://www.isoc.org/oti/articles/0201/rao.html [accessed 27 August 2012].

Reinhard, U. 2010. Talking about a Revolution: Tunisia. *Ulrike Reinhard* [Online]. Available at: http://www.ulrikereinhard.com/2010/12/31/talking-about-a-revolution-tunisia/ [accessed 27 August 2012].

Reporters without Borders. 2008. Press law amendments hailed but journalists still face jail and websites risk closure, July 3. Available at: http://www.rsf.org/article.php3?id_article=27741.

Reporters without Borders. 2010. *Press Freedom Index* [Online]. Paris, France. Available at: http://en.rsf.org/spip.php?page=classement&id_rubrique=34 [accessed 8 April 2011].

Reporters without Borders. 2011. *Press Freedom Index* [Online]. Paris, France. Available at: http://en.rsf.org/press-freedom-index-2011–2012,1043.html [accessed 22 March 2012].

Reporters without Borders. 2012. *Enemies of the Internet Report 2012*. Available at: http://en.rsf.org/beset-by-online-surveillance-and-13-03-2012,42061.html [accessed 9 September 2012].

Rizzo, H.M. 2005. *Islam, Democracy, and the Status of Women: The Case of Kuwait.* New York: Routledge.

Roy, S. 1987. The Gaza Strip: A Case of Economic De-Development. *Journal of Palestine Studies* 17(1), 56–88.

RSF. 2005. The 15 enemies of the Internet and other countries to watch. *Reporters without Borders* [Online]. Available at: http://en.rsf.org/the-15-enemies-of-the-internet-and-17-11-2005,15613.html [accessed 8 August 2012].

RSF. 2009. Massive censorship accompanies Ahmadinejad "victory." *Reporters without Borders* [Online]. Available at: http://en.rsf.org/iran-massive-censorship-accompanies-13-06-2009,33397.html [accessed 27 August 2012].

RSF. 2012. Countries under surveillance: Tunisia. *Reporters without Borders* [Online]. Available at: http://en.rsf.org/surveillance-tunisia,39747.html [accessed 27 August 2012].

Rugh, W.A. 2004. *Arab Mass Media: Newspapers, Radio, and Television in Arab Politics.* Westport, CT: Praeger.

Ryan, Y. 2011. Transforming Tunisia's internet agency. *Al Jazeera* [Online]. Available at: http://www.aljazeera.com/indepth/features/2011/10/2011105124516751900.html [accessed 20 August 2012].

Ryan, Y. 2011. Tunisia's bitter cyberwar. *Al Jazeera* [Online]. Available at: http://www.aljazeera.com/indepth/features/2011/01/20111614145839362.html [accessed 30 August 2012].

Saigol, L. 2011. Foreign companies face Arab spring fallout. *The Financial Times* [Online]. Available at: http://www.ft.com/intl/cms/s/0/99a5bcc6-e917-11e0-9817-00144feab49a.html#axzz266sX4hSy [accessed 27 August 2012].

Salamey, I. 2009. Middle Eastern Exceptionalism: Globalization and the Balance of Power. *Democracy and Security* 4(3), 249–260.

Salamey, I. and Pearson, F. 2012. The Collapse of Middle Eastern Authoritarianism: Breaking the barriers of fear and power. *Third World Quarterly* 33(5), 931–948.

Salamey, I. and Tabar, P. 2012. Democratic Transition and Sectarian Populism. *Contemporary Arab Affairs* 5(4).

Salem, P. 2008. Kuwait: Politics in a participatory emirate, in Ottaway, M. and Choucair-Vizoso, J. (eds) *Beyond the Facade: Political Reform in the Arab World.* Washington, DC: Carnegie Endowment for International Peace.

Salemink, O. 2008. Enclosing the Highlands: Socialist, Capitalist and Protestant Conversions of Vietnam's Central Highlanders, RCSD Conference "The Politics of the Commons" (co-hosted by IASCP), Chiang Mai University, 11–14 July 2008 (invited plenary speaker). Available at: http://dlc.dlib.indiana.edu/dlc/handle/10535/1787.

Samti, F. 2012. Tunisia Joins "Freedom Online Coalition." *Tunisia Live* [Online]. Available at: http://www.tunisia-live.net/2012/09/07/tunisia-joins-freedom-online-coalition/ [accessed 7 September 2012].

Satter, R. 2012. Syria Crisis: WikiLeaks Reveals Syrian Security Got Communications Equipment From West. *Associated Press*, July 16. Available at: http://www.huffingtonpost.com/2012/07/16/syria-wikileaks-security-commu nications-west_n_1675730.html [accessed 15 October 2012].

Schiffrin, A. 1997. Vietnam's Restless Countryside. *Asian Wall Street Journal*, 25 November.

Schiffrin, A. 2002. Assignment: Vietnam. *American Prospect*. Available at: http://prospect.org/article/assignment-vietnam [accessed 2 October 2012].

Schiller, D. 1999. *Digital Capitalism: Networking the Global Market System*. Cambridge: MIT Press.

Schmitt, C. 1985. *Political Theology: Four Chapters on the Concept of Sovereignty*. Cambridge, MA: MIT Press.

Seib, P.M. 2007. *New Media and the New Middle East*. New York: Palgrave Macmillan.

Sheikholeslami, A. 2009. Iran blocks Facebook, Twitter, before elections (update 1). *Bloomberg* [Online]. Available at: http://www.bloomberg.com/apps/news ?pid=newsarchive&sid=anh.uW3gNZp4 [accessed 16 August 2012].

Shumate, M. 2006. Trouble in a Geographically Distributed Virtual Network Organization: Organizing Tensions in Continental Direct Action Network. *Journal of Computer-Mediated Communication* 11(3) (April), 802–824.

Sidorenko, A. 2011a. Russia: Election day DDoS-alypse. *Global Voices Online* [Online]. Available at: http://globalvoicesonline.org/2011/12/05/russia-election -day-ddos-alypse/ [accessed 9 September 2012].

Silver, V. 2011. Post-Revolt Tunisia Can Alter E-Mail with "Big Brother" Software. *Bloomberg* [Online]. Available at: http://www.bloomberg.com/news/2011–12–12/tunisia-after-revolt-can-alter-e-mails-with-big-brother-software.html [accessed 20 August 2012].

Snider, E.A. and Faris, D.M. 2011. The Arab Spring: Democracy Promotion in Egypt. *Middle East Policy* 18(3), 49–62.

Somaiya, R. 2011. Hackers Shut Down Government Sites. *New York Times*, February 2. Available at http://www.nytimes.com/2011/02/03/world/middle east/03hackers.html [accessed 25 August 2012].

Sonne, P., et al. 2011. U.S. Products Help Block Mideast Web. *Wall Street Journal* [Online]. Available at: http://online.wsj.com/article/SB10001424052748704438104576219190417124226.html [accessed 20 August 2012].

Sotloff, S. 2010. Bahrain's Shia Crackdown. *Foreign Policy*, September 10. Available at: http://mideast.foreignpolicy.com/posts/2010/09/09/bahrain.

Sreberny, A. and Khiabany, G. 2010. *Blogistan: The Internet and Politics in Iran*. New York: I.B. Tauris.

Sreberny-Mohammadi, A. and Mohammadi, A. 1994. *Small Media, Big Revolution: Communication, Culture and The Iranian Revolution.* Minneapolis: University of Minnesota Press.

Steavenson, W. 2011. Letter from Damascus: Roads to Freedom. *The New Yorker*, August 29. Available at: http://www.newyorker.com/reporting/2011/08/29/110829fa_fact_steavenson [accessed 25 August 2012].

Stecklow, S. 2011. Nokia Siemens venture to reduce its business in Iran [Online]. Available at: http://online.wsj.com/article/SB10001424052970203430404577096503401073904.html [accessed 15 October 2012].

Stepanova, E. 2011. The Role of Information Communication Technologies in the 'Arab Spring' Implications Beyond the Region, PONARS Eurasia Policy Memo, No. 159, May.

Still, B. 2005. Hacking for a cause (computer file). *First Monday (Online)* 10, no. 9 (September 5), 1.

Street, D. and Leggett, J.C. 1961. Economic Deprivation and Extremism: A Study of Unemployed Negroes. *American Journal of Sociology* 67, 53–57.

syrianona. 2011. Anonymous' message to the people of Syria. *YouTube.com*, August 7. Available at: http://youtu.be/F1Sn9EpBGn8 [accessed 30 August 2012].

Tarrow, S. 1998. *Power in Movement.* New York: Cambridge University Press.

TCI Website. *History of Telecommunication in Iran* [Online: Telecommunication Company of Iran]. Available at: http://tci.ir/about/index.aspx?lang=En [accessed 31 August 2012].

Tehrani, H. 2009. Iran's revolutionary guards take on the internet. *Internet and Democracy Blog* [Online]. Available at: http://blogs.law.harvard.edu/idblog/2009/01/08/irans-revolutionary-guards-take-on-the-internet/ [accessed 31 August 2012].

Tesquet, O. 2011. Ben Ali: Les Compromissions d'Orange en Tunisie. Owni.fr [Online]. Available at: http://owni.fr/2011/03/03/ben-ali-les-compromission-dorange-en-tunisie/ [accessed 27 August 2012].

Tétreault, M.A. 2000. *Stories of Democracy: Politics and Society in Contemporary Kuwait.* New York: Columbia University Press.

Tétreault, M.A. 2006. *Kuwait's Annus Mirabilis* [Online]. Available at: http://www.merip.org/mero/mero090706.html [accessed 25 January 2011].

Thayer, C. 2007. Vietnam: The Internet Turns Ten. *Radio Singapore International.*

Thayer, C.A. 2009. Political Legitimacy of Vietnam's One-Party State: Challenges and Responses. *Journal of Southeast Asian Affairs* 28(4), 47–70.

Tilly, C. 1978. *From Mobilization to Revolution.* Reading, MA: Addison-Wesley.

Toumi, H. 2010. Bahrain Imposes Gag Order on Media Coverage of Terror Network. Gulfnews.com, August 28. Available at: http://gulfnews.com/news/gulf/bahrain/bahrain-imposes-gag-order-on-media-coverage-of-terror-network-1.674126.

Tufecki, Z. and Wilson, C. 2012. Social Media and the Decision to Participate in Political Protest: Observations From Tahrir Square. *Journal of Communication* 62, 363–379.

Ulbricht, M. 2012. How Media-Savvy Activists Report from the Front Lines in Syria. PBS.org, March 27. Available at: http://www.pbs.org/idealab/2012/03/how-media-savvy-activists-report-from-the-front-lines-in-syria085.html [accessed 25 August 2012].

Ulfelder, J. 2005. Contentious Collective Action and the Breakdown of Authoritarian Regimes. *International Political Science Review* 26(3), 311–334.

UNECA. 2012. National Information and Communication Infrastructure: Tunisia. Available at: http://www.uneca.org/aisi/nici/country_profiles/tunisia/tunisinter.htm [accessed 27 August 2012].

UNESCO. 1993. Informafrica: Meeting of High-Level Informatics Experts in Africa and of RINAF. Available at: http://unesdoc.unesco.org/images/0013/001389/138974eo.pdf [accessed 27 August 2012].

VanHemert, K. 2011. How Egypt Turned off the Internet. Gizmodo.com, January 28. Available at: gizmodo.com/5746121/how-egypt-turned-off-the-internet [accessed 25 August 2012].

Varnelis, K. and Friedberg, A. 2008. Place: Networked Place, in Karzys Varnelis (ed.) *Networked Publics*. Cambridge: MIT Press.

Wagenseil, P. 2011. Anonymous "Hacktivists" Attack Egyptian Websites. *Tech News Daily*, January 26. Available at: http://www.technewsdaily.com/6555-anonymous-hacktivists-attack-egyptian-websites.html [accessed 28 August 2012].

Wagner, B. 2009. Deep Packet Inspection and Internet Censorship: International Convergence on an "Integrated Technology of Control." *Global Voices Advocacy* [Online]. Available at: http://advocacy.globalvoicesonline.org/wp-content/uploads/2009/06/deeppacketinspectionandinternet-censorship2.pdf [accessed 20 August 2012].

Wagner, B. 2012. Push-button-autocracy in Tunisia: Analyzing the role of Internet infrastructure, institutions and international markets in creating a Tunisian censorship regime. *Telecommunications Policy* [Online], 36(6), July 2012, 484–92. Available at: http://www.sciencedirect.com/science/article/pii/S0308596112000675 [accessed 8 August 2012].

Waisbord, S. 2002. Antipress Violence and the Crisis of the State. *The Harvard International Journal of Press/Politics* 7, 90–109.

Washington Times. 2009. Editorial: Iran's Twitter revolution [Online]. Available at: http://www.washingtontimes.com/news/2009/jun/16/irans-twitter-revolution/ [accessed 8 August 2012].

Watson-Boles, A. 2004. Without a Net. *Committee to Protect Journalists* [Online]. Available at: http://cpj.org/reports/2004/10/yahyaoui.php [accessed 20 August 2012].

Weddady, N. 2010. Online Activism Meets Real World Activism: A Day against Censorship. *Dekhnstan* [Online]. Available at: http://dekhnstan.wordpress.

com/2010/05/23/online-activism-meets-real-world-activism-a-day-against-censorship/ [accessed 27 August 2012].

Wedeen, L. 1999. *The Ambiguities of Domination: Politics, Rhetoric, and Symbols in Contemporary Syria.* Chicago: University of Chicago Press.

Weingast, B.R. 1997. The Political Foundations of Democracy and Rule of Law. *American Political Science Review* 91(2), 245–263.

Weizman, E. 2009. Lawfare in Gaza: Legislative Attack. *OpenDemocracy*, March 1. Available at: http://www.opendemocracy.net/article/legislative-attack.

Wells-Dang, A. 2010. Political Space in Vietnam: A view from the rice-roots. *The Pacific Review* 23(1), 93–112.

Wheeler, D.L. 2006. *The Internet in the Middle East: Global Expectations and Local Imaginations in Kuwait.* Albany: State University of New York Press.

White, G. 2011. This is the Wikileak that Sparked the Tunisian Crisis. *Business Insider* [Online]. Available at: http://www.businessinsider.com/tunisia-wiki leaks-2011-1 [accessed 11 October 2012].

WikiLeaks. 2012. Syria Files. WikiLeaks.org. Available at: http://wikileaks.org/syria-files/ [accessed 31 October 2012].

Wilson, R. 2011. Economy: The Root of Uprising, in *the Arab Spring Implications for British Policy*. Conservative Middle East Council, 49–53.

World Bank. 2010. Internet users (per 100 people) [Online]. Available at: http://data.worldbank.org/indicator/IT.NET.USER.P2 [accessed 20 August 2012].

World Bank Group. 2008. *West Bank and Gaza Telecommunications Sector Note: Introducing Competition in the Palestinian Telecommunications Sector*, Report No. 42987. Available at: http://www-wds.worldbank.org/external/default/WDSContentServer/WDSP/IB/2008/03/20/000333037_20080320052257/Rendered/PDF/429870WP0GZ0Te10Box327342B01PUBLIC1.pdf.

Yahyanejad, M. and Gheytachi, E. 2012 Social Media, Dissent, and Iran's Green Movement, in *Liberation Technology: Social Media and the Struggle for Democracy*, edited by L. Diamond and M.F. Platter. Baltimore: The Johns Hopkins University Press.

Yang, G. 2009. *The Power of the Internet in China: Citizen Activism Online.* New York: Columbia University Press.

Yeganeh, B. 2010. Types of centers, groups, and organizations, all for controlling the Internet. *Radio Farda* [Online]. Available at: http://www.radiofarda.com/content/f35_Iran_Internet_Under_Control/1958457.html [accessed 27 August 2010].

Yurchak, A. 2005. *Everything was Forever, until it was No More: The Last Soviet Generation.* Princeton, NJ: Princeton University Press.

Zuckerman, E. 2005. WSIS—The Citizen's Summit [Online]. Available at: http://www.ethanzuckerman.com/blog/2005/11/17/wsis-the-citizens-summit/ [accessed 20 August 2012].

Zuckerman, E. 2007. Democrats invent the remix, only three years after the Tunisians [Online]. Available at: http://www.ethanzuckerman.com/blog/

2007/04/07/democrats-invent-the-remix-only-three-years-after-the-tunisians/ [accessed 20 August 2012].

Zuckerman, E. 2008. *Bridgeblogger and Xenophile, a Tale of Two Bloggers* [Online]. Available at: http://www.ethanzuckerman.com/blog/2008/12/05/bridgeblogger-and-xenophile-a-tale-of-two-bloggers/ [accessed 9 September 2012].

Zuckerman, E. 2011. The First Twitter Revolution? *Foreign Policy* [Online]. Available at: http://www.foreignpolicy.com/articles/2011/01/14/the_first_twitter_revolution [accessed 22 October 2012].

Index

For Product Safety Concerns and Information please contact our EU
representative GPSR@taylorandfrancis.com
Taylor & Francis Verlag GmbH, Kaufingerstraße 24, 80331 München, Germany

www.ingramcontent.com/pod-product-compliance
Ingram Content Group UK Ltd.
Pitfield, Milton Keynes, MK11 3LW, UK
UKHW011012180926
475701UK00004B/691

* 9 7 8 1 1 3 8 2 5 0 1 0 9 *